YOUR
TIME
STARTS
NOW

Also by Julie Goodwin

Our Family Table
The Heart of the Home
Gather
Julie Goodwin's Essential Cookbook
Julie Goodwin's 20/20 Meals
Homemade Takeaway
Classic

JULIE GOODWIN

YOUR TIME STARTS NOW

FOOD AND FAME, FAILURE AND FREEDOM: THE LIFE STORY OF AUSTRALIA'S FIRST MASTERCHEF

EBURY
PRESS

EBURY PRESS

UK | USA | Canada | Ireland | Australia
India | New Zealand | South Africa | China

Ebury is part of the Penguin Random House group of companies
whose addresses can be found at global.penguinrandomhouse.com

First published by Ebury in 2024

Copyright © Julie Goodwin 2024

The moral right of the author has been asserted.

All rights reserved. No part of this publication may be reproduced, published,
performed in public or communicated to the public in any form or by any means
without prior written permission from Penguin Random House Australia Pty Ltd
or its authorised licensees.

Cover photography by Steve Brown
Cover design by Adam Laszczuk © Penguin Random House Australia Pty Ltd
Internal design by Midland Typesetters, Australia
Typeset in 11/17 pt Sabon by Midland Typesetters, Australia

Printed and bound in Australia by Griffin Press, an accredited
ISO AS/NZS 14001 Environmental Management Systems printer

 A catalogue record for this book is available from the National Library of Australia

ISBN 978 1 76134 115 1

penguin.com.au

We at Penguin Random House Australia acknowledge that Aboriginal and
Torres Strait Islander peoples are the Traditional Custodians and the first
storytellers of the lands on which we live and work. We honour Aboriginal and
Torres Strait Islander peoples' continuous connection to Country, waters, skies
and communities. We celebrate Aboriginal and Torres Strait Islander stories,
traditions and living cultures; and we pay our respects to Elders past and present.

CONTENTS

Prologue	1
1. It's only the beginning	5
2. Hip to be square	20
3. Crazy little thing called love	29
4. White wedding	51
5. Hot potato	65
6. Taking care of business	75
7. Hot and cold	94
8. This is me	108
9. Under pressure	124
10. The final countdown	139
11. Changes	152
12. Dance monkey	172
13. A whole new world	194
14. Where everybody knows your name	209
15. Going under	227
16. How do you mend a broken heart?	258
17. Learn to fly	281
18. Mad world	298
19. All you need is love	314
20. Times like these	345
Acknowledgements	357

For Mick
a love story

PROLOGUE

I'd been a contestant on the first season of *MasterChef* Australia for seven weeks. You couldn't say we'd settled into a routine; there was no routine to it at all, really. But I'd been a part of the show long enough to have participated in some weird and wonderful challenges. With my fellow contestants I had manned a sushi train, cooked for thousands of punters at the Royal Easter Show and gone deep-sea fishing for ingredients to cook on a Sydney pier. Nothing, however, had prepared me for the shock of Adriano Zumbo walking into the kitchen with a croquembouche almost as tall as me. At the time, Zumbo was not a familiar name to most Australians; that was about to change.

I'd landed in this particular pressure test after a two-course meal challenge. I had been teamed up with my friend and roommate, Tom, and our dishes had not made the grade. Tom was a lawyer, a Torres Strait Islander, a gentle spirit and wildly funny human who became my best friend and my rock inside the *MasterChef* house. On croquembouche day, we were competing against each other, as well as against Poh and Chris, who had also landed in the bottom four the day before. Chris was the hat guy, the beer guy, the nose-to-tail cooking guy. He was the very confident guy. He was, however, like myself, not the dessert guy. Poh, an artist from Adelaide, was an adventurous cook, taking risks that sometimes fell short of the mark but more often resulted in brilliance. The Poh-lercoaster, she became known as, and it was a fitting name.

I'll never forget the sight of Adriano carrying in that monstrosity of a pastry. We may not have known who he was, but I knew a giant pile of pain when I saw one. (The croquembouche, not Adriano.)

I spent the entire time that Adriano was explaining the pressure points of this dessert staring at it dumbstruck and wondering when they were going to pull out a miniature one from under a cloche to demonstrate the size we would have to make. Because surely, *surely* we weren't making one like his. It was the height of a human child. I even asked, right before they kicked off the challenge, 'But how *big* does it have to be?' Gary looked at me a bit quizzically, gestured at Adriano's croquembouche and said, 'That big!' As though it should have been obvious.

Judge Gary Mehigan said, 'Your two hours and forty-five minutes start ... now!' What followed were possibly the most frantic two-plus hours of my life. I didn't have time to look up so I didn't know how anyone else was going. I was in shock that my choux pastry worked and that suddenly everything seemed to be coming together beautifully, though creating spun sugar is not something I would recommend to anyone who values their fingers, or their polished timber floors. That stuff burns on contact, sinking into flesh (and floorboards) like a hot knife into butter.

Assembling the croquembouche involved dipping our custard-filled choux buns into molten sugar and stacking them inside a metal cone to create the tower shape. The profiteroles were meant

PROLOGUE

to stick to each other, not the metal, and when the cone was inverted they were meant to glide out effortlessly and stand proudly on their toffee base. Sadly, I kind of glued my pastry into the cone, and when it was time to unmould, the top of my profiterole tower snapped clean off the bottom. The word I said next was bleeped out for television. I had just enough time to toffee-coat a few of my spare choux buns and stick them on top, but mine was a very stumpy little croquembouche compared to Poh's, Chris's and Tom's.

Not for the first time in this kitchen, and most certainly not for the last, I sat in a room with my fellow contestants, waiting for my efforts, for my heart, soul and food, to be consumed, dissected and judged; and for my fate to be decided.

CHAPTER 1

IT'S ONLY THE BEGINNING

For nearly every baby born, there is a bewildered adult holding them with awe, fear, and a deep curiosity about who it is they are meeting for the first time. Who do they look like? Who will they *be* like? What will they be good at? What will they become? Whatever my mother's dreams and hopes were for me on 31 October 1970, she couldn't have had a single inkling of what was ahead for us. For one thing, *MasterChef* wasn't invented yet.

Marlene Mary Joy McComish (nee White) gave birth to me at St Margaret's Maternity Hospital in Darlinghurst, Sydney. My father, David McComish, had dropped Mum at the hospital and upon being told it would be a long wait, went home. The details of where he was for the next couple of days are blurry, but by the time the hospital finally tracked him down and told him he had a daughter, he had some news of his own to share. There had been a catastrophe while he was out: our little unit, our home in San Souci, had caught fire. The record player, left on, had started the inferno; the lounge room was incinerated but the nursery, filled with hand-knitted bootees and jackets, was miraculously untouched. I was roughly two hours old when my newly minted parents, only in their twenties, had this conversation. They named me Julie Kathleen.

The flat was rebuilt and I spent my first two years there, then we moved to a house in Normanhurst, near Hornsby, in the north-western suburbs of Sydney. Mum worked in insurance, and my father, who was born in Ireland but had lived in Australia since his early childhood when his parents had emigrated, was an air traffic controller at Sydney Airport.

Mum's mum, my nan, was always a big part of my life. My first two months were spent with her and my parents, after the fire had destroyed our home. She lived in Ryde in the house her husband had built. Poppy Roy, as I have always referred to him, died when Mum was sixteen, after a brief duel with stomach cancer. Nan was in her forties when he died, and she didn't look at another man for the rest of her life. Poppy was never far from the conversation, though. He was a practical joker, a larrikin, a skilled carpenter, a doting dad. He was remembered with such lovingly told, detailed stories that although I never met him, I felt his presence in my life.

My paternal grandmother was less involved but still came to family occasions. My father was often away from the house for long periods of time. I don't remember much about that but I do have very early memories of lying on the carpet in the front hall, by the door with the beer-bottle glass, waiting for him to get home. Mum trying to convince me to come into the lounge room, away from the front door; that he was at work and we weren't sure when he would be home. He wasn't at work; Mum didn't know where he was, but that's how she explained it to me.

One of my earliest memories is from when I was three. My father had not been home for a long time. Being three, I didn't understand why. Years on, I knew that my parents' marriage had broken down and he had moved out. Some time after he had left, he came back to collect his things. I was so excited to see him. Being three, I must have been excited enough to need a quick wee. When I came back from the bathroom, he had left, apparently unable to handle saying goodbye to me. I didn't see him again, and then only briefly, until I was fourteen.

Mum was pregnant when he went. She was left paying the mortgage along with a bunch of other money that had to be repaid on my father's behalf. Back in those days, you could not claim any kind of assistance for six weeks after being abandoned – that was the word that was used – and during those six weeks, people from the government knocked on the door at odd hours to make sure Mum was really a single parent now. My father was untraceable so child support was not an option. I only found out about these things many years later.

I was very pleased about Mum's pregnancy, convinced I was going to have a little sister. Mum tried to talk me into being just as excited for a little brother, in case that's what we ended up with, but I was not having a bar of it. My last words to her as she went off to the hospital were, I'm told, 'Don't bring home a boy one!'

She did not bring home a boy one, she brought home Debbie Maree, my pride and joy, my new baby, my little sister. Debbie's first steps were later than they might have been if I hadn't cried out in panic every time she got on her feet, afraid she would hurt herself. She had the most amazing dimples and when her hair came, it was in golden ringlets. She was, not just in our eyes but also to the many strangers who stopped us on the street to comment, breathtaking. She was the spitting image of Shirley Temple and she won hearts everywhere we went. I was so fiercely proud to be the big sister of such a bright, shiny little person.

Although I don't think it was ever said out loud to me, I knew from a young age that I was the clever sister and Debbie was the cute one. It wasn't a sore point, it was just a fact. It became a sore point in adulthood when Debbie got her master's degree in Social Change and Development, thus becoming the clever one *and* the cute one. Rude.

Back in those days Mum had to work two jobs to keep up with the house and the bills. She had given up her job in insurance to be able to look after us girls. She was a house cleaner by day, taking Debbie with her while I was at school, and a waitress by night. Nan would come and look after us on the nights Mum waitressed. I'm not sure how we came to the attention of St Vincent de Paul around that time – Mum didn't go to them – but they came to visit. I remember being asked by two kind old men (they probably were not old but they seemed so to me) what I wanted for Christmas. I asked for batteries. I had this fluffy little white dog that would bark and sit and do flips, and I played with it so much that it didn't take long for its batteries to go flat, and batteries were really expensive. So I was indeed given batteries, and we were also given a big Christmas hamper. Mum told me a long while later that she was stricken by being the recipient of charity but at the same time so grateful to have nice things for Christmas.

Being a little kid, I had no idea of any financial difficulty, and no sense of the logistical challenge it must have been for Mum and Nan, both working, to juggle us girls between them. I loved my mum very much, and have clear memories of us colouring in together and cooking pikelets on the stove. I loved my nan too, and remember warm afternoon walks on leafy streets holding her hand, and sitting by her side as she pedalled her pianola and we sang songs together. I adored my little sister, my playmate and best friend. I missed my father, more some days than others, but my main memories of those years are of being safe, and clean, and fed, and adored by the people in my life.

IT'S ONLY THE BEGINNING

Mum eventually joined a social group called PWP – Parents Without Partners. In the 1970s being a single parent probably wasn't as common as it is now. I certainly recall feeling a bit different, only having a mum and not a dad. I don't remember ever being picked on for it, or singled out, but I was aware of the difference. A group like PWP gave single parents a social outlet – for themselves, and for their kids. I have really fond memories of the things we used to do – picnics at Crosslands Reserve in Berowra, bonfires, camping weekends. And it was in this group, in 1975, that Mum met Tony Hunt, the man who would become my beloved dad and still is, nearly half a century down the track.

Tony had lost his wife, suddenly and awfully, leaving him the single dad of two very small children. Debbie and I loved Tony, and we loved his two kids as well, a boy and a girl just slightly older than me. I loved going out in Tony's car, a blue Kingswood station wagon, which always stank of petrol. We would roll around in the back of the wagon, no seatbelts, moments away from exploding in petrol-fuelled flames, either suffocating from heat exhaustion or succumbing to hypothermia, depending on the season.

I would ask Mum on the regular, 'Why can't you and Tony get married?' and she would tell me she had to wait to be asked. I wanted to know why she couldn't ask Tony, and I was always told that it's not how it works. Even as a young child I thought this convention was stupid.

It turns out that Tony had already proposed to Mum twice in the previous eighteen months, and she had declined. She was madly in love, but skittish about the possibility of putting her kids through another relationship that might not last. But seeing how much we loved Dad, and how much he loved us too, she finally said yes. The two of them gathered us all together to announce the news and I said, to Dad's confusion, 'Tony, I thought you'd never ask!'

I was six and Debbie was two. We were thrilled beyond words and looked forward to a Brady Bunch-style situation with our new dad and siblings. But of course, the Brady Bunch was utterly fictitious, fluffy televised storytelling, where any problems are sorted out in the space of an episode. Families aren't like that. And ours was starting its journey with four very young people already damaged by life: two little kids who had lost their mother, and two little kids whose father was lost to them.

I am sure that these days there are resources for helping families to blend as harmoniously as possible; there are counsellors and psychologists and programs and just a lot more understanding around the impact of trauma on children. And on parents, too. But those resources weren't readily available in the 1970s. Even if they were, my parents were of a generation and mindset that didn't ask for help. Added to the mix was a complex extended family situation, a cast of characters who all played a role in the shape and texture of our new family life.

Dad sold his house in Berowra and our Normanhurst house was extended so us kids could each have our own room. We ate dinner together at the table nightly and watched *A Country Practice* every week. The TV guide was in the newspaper, and there was no such thing as a remote control. We attended Mass on Sunday nights and sometimes afterwards Dad would stand in the church car park pointing out constellations, which should be a heartwarming memory, but in reality was mostly annoying as we were impatient to get home to dinner and the telly. I can still name most of the constellations, though.

Mum loved to entertain, loved to throw a dinner party. Certain things were always on the party buffet – strawberry shortcake, cream horns, devils on horseback. Sherry log. Cabanossi with cheese cubes, and watermelon served in a basket cut out of the watermelon itself.

IT'S ONLY THE BEGINNING

We went on camping holidays down the New South Wales south coast, in Dalmeny, where my nan and Poppy Roy had bought a piece of land in the 1950s. Eventually a house was built on the land and we upgraded from our caravan and tents to four walls and running water. We spent nearly every Christmas holiday there, and most other school holidays as well. We were allowed more freedom to roam when we were on holidays, and I would spend hours wandering the beaches, adding to my rock collection and embedding myself in this place as it became embedded in me. There has always been something very special about that pristine coast. Back then, it was probably a combination of the vastness of the sea and sky, with idle hours to explore and daydream, and a slower pace with fewer rules. Simple meals, that raging hunger you get from being in salt air all day, sun-warmed skin and multiplying freckles, the sound of the ocean as I fell asleep – all of this made it the place I loved most in the world.

During school term, life went along as life does. Us kids attended Normanhurst West Public School, a fifteen-minute walk from home. I liked school, I enjoyed having fresh pencils and paper and especially those rare days when Mum would put some coins into a brown paper bag for a lunch order. We did our homework and our chores, we took jazz ballet lessons and learned a musical instrument. Music was – is – a big part of my life. I started to learn the clarinet when I was eight. I joined the primary school band and, not long after, Hornsby Concert Band, which met in a local school hall one night a week. I was in the band until I was sixteen years old, when it became a marching band and my distinct lack of coordination ruled me out. Up until then we competed in band championships, played at nursing homes and outside shopping centres, and went away on band camps. It was pretty much the biggest part of my social life up until I joined Antioch, the church youth group.

Along with clarinet I learned piano, which I loved because you could sing along to it. If there was a choir going I joined it. For my sixteenth birthday I got a guitar, and started writing my own songs.

When I was in primary school I used to have my clock radio tuned to a classical station. The music made me feel like I was in a film – one minute exciting and loud, then kind of slow and mournful, then bright and upbeat. Mum, in what was probably a desperate attempt to give me some kind of street cred, eventually suggested that I tune in to a commercial station once in a while. I did, and got up to speed with what all the cool kids were listening to. I still love having music in my ears – what kind depends on my mood. At the moment I quite enjoy putting on a chill piano playlist and walking around like my life is a scene from a 1980s made-for-television movie. Try it – like the old Crunchie ad says, it'll change the colour of your day.

Music was my jam. Dance, however, was another matter. I was spectacularly awful at jazz ballet, with my lack of coordination, grace or style. Sometimes the teacher would stop the music, stop the class, and say, 'Julie, do that part again,' while telling the others in the class, 'Observe the incorrect way to dance!' I had largely forgotten about such remarks until I came upon my exam reports, which have comments such as 'Lacks coordination', 'Needs better control of arms' and, generously, 'Has a nice smile?'

I was a pretty scruffy little creature all round. Despite Mum's best efforts, I didn't seem to stay clean and tidy for long. It was like I had an auto-dishevel function. My hair was untameable, my knees scabby and my clothes always covered in mud or paint or whatever I'd just eaten. I never walked if I could run, and did everything full tilt. I was accident-prone and unwieldly. Not much has changed, to be honest – my husband, Mick, lovingly calls me his little ballerina as I crash around the house, knocking things over and stubbing my toes on the furniture.

I was good at school though, both in behaviour and in achievement. My second-grade report card reads, 'Julie is very enthusiastic. She usually works at a very high level except when she gets excited.' I can't remember what kind of stuff I was getting excited about but it must have been big.

According to the testing that was done on kids in the 1970s and '80s, I was in the top 5 per cent of fourth graders, brain-wise, which meant I was given the opportunity to go to a different school to be in an Opportunity Class, or OC. These classes were offered in a few schools across the state, the idea being to gather high-achieving children together to improve their performance and opportunities. Even back then there were questions about whether this was beneficial to anyone. I think it was beneficial for me – I remember the shock of suddenly not being automatically at the top of the class but having to work a lot harder to stand out. I think that when teachers expect kids to be smart and do well, that it comes to pass. I also think that when teachers expect kids to struggle and behave poorly, that also comes to pass. So I do wonder about the effect on the kids left behind of some of their classmates being yanked out to be fast-tracked. I wonder about the effect on the kids in what was then called the OA class, the ones whose parents were told they were in the lowest group of achievers who needed to be isolated from the mainstream for their own benefit. After studying education and raising three very different sons, I prefer an integrated approach to schooling while still recognising that some children have particular needs that can't be met in a mainstream classroom. I'm pleased that IQ testing isn't relied on as it was back then – there are so many more illustrative ways to assess children, and better tools to appreciate and nurture them.

So for fifth and sixth grade I moved from Normanhurst West to Hornsby Public School. I don't remember being nervous about this move, but I was definitely happy that my best friend, Lyndal, was coming with me to the new school.

One thing I recall clearly about the long summer break before I headed off to the new school was Mum sitting me down and telling me that Santa Claus wasn't real. Not only had I not twigged, but I was a fierce and vocal defender of Santa, so she didn't want me arriving at smart-kid school holding on to this passionate belief. I cried floods of tears at the news, which only intensified when it occurred to me that this must apply to the Easter bunny, and the tooth fairy, too. For a smart kid I was slow on the uptake.

My sadness was so great that I promised myself I would never do this to my own children – and I haven't. They are now in their twenties and we have never had That Conversation. On Christmas Eve we still put out Santa sacks and carrots for the reindeer. I suppose I will have to let them know eventually. I hope they take it better than I did.

I had to catch the train to my new school by myself – at ten years old! It was thrilling and scary at first but soon it became routine. Mum took me on a couple of practice runs, and made sure I had a twenty cent piece in my little plastic wallet in case I needed to phone home. In my fresh new uniform and shoes, with my new train pass and lunch box, I went off to my big new school.

I liked these middle years at school and I liked the work. I idolised my fifth grade teacher, Mr Schultz, who taught us poetry and art along with the basic subjects. Lyndal and I had a little group of mates in no time. Our friends were, like me, a bit left of centre. We dubbed ourselves the Weirdo Gang and would march around the oval at lunch time singing songs with names like 'There was a paratrooper from the forty-ninth brigade' to the tune of 'Glory, Glory, Hallelujah'. In the high school to which we all moved in due course, the Weirdo Gang developed into the Far Out Brussels Sprouts, and we would enter school talent quests dressed in green garbage bags and singing acapella parody songs, mostly about the teachers. But for now, our musical gifts were confined to our lunch-time marches.

We were allowed to leave school grounds at lunchtime if we had lunch money, and go down the main road of Hornsby to the shops. I can't imagine Years 5 and 6 having this privilege now, but it was 1981 and kids were fairly free-range. The most popular shop was the fish and chip shop. Salty hot chips wrapped in newspaper could be had for less than a buck. The more cashed up among us – not me – could afford a hamburger. Then a kebab shop opened a couple of doors down, and Mum gave me extra money so I could try my first doner. I had never eaten anything like it, and I reckon it was the first time that the memory of something I ate came back to visit me over and over again.

I think that for the most part younger kids go about their business without too much of the adult world filtering through. But in 1982 the Cold War was permeating our consciousness and conversations. We were genuinely powerless in this situation, which seemed at the time likely to bring about the actual end of the world. We talked about nuclear bombs in class; we wrote poetry about it all. We wrote letters to Mr Reagan and Mr Brezhnev, asking them to make friends. I wonder what effect that bleak era had on our young minds. What was the impact of that sense of danger, of imminent disaster, on our future selves? I wonder the same thing about the effects the pandemic and climate crisis will have on this generation of kids. I wonder if we'll ever really know.

YOUR TIME STARTS NOW

I started my first business almost by accident, when I was ten. I wanted a camera and knew that I needed to earn the money to buy it. Nan would bring home offcuts of cardboard from the Australian Gaslight Company where she worked, and I turned them into gift tags. Using an inkpad (also, I believe, 'requisitioned' from the gas company), I would put a fingerprint on the card – a whole one for a body, and a fingertip for the head – and use a pen to turn these little prints into characters. Clowns, lawn bowlers, golfers, nurses, nuns.

When I had exhausted all our extended family members and friends of my parents as potential clients, I hit the shops. I went door-to-door throughout Hornsby selling my little cards after school. I recall the lady in the framing shop saying, 'I have no need for gift cards, we don't sell those.'

'But people buy picture frames as presents, so maybe they would like a gift card to go with them,' I replied. She bought the discount bulk pack.

The owner of the toy store bought a pack of cards, told me I could sell ice to Eskimos and asked me to come back and see her when I had made my first million. I had visions of rolling up to her store in a stretch limo, wearing sunglasses and probably a cloak, and sweeping in the door asking, 'Remember me?' She couldn't possibly have known how encouraging her words were, and how many eye-rolls and impatient rejections they would see me through.

I did eventually save enough for my camera. I'd earned it and I treasured it. That camera represented a reward for creativity and proactivity; it was a lesson that I carried through many chapters of my life.

In sixth grade, when I was eleven, Mum and Dad took us kids out of school for three months and we did a camping trip around Australia. They had been saving for this trip for years, and waiting for Dad's long service leave. We took a caravan that Poppy Roy had built in 1956, that beautiful plywood work of art, and a couple of tents.

We set off in a northerly direction, heading for Queensland. A routine was quickly established: we'd wake up early, travel a few hundred kilometres in the morning, then set up camp and head off to explore whichever new place we had landed in.

My sixth-grade teacher, Mrs Chiswell, was very cool. She only set me two tasks to complete while we were on our trip: to work through certain chapters in our maths textbook, and to write letters to the class at least once a week. I did the latter with great gusto, including my poetry, my sketches, and wildly elaborate descriptions of every place we went. At the end of my trip Mrs Chiswell handed me an enormous stack of letters tied with ribbon. I still have them.

Years later, a girl I went from primary to high school with told me that when one of my letters arrived, the whole class would groan because it meant a supremely boring afternoon of listening to every bloody detail of my every bloody day. I was quite taken aback, assuming that my highly descriptive letters would have been the highlight of everyone's week.

The trip was extraordinary. We went down mines and up mountains, camped by rivers and oceans and in the middle of deserts. We squelched through the mud flats of Mackay, went to the apple canning factory in Leeton and swam in the Ord River dam, which gave us all violent diarrhoea. We stayed at Uluru – Ayers Rock as it was known then – and I felt in my bones how ancient and sacred this place was. I had my cozzies nicked off the campground clothes line in Darwin. We saw the sun rise over the beach in Broome, snorkelled in Carnarvon and met the wild dolphins of Monkey Mia. We drove across the Nullarbor Plain. Petrol in the outback was fifty cents per litre, which was truly shocking. It was only thirty-six cents at home.

We wore out our one music cassette, the hits compilation '1982 with a Bullet', to which I still know every word of every song. Kim Wilde, Toni Basil, The J. Geils Band, Moving Pictures – these artists provided the soundtrack of our road trip.

Eating on the road provided some challenges. Fresh fruit and vegetables were few and far between, especially in the outback. Breakfast was always Weet-Bix, and lunch was Vegemite or peanut butter sandwiches. For dinner, we ate a lot of what Mum called 'surprise rice'. This consisted of salty boiled rice paired with things that didn't need refrigerating, such as dehydrated peas and hard-boiled eggs. It was on the menu several times a week, rendering it utterly unsurprising.

Just outside the Northern Territory's Tennant Creek, on an infinitely flat, straight stretch of road, a road train somehow sucked us into its vortex as it passed and our caravan flipped onto its side, raising the tailgate of the station wagon high into the air. Nobody was hurt but we spent a week in Tennant Creek getting the van repaired. Mum and Dad did all the work on the van, thanks to the kindness of a mechanic who lent them space in his workshop and the tools to do the job. We kids spent those hours hanging out in the onsite van we'd rented, doing homework, squabbling and waiting for Mum or Dad to duck back and take us for a swim in the tiny, tepid caravan-park pool.

It was an extraordinary trip. I remember more, and learned more, from those three months on the road than I possibly could have in a classroom. This vast country with its breathtaking landscapes, its wild contradictions, its incredible variety of wildlife and its endlessly fascinating people, was stitched onto my heart and into my very soul in those months. My yearning to get out there, to the wild places and the remote places, has never left me.

IT'S ONLY THE BEGINNING

Pikelets

This is the ideal recipe to introduce your children to cooking. The kids can contribute to measuring and stirring, and even to the flipping with a spatula when they are big enough. Of course, the best part of any cooking you do with children is the time and attention you give to them. The mess is temporary and the food is secondary.

Prep time: 5 minutes
Cooking time: 10 minutes plus 30 minutes resting time
Makes enough for afternoon tea

1 cup self-raising flour
1 tablespoon caster sugar
1 egg
¾ cup milk
4 tablespoons melted butter

Place flour and caster sugar into a medium bowl, and run a wire whisk through the mixture to break up any lumps.

Lightly beat the egg in a small bowl and add milk.

Make a well in the centre of the dry ingredients and add the wet ingredients, stirring well. Make sure there are no lumps.

Rest for 30 minutes. (This may not work when cooking with small children, so you can ignore it if you need to.)

Heat a non-stick frying pan to medium heat and brush with butter (or just run your block of butter over the hot pan). Drop tablespoons of mixture into the pan. Only make about 6 pikelets at a time and leave plenty of room to turn them over.

Cook over a medium heat until bubbles appear on most of the surface.

Turn and cook on the other side for just a minute, or until golden brown.

Pikelets should be eaten the day they are made. Serve them hot with butter and golden syrup, or cold with butter and jam or jam and whipped cream.

CHAPTER 2
HIP TO BE SQUARE

As 1983 began, so did my high school years, at Hornsby Girls. 'Faith with fortitude' was our motto, Minerva our muse, beige our uniform. I loved the school's old buildings and polished floors, the hall with the stage and piano. Compared to primary school it all seemed very grand. I think the butterflies in my gut were a little bit of nerves mingled with a lot of excitement. The place seemed full of possibility. Hornsby Girls was always a high-achieving public school but probably more so now that it is selective. Back then it was not – they'd take any old scrubber, I like to say.

Most of my friends had moved from Hornsby Public to Hornsby Girls, and in the first couple of terms our little group added a few new, like-minded girls along the way. My friendship group was mainly studious and musical. We weren't very social outside of school, and we weren't particularly athletic. When it came time to choose sports, we usually opted for tenpin bowling or swimming – whichever option meant we didn't have to get too hot and sweaty.

I did well in class, and threw myself into all the extracurricular stuff I could. I don't recall ever being pressured to do this. I do remember having enormous enthusiasm for just about everything, especially if it involved music or talking. Choir, band, ensemble, the school musicals when they were on; public speaking comps, debating, and in later years mock trials and massed choir events with other schools. I was even in the computer club, where we learned to program in MicroBee. I was fiercely competitive in all these endeavours – not only with my academic grades but also in any musical or speaking competition. Whatever I was doing, I wanted to win. I hated not to win.

I attended Catholic scripture while most of the year was at Anglican scripture classes. Scripture in our state school was only held once a term, which was fine by me. Our family was still attending Mass regularly so I didn't like or need this unwelcome instruction from Sister Margaret. I had the same nun taking my classes all the way from fifth class to Year 12, and I knew even as a teenager that some of her takes were pretty dreadful. She didn't like to be challenged on them, either. One day she read a Bible passage about women who remarry being adulterous. I said to her, 'What about my mum? She was remarried to my dad.' She shrugged and said, 'She's an adultress.' I certainly couldn't find anything compassionate or Christ-like in her answer or her demeanour towards me. I hated scripture.

Outside of school I was still in Hornsby Concert Band and was part of the music ministry at our church, playing clarinet until I switched to guitar. In Year 10 I joined Antioch, the church youth group. The group met on Sunday nights after Mass, but as everyone was good friends there were plenty of weekend outings as well. Trips to the beach, the shops, or hanging out at each others' houses were all on the agenda. As wholesome as it all sounds, there were hook-ups and not-for-parental-viewing activities going on. I was the youngest in the group for a while; you were meant to be sixteen to join but because I knew a bunch of them through the church music group I was allowed in at fifteen. I had a reputation for being a goody-two-shoes, so I was often left out of the more nefarious schemes. In hindsight, I'm kind of glad – I don't even want to know where I would have ended up if I'd have started with anything too heavy back then. Probably dead in a ditch a long time ago – I don't do moderation very well. As a result of being excluded from the wilder parties and gatherings, I've actually never taken an illicit drug. I ended up being able to drink for Australia, but pot or anything harder have just never been offered to me. Not even at the Logies, which I believe puts me firmly in a minority.

It was with this youth group that I had my first real encounter with alcohol, at seventeen years of age. It was somebody's eighteenth and my friends brought me a hip flask of overproof rum. Dangerous stuff, especially if you don't know how to mix drinks or pace yourself. I don't remember a whole lot about that night except lying on someone's driveway looking up at faces and streetlights spinning above me. I don't think I had ever felt as crook as I did the next day, when I had to leave work early. With hindsight, it's probably the first time I ever felt alcohol-induced shame. I rang the parents who threw the party and apologised for my behaviour. They were slightly bemused – I probably wasn't the only one who'd got into a state that night but I was possibly the only one who'd phoned up to say sorry. I was well and truly over the legal age before I touched alcohol again.

The day I turned fourteen and nine months, legal working age back then, I went from store to store in Northgate Hornsby asking for work. I was given a job in Noni B, the fashion store, on Thursday nights and Saturday mornings. I loved this job. I had the best manager, who taught me how to make the dresses look nice on the racks and how to tie a proper bow. I enjoyed helping the customers too, especially men looking to buy for wives and girlfriends, who would hang about looking awkward until one of us could guide them to a good choice.

From there I went on to be receptionist for a local GP, a rude and sexist man, and then I landed a job at Bowden Brae nursing home as a domestic. My job was to serve meals in the dining room and to bed-bound residents, to pour the tea and cut up food where necessary, collect the trays and wash the dishes.

This job would see me through the rest of high school and into my university years. It paid for my first car, train tickets, books, my social life. The money was great, especially on a Sunday, when I could earn $120 in the hand for an eight-hour shift. I enjoyed the work too. It was physical and timed to the minute, but I liked working with the residents and got to know them very well over the four years I was there.

Lots of these elderly people had nobody to visit them so I would stay behind on my Sunday shifts to chat. I heard the most incredible stories. There were fascinating lives locked up in the ageing bodies inside that building. One old lady in particular, Mrs Hill, tiny and frail as a sparrow, would talk in a half-dream state about her sisters and their childhood. I'm not sure that she knew who I was at all. We'd talk and I'd brush her hair and buy her marshmallows, which were her favourite. She was much older at that time than my nan was, but she was like my nan and it made me sad, and angry actually, that nobody came to visit her. I was determined that my beautiful nan would never be left on her own like this, not while I had breath in my body to prevent it.

I only had a few boyfriends during my school years. One was in a hurry to go where I wasn't ready to go; one was a beautiful guy, sporty and funny with a great family; one was an arsehole who turned out to have another girlfriend on the side the whole time.

Or maybe *I* was the girlfriend on the side. Each relationship only lasted a few months. Each experience left its own imprint.

When it was time to arrange work experience in Year 11, I was overjoyed to be selected to go to 2GB radio, and to a law firm in Sydney. I had decided I wanted to be either a journalist or a criminal lawyer. I had no reason to believe that I couldn't achieve the necessary marks to get into the courses I wanted. I had no way of knowing how pear-shaped all these plans were about to go; I wouldn't know for years and years what the reason was. It is only now, as I am laying out the chronology of my life, that I can appreciate the cause and often devastating effect of what happened next.

It was while I was sixteen that I accidentally uncovered a buried memory. My seven-year-old self wanted to be heard. I don't know why the memory appeared at that particular moment. You'd think that if something hasn't crossed your mind for nine years then it can't have been that formative, or traumatic, or even important. But there it was one afternoon, a dusty old library book in my brain. I took it down from the shelf, and I read it, and that is how I remembered: I had been sexually abused when I was seven. Those weeks – months – laid out in front of me, in detail, in that dusty old book.

I had no idea what to do with this realisation and no idea why it came to me like it did, and when it did. So I banished that seven-year-old. I jammed that book back onto its shelf and I put my sixteen-year-old back against it, and I braced my sixteen-year-old legs and I held it there the very best I could.

I want to say right now that these are all the details I will share – other than to make very clear that what had happened was completely unknown, until recently, to Mum and Dad. In this instance, there is nothing to be gained from naming, shaming, disseminating, picking over the tawdry minutiae of what happened. Only that it happened.

HIP TO BE SQUARE

There is, in fact, only one reason to write about something this personal, this painful, this sickening, humiliating, frightening, at all. And if you need to hear it, then you are the reason. Here it is: shame dies in daylight. If there is a part of you that is hurt and exiled, if you can reach that part of you – that boy or girl, that woman or man who is cowering in the darkness, covered in shame and terrified to be seen; if you can gently reach out to them and bring them into the room where all the other parts of you are waiting; if you can put your arms around that broken part and tell them, 'You're safe now,' then perhaps you can start to heal.

It is only now as an adult in my fifties, and having gone through quite the wringer and lots of work, that I am able to say to my seven-year-old self: *Come in from the cold. The shame isn't yours to carry. It never was.*

―

At the end of Year 11, I was elected by my peers as school captain. Or head prefect as it was called at Hornsby Girls. I guess Huey Lewis and the News was telling us it was hip to be square. My best friend was made vice captain and my friendship group made up basically half the prefects.

I would say that my approach to being the school captain was similar to my approach to schoolwork and pretty much everything I did. I was driven, uncompromising, and had high expectations of myself and everyone around me. I threw myself full tilt into the role of school captain, probably to the detriment of my marks.

At some point in Year 12 I decided that I was not going to get the tertiary entrance score I needed to pursue the careers I wanted. I don't remember what prompted this realisation at the time. Nobody told me; I just decided that it was true. Again with the benefit of hindsight, from the safety of my fifties, I can see the slide that began when that memory came back. At the time I was right back in forget-and-deny mode, so I didn't connect those dots. I can connect them now.

I set my sights on teaching. I'd always loved school and if I couldn't be a Pulitzer Prize–winner or Clarence Darrow, I could at least be like Mr Chips. A Bachelor of Education needed a much lower mark than journalism or law – supply and demand, I guess. Until the people tasked with educating our kids are as highly valued as other professions, there will always be a shortage of people drawn to teaching. I hope this changes in my lifetime. Hurry up, eh?

It was during Year 12, when I was seventeen, that I first tried to kill myself. I know that this will come as a shock to the people who knew me. It certainly came as a shock to my parents. I can't really explain what led me to do what I did. It was a Sunday in the middle of the year, and I was studying for a trial HSC exam the next day. History, I think. I didn't expect to end up having my stomach pumped that afternoon. I just remember having an overwhelming sense of dread, as though everything was coming to an end. I couldn't face the exams, nor could I face whatever came after them.

I spent a couple of days in hospital, during which time a social worker came and asked me if I was going to do this again. I said no, and was discharged. No follow-up, no psych assessment. Just a kind of eye-roll at this attention-seeking teenager, and a bit of a slap on the wrist. Of course, this is so different to the way things are handled now. There was no intervention, there was no real understanding of suicidal ideation or depression in kids. I know that my parents were at an utter loss as to what to do.

Had my intention been to seek attention, it failed dismally. A decision was made as a family that we would not speak of it again.

We wouldn't tell anyone; we wouldn't even discuss it among ourselves. The shame was too great. I would surely lose my position as school captain; I would never be able to scrub off the stain it would leave on my reputation.

Was this decision correct? Probably not. But I believe with every fibre in my being that it was made to protect me.

I went back to school. The exams I had missed were rescheduled and I got on with them.

More than a year later, I shared this dark secret with my boyfriend. Maybe I wanted to test him, to see if he could love me even with this twisted part of me inside. He made me promise to never do that again. I kept that promise for as long as I could. I kept it for thirty-two years.

Strange as it may seem, considering how Year 12 unfolded, I look back on my school days mostly with fondness. We were all so different, we girls, but as the years went on we all had, I think, a healthy respect for each other's differences. Now, through the magic of social media, I catch glimpses of our lives. We are doctors, professors, lawyers, town planners, CEOs. We are mothers and grandmothers, daughters and lovers. We are cancer survivors and entrepreneurs, artists and activists and travellers. We have lost parents, partners, friends and children. We've strived and achieved, struggled and grieved, worked and played. We've faced the whole spectrum of what life has to give and to take away, and prevailed. We are fucking glorious.

YOUR TIME STARTS NOW

Crumbed cutlets

When lamb is inexpensive, this is a lovely treat for the family and may just become their favourite dish.

Prep time: 15 minutes
Cooking time: 20 minutes
Serves 4

12 lamb cutlets (1.2 kg)
1 cup plain flour
1 teaspoon salt
¼ teaspoon ground white pepper
2 eggs
2 cups fresh breadcrumbs
Oil, for shallow frying

With a meat mallet, gently hammer the lamb cutlets until they are just less than 1 cm thick.

Combine the flour with salt and pepper in a shallow dish. Beat the eggs with ¼ cup water in another shallow dish. Place crumbs in a third shallow dish.

Set up the cutlets to the left of the other three dishes, to create a production line. Dip the cutlet into the flour, then bathe in the egg mix, and toss generously in the breadcrumbs. Place onto a clean plate.

Meanwhile, heat 3 mm of oil in a large heavy-based chef pan.

Cook 6 cutlets for 4 minutes each side or until golden brown and cooked to medium.

Clean out the pan, add more oil and cook the rest of the cutlets.

Rest the cutlets for 5 minutes or so before serving.

CHAPTER 3
CRAZY LITTLE THING CALLED LOVE

As I'd hoped, once I'd let go of the idea of law and the media, I was accepted into a Bachelor of Education at the University of Sydney, also taking English, history and psychology. Now that I had changed my focus and direction, I was excited for what lay ahead.

In the weeks between school ending and university beginning, I ran into Chris M, a friend who had been the school captain of St Leo's Catholic College, not too far from Hornsby Girls. I'd met Chris via a few school-captainy events and also seen him at church. When I asked him if he was as bored as I was waiting for the year to kick off, he told me he was flat-out with a new youth group that he had started under the banner of St Vincent de Paul. St Vinnies groups were mostly for the more senior among us, but Chris had started this group, with St Vinnies' blessing, especially for young people. I asked if I could come along and see what it was about. It's not hyperbolic to say that this conversation changed the whole course of my life.

I rocked up to my first meeting of the Vinnies youth group in January 1989. The other people in the room were all guys who had gone to St Leo's, and what an interesting group they were. There were about ten of them; a ragtag group including, randomly, a boy who had been in my class at Hornsby Public School. Notably, there were two Micks, who were referred to as Micky C and Micky G; Micky C set fire to small things with his lighter throughout that first meeting. Micky G was the tallest boy I think I had ever met, standing at six foot seven inches – two metres. There was colourful language and boisterous laughter. These guys were rough as guts, but here they were organising blanket and food drives for local people who were struggling. They were volunteering to paint houses and look after gardens for tenants who couldn't manage, who had fallen afoul of their landlords. They were distributing sandwiches in Sydney city in the dead of night. They had hearts of pure gold, and they became my people. Some of them are still my best friends. One of them – Micky G – became far more than that.

What with uni, work at the nursing home, a second job at the Swiss Deli in Glebe and our Vinnies group, I didn't have a whole lot of spare time up my sleeve, but Friday nights were made to party. Our group would go to Hornsby RSL – free before 9 p.m. and with dollar drinks to boot. If I had ten bucks left at the end of the week after all my expenses, I was in for a good night.

Saturday nights we were on a roster to do dawn patrol in the city. We would go to the Matthew Talbot Hostel at 1 a.m., pick up sandwiches and a huge urn, and go to the places where homeless people slept. We covered Central, Town Hall and Wynyard stations; Kings Cross, Circular Quay, the Rocks, Hyde Park. We'd find mostly men, occasionally women, sleeping in doorways, on benches, in boxes and on stairs. Usually they were thankful for some sustenance; sometimes we got yelled at for waking someone up. Once, at Central Station, we were berated by the police for feeding people when they should not be sleeping there. As though they had some kind of choice.

In May 1989, I received a phone call from one of the guys in the Vinnies group. He was distraught – Chris and Micky G had been in a car accident. They had been on their way to Kogarah Oval to see their respective NRL teams play – Chris was a Dragons supporter and Mick was a Western Suburbs Magpies fan. Chris had had to brake suddenly as traffic ahead of him came to a sudden halt. Their minivan veered onto the wrong side of the road and crashed head-on into a four-wheel-drive with a bull bar. The jaws of life were required to get them out. The traffic jam it caused was on the news. Both boys broke both their legs. The other driver was thankfully unhurt.

Chris and Mick were rushed to Westmead Hospital, which happened to be on the same train line as Redfern Station, where I got off to walk to uni. Over the next weeks, it's not a stretch to say that I more often stayed on the train to Westmead and visited the lads than got off at Redfern and went to my lectures and tutorials. Mick, with the more severe injuries, was in hospital for over a month. One of his legs had been broken below the knee. The fibula and tibia in the other had both snapped. His thigh bone required a stainless steel pin, which had to be tailor-made because his legs were so freaking long. I don't think the doctors had ever had a broken-legged six-foot-seven patient before.

One day I walked into Mick's room to see his leg – the worse of the two – on a machine that kept it moving. Up and down, bend and stretch. It looked incredibly painful. The bruises and cuts on his face were healing but his legs would take a lot longer.

'I'm going home on Friday!' he said in a cheerful voice.

I was flabbergasted. 'How? Surely not? Did they say that?'

'No,' he said. 'They said I'll be here for a while yet. But I am going to think positive and get myself out of here.'

And so I began to learn about this extraordinary boy. I already knew he had a beautiful heart, because of how we had met. Over the weeks he was in hospital, while he was a captive audience to this crazy girl who kept skipping uni to visit, I learned everything else I needed to know to fall in love.

Mick was one of six kids, the second eldest, and he lived in Berowra Heights with his mum and dad and siblings. They were another Catholic family, his mum one of eleven kids and his dad one of thirteen. His mother was a seamstress and a quilter, his father a wharfie on the docks in Sydney.

Mick was attending Tech in St Leonards, studying to become a telecommunications trade officer. He was working for OTC, the overseas arm of Telecom, which has since become Telstra. He loved working with his hands and swore he would never have a job that required him to wear a tie. He had an earring and a wicked mullet. He was extremely tall, extremely skinny, he played guitar and he was cool. Way too cool for me, I thought, but the heart wants what it wants.

It was four whole months after his accident that Mick finally cottoned on that I was crushing on him. Or 'had the hots' for him, as we said in the day. Too nervous to make any moves myself, I continued to hang around with the group, waiting and hoping. This was a frustrating time, I remember; for someone so smart in other ways, he really was a bit dense in matters of the heart. Occasionally when we were hanging around with our friends at the RSL, he'd point out girls to me and say, 'She's quite tall, maybe she could be the one?' Once, I lost my patience with him. I drew myself up as tall as a short person can and snapped, 'And why does she have to be tall?' He replied with astonishment, 'Uh – I dunno, just that I'm tall?'

And then, on the night of his nineteenth birthday, 1 September 1989, he pulled off a move that his mates have never let him live down – but to me was perfect. He did The Yawn. Right there in Celebrations nightclub at Hornsby RSL, after a few dollar drinks, he yawned, and stretched, and when his arm came down it was resting tentatively on my shoulder. And the rest, as they say, is history.

I was struggling at uni. I'd gone from a school where everyone knew my name to this giant place with so many faces but none familiar. All the confidence I'd had for most of my high school years ebbed away. I joined no extracurricular groups. I made no friends. I spent my days drifting from lectures to the library to the student union, where I bought hot chips with gravy for a dollar and ate alone. I felt like a ghost impersonating a live person. I would often realise, upon arriving home, that the words I spoke to my parents were in fact the first words I had spoken all day. I was small, invisible and lost. I didn't know what help I needed or how to ask for it. About halfway through my second year I deferred. I never went back.

After I left uni I took a job with Village Roadshow in Pyrmont. I was a booking clerk, which meant I physically booked the big reels of film coming in from overseas studios to be shipped to cinemas around New South Wales. I didn't much enjoy the office environment but the work was undemanding. My boss looked exactly like Glenn Close in *Fatal Attraction*, and she loathed me. I don't know why; at the time I just assumed I was annoying in the awkward, undefined way I felt I had always been. When I was a primary-schooler I dealt with this feeling by marching around the oval singing loudly and declaring my weirdness; now that I was a grown-up person in a grown-up job I tried to tone things down a bit and just get along. This boss wasn't having a bar of me.

The thing I loved about the job was its proximity to the movies. How I loved the movies. There was a theatrette in the Village Roadshow building and sometimes we would get to go to pre-screenings of a big new release. One afternoon there was a screening of *Blood Oath*, the new Bryan Brown film. I'd talked all morning about how much I loved Bryan Brown, and how excited I was for the screening. When it came time to go downstairs, however, my boss told me to stay behind and attend to the phones. I was disappointed, but not as much as I was the next day when I found out that Bryan Brown himself had made a surprise appearance to watch the movie. I was gutted, and I never quite forgave my boss. Still haven't, if I'm honest.

The best part of working at Village Roadshow was the two double passes to the movies up for grabs every week. We were a small office within the organisation, and more often than not I was the only one who wanted the tickets. Mick would come into town after Tech and we'd go see a movie – whatever was on, it didn't matter. It was free! Sometimes if we had extra cash we'd go to a pub in Darling Harbour afterwards, where there was a giant grill to cook your own meat, and an all-you-can-eat salad bar. Happy days.

Mick and I were spending more and more time together. Talking with him was so easy. He would ring me up and tell me the most minute details of his day: who he had sat near on the train, what song he was liking, what he had for lunch. And he listened with rapt attention as I told him the smallest of details about my day too. We laughed at the same stuff. We had some pretty robust conversations about football (me a Balmain Tigers girl, he a Magpies boy), politics, bands. Ours were both blue-collar families; we didn't agree on everything in politics but our views and values were aligned.

Mick had been in a band in high school with a few of his mates, playing covers of the rock acts of the day. The music back then was the best – Chisel, the Oils, the Angels, Aussie Crawl. One night Mick and I were driving along Pennant Hills Road, right outside Loreto Normanhurst, when The Angels' 'Be With You' came on the radio. Mick was not given to displays of affection – it was an effort to get him to hold my hand back in those days – so when he said, 'This is my song for you,' I felt it in my chest and my fingers and toes. It's still up there on my list of favourite songs, and favourite moments.

The first time I had dinner at Mick's house, I was in for a bit of culture shock. For a start, there were so many of them. Brian, Mick's father, and Kath, his mum; Paul, the eldest, and Anthony, just younger than Mick; Elizabeth, Rebecca and baby Ben – the kids ranged in age from twenty to six years old. In my house, nobody began to eat until everyone was ready. The table was set and we said grace. At Mick's place Kath dished the dinners up at the kitchen bench, and one by one everyone would grab a plate, sit down at the table and start eating. The first takers had often finished before Kath had sat down herself. It was rowdy and rambunctious. We served ourselves salads right from the Tupperware on the table. Unfortunately this would be my undoing, the first impression I would leave on this family that I wanted to be a part of. I was trying to get the lid off the tall narrow container of beetroot. What I did not know was that it was a strainer-type thing, where you lifted the handle and the juice drained away so you could take a slice of beetroot off the top without dripping purple juice everywhere. I pulled the handle a bit too hard and beetroot and juice were flung out of the container all at once, flying across the table and landing in a stained purple arc. There was a moment of shocked silence, then roaring laughter. I still get hassled about it at family functions. Build a bridge, guys.

The food at Mick's place had plenty in common with the food at my place, with a few notable differences. In the late '80s, in ordinary suburban families, we were eating a lot of lamb chops – lamb was the cheap meat back then, if you can believe it. Sausages as well. Steak was less usual, being more pricey, and chicken wasn't on the menu as much either in those days. Of course, now that it's more intensively farmed and cheaper to produce, chicken is the cheap meat. Being Catholic, it was fish on Fridays or just no meat at all, a most disappointing day of the week. Meat and three veg was the go-to dinner, with occasional pastas, and curries made with Keen's curry powder creeping into the rotation.

Mum used to read magazines and tried to be extra creative on occasion. Once, she made lentil burgers, which were supposed to be healthy and probably were, but which to my childhood palate were the worst thing I had ever had put in front of me – except, maybe, brussels sprouts. Mick's least favourite meal was, and remains, boiled corned beef with white sauce and cabbage. My favourite meal was crumbed lamb cutlets with mash. It's still up there in the top twenty, I reckon. Mick's favourite, then and now, is lasagne.

One of the notable differences between our two homes was that in Mick's house dessert was always on the menu. Ice cream with tinned or stewed fruit, ice cream with Milo, ice cream with topping; or one of the many beautiful things Kath baked regularly. We weren't a big dessert family at my house, unless Mum was having a dinner party. Then she would roll out those faves of hers: strawberry shortcake, cream horns, sherry log.

Mick's and my social life consisted of going out together, hanging at each others' houses, or getting about with the Vinnies group. Two of Mick's best friends from school and Vinnies, Adam and Daniel, tagged along with him and me so often that Dad would joke he was never quite sure which one of the three was my boyfriend. We went to backyard parties, barbecues, the beach, bushwalks, camping trips.

One night, Mick dropped me home after we'd been out, kissed me goodbye (standing two steps down from me so I could reach his face) and made the fifteen-minute drive back to his house. Then our phone rang – the big curly-corded unit in the front hallway, positioned so that everyone could hear every bloody word you said. It was Mick. 'Go outside,' he said. 'Look at the moon! It's huge! You should see the colour of it! You'll love it!'

There was something about this call that settled around me, soft, like a blanket. An understanding, a realisation. A certainty. This nineteen-year-old boy, awed by the moonrise and wanting to share it with me – he was my human being. Here he was.

These are the years I look back on with rose-tinted nostalgia; the ones when everything felt exciting and a little bit dangerous, where anything could happen, where I'd laugh till I cried and couldn't believe my life. How had I ended up belonging to this incongruous bunch? Guys who hung out at pubs and smoked and swore, and tended to the gardens of the elderly and collected donations, and gave up their weekends to feed people sleeping in the street. It was a far cry from my high-school life. Leaving uni didn't feel like a regret, but a relief; for the first time I wasn't striving to achieve good marks or trying to outperform my peers. I felt free. I freaking loved it.

I had a little white Mazda 626 and Mick had a red VK Commodore. Since his accident, when he had been a passenger, he far preferred to be the driver, so we spent way more time in the Commodore. That thing saw some action. They don't make suspensions like they used to. I mean, they might. I wouldn't know. I haven't tested any car suspensions in a while. I'll pop it on my to-do list.

While I was working in Pyrmont I moved into a share house in Wollstonecraft. I was nineteen and ready for my own space. The best thing about this, besides the proximity to my work and Mick's Tech, was an all-you-can-eat pasta restaurant at Crows Nest, a walk away from my door. It had plastic chequered tablecloths and free jugs of cordial, and you ordered the shape of your pasta and the sauce you wanted, as much as you wanted, for eight bucks. It was the kick-off point for a few good nights out.

It was while I lived out of home that I first really got a taste for cooking – and cooking on an extreme budget, too. I could turn a couple of dollars into a really decent feed. Working at the Swiss Deli, I got staff discount on the smallgoods, so I would bring home little parcels of mortadella, or olives, or soft, ripe brie, or marinated artichokes, and turn them into a meal. The first thing I practised regularly was pasta. Before too long Mick didn't want to go to the pasta place anymore as he liked mine better.

It was in this share house that I really started to cook regularly. At home, Mum had mostly taken care of meals except on the thankfully rare occasions that Dad would give it a crack. I was, for the most part, deemed too messy to be in the kitchen, a sentiment that would be echoed many years later by the *MasterChef* judges. It wasn't until I moved up the Central Coast, into my own house with my own kitchen, that things really got underway; but the quest to make yummy dinners really started in that big old Wollstonecraft house.

Mick loved it. He still lived at home but spent a lot of time at my place, not far from where he attended TAFE. We had some great date nights in that house, eating whatever I had rustled up and watching the TV that my dad had rescued from a council pick-up pile. The picture tube was nearly gone so I had to turn it on half an hour before we wanted to watch anything, and the pictures were almost black and white but in shades of green. It did the job.

After about nine months with Village Roadshow I decided to look for something else to do for a living, preferably not in an office. Without a degree I couldn't pursue teaching. I still loved the idea of working with young people but just couldn't find my way back to university. Fortuitously, around this time I received a phone call from environmentalist, teacher, musician and ex-nun Monica Brown. She had become aware of me through my music at church, and was looking for someone to work in her music ministry, delivering workshops to kids in primary school.

Anyone of my vintage will remember the 1980s TV commercial featuring a little boy singing 'Hello, My God'. That was Monica's. Emmaus Productions, her company, went into primary schools and presented environment, peace and justice workshops, using music, storytelling, clowning and drama. For the really little kids I would take Alexander Monkey, my beloved hand puppet, to talk about kindness to each other and caring for the earth.

It was the early 1990s and the biggest issues facing the environment at that time in the public's consciousness were the hole in the ozone layer, oil spills in the ocean and global warming caused by air pollution. Emmaus Productions workshops empowered primary-school kids to reduce their own impact on the planet by not littering, and to talk to their parents about the importance of reducing the use of cars and the incinerator in the backyard, and about the harm caused by pouring oil down the sink.

Recycling had just started in my area, but it was limited to newspapers, which had to be tied with string and left on the kerb for collection by the council. The term 'carbon footprint' hadn't been invented. Back then, caring about the environment was a bit of an out-there, hippy, tree-hugging way to be. It certainly wasn't mainstream – Monica was well ahead of her time in that regard. And all these years later, all this science and knowledge and proof later, there are still people who refuse to get it.

Monica's ministry spanned New Zealand, Ireland, the UK, the US and Canada, and in 1992 Monica and the Emmaus team took her music on the road. I was her backing vocalist for the trip. We went to England and Ireland, Canada and the USA on a ten-week tour. It was mind-blowing to start a song and have hundreds of kids take up the tune and know every word.

There wasn't a whole lot of money in this line of work. Not much at all, to be honest, but it was work I believed in. It had purpose. It was good. But with bills to pay, I took on a second job waitressing in Pennant Hills. The Black Stump was an iconic restaurant chain back in the 1980s and '90s. It was pretty much the go-to if you wanted a decent restaurant meal, billing itself as 'providing quality service, great steak dishes and fine wine'. It had classics like prawns wrapped in bacon, steak Diane, the New York cut. Your steak came with chips or jacket potato, roast tomato and corn on the cob. Once your plate landed I'd be there asking if you'd like butter or sour cream with your potato, French or hot English mustard for your steak. Filtered coffee was bottomless, topped up as many times as you wanted. Or you could order a cappuccino, which we were trained to make with the froth popping right up over the rim of the cup, like a soufflé.

The kitchen was a reflection of how kitchen culture generally was back then – fast, hot, crude, rough. The divide between back of house and front of house was real. The banter was cutting. The pace was lightning quick and the steaks were great. It wasn't for the faint-hearted and most certainly wouldn't fly today, but I wasn't faint-hearted and mostly enjoyed the adrenalin, the verbal fencing and even the dull ache in my legs at the end of a busy shift.

CRAZY LITTLE THING CALLED LOVE

I worked at the Black Stump for four years, long enough to see the transition from the chain's heyday to the beginning of the end. Once shop-a-docket, 2-for-1 deals hit the tills, cost-cutting measures were inevitably taken. I was sad to see the drop in standards. Salad dressings, once prepared fresh, began to arrive in huge plastic bags. No longer could we offer tomato and corn, now the customer had to choose one or the other. Plates got smaller. It must have been noticed by the public too, as, one by one, the restaurants closed down.

After I'd been working with Monica for two years, she changed focus in her ministry and those of us on her school teams were given her blessing to create a similar business to fill the gap. We called ours Karis, and there were five of us. For the next two years I worked on a team with Chris D, a mad musician and guitarist with a rich history to offer the high-school kids. We were booked by Catholic schools to run their retreat days and school camps. We travelled all over Australia to schools and venues, working with boys, girls and co-ed schools, facilitating conversations about peers vs parents and social justice issues. It was challenging much of the time – it's no small feat to stand in front of a hall filled with Year 10 boys staring sullenly at you as you try to get them enthused about a day of group activities and reflections. Chris played the electric guitar and I played the bass guitar. Music was how we got the kids into it – we played whatever was current at the time. In a boys school, it would take quite a while before we could break through to them and get them motivated and involved. In a girls school, within one millisecond of their favourite song kicking off, they'd be on their feet dancing and having a blast. Teenage girls were, and I'm guessing still are, much easier to engage in that sort of thing. Less inhibited, when it came to music and performance, by what their peers thought of them; more willing to put it all out there and have fun. I decided back then, long before I had my own family, that if I ever had sons they'd go to a co-ed school.

In between my work in schools and at the Black Stump, I sought out daytime weekend work as well. I acquired my own sound gear so I could sing at weddings and funerals. Using Cubase, a brand of musical production software, I programmed my own backing music on the computer. I had to save my pennies for the equipment; I had a beautiful Korg sound module, which could transform a simple keyboard into an orchestra or a drum kit or a fanfare of trumpets. I composed and recorded bespoke songs for brides. I clowned at kids' parties. I did calligraphy for wedding invitations and place cards, back before every household had a printer. This work came as a result of hand-made and photocopied flyers, which I dropped into shops and letterboxes, and eventually through word-of-mouth. I also started house cleaning and had a couple of regular families.

I did a few gigs as a roadie as well, as part of a crew that pulled down concerts when they were finished. We usually caught the second half of the show before we had to start working, seeing some great acts this way. My favourite and the most memorable was the 1992 Prince 'Diamonds and Pearls' concert at the Sydney Cricket Ground. After everyone left, the oval was a sea of empty Southern Comfort bottles.

Roadie work was heavy and tough but I had become pretty tough myself. I'd developed muscles and calluses from the heavy lifting; and I'd grown a tough hide from dealing with blokes in a blokey work environment. The money was good and because the work happened late at night, it didn't interfere with my other commitments. Sleep was for suckers, anyway.

Put all together, these jobs almost added up to a living wage.

CRAZY LITTLE THING CALLED LOVE

When Mick and I had been together for nearly four years, I tentatively raised the subject of The Future with him. I was twenty-two, after all. I wanted to know what he saw as happening next for us. Mick kind of batted away the question, which was not the response I was seeking. When I pressed him on the subject, he told me he wasn't ready to talk about it. I suggested that he get ready. I was giving him my prime years, dammit – were we headed somewhere?

What I didn't know was that he already had an engagement ring on lay-by and was waiting for his tax return to pay it off. I reckon he'd have been within his rights to tell me that and put an end to my hectoring. But he kept his poker face and let me believe that I was possibly putting all of my love and hopes and expectations into someone who might not ever want to commit. At the end of the day, though, he was my person. I couldn't make a picture in my head of life without him.

I didn't have to wait too long. For our four-year anniversary, Mick took me out to dinner at the revolving restaurant at the top of Centrepoint Tower. It was a big deal, a special occasion. We had placed our order. I can't remember exactly what it was but I recall that the restaurant served Australian native foods and Mick ordered an emu and kangaroo entrée, prompting a joke about eating the coat of arms. The city spun by ever so slowly in the window. Four years. All my adult life.

'Jules,' Mick said. His face in the dim lights was whiter than usual. He had something in his hand. 'I love you, and I want to spend my—'

'Your champagne, sir!' came an enthusiastic voice, from a waiter bearing a bottle. Mick looked up at him, stricken, then back to me. Not to be deterred, he took a deep breath and continued: '—and I want to spend my life with you.'

The poor waiter, still holding the champagne, tiptoed backwards with cartoon-like exaggeration, and disappeared from sight.

'Will you marry me?'

I didn't need time to think it over. I did, however, need to go to the bathroom and soap my knuckle to get the ring on. A sparkling diamond with two tiny diamonds nestled to one side, it was the most beautiful thing I had ever seen. I couldn't take my eyes off it and for many weeks used exaggerated hand gestures so that people would notice it.

It was ages before the waiter came back, bearing the bottle once again, and asked tentatively, 'So . . . are we . . . is it . . . do we want the champagne, sir?'

I think our goofy, relieved, ecstatic grins answered that question. And champagne was had.

It's such an exciting time, getting ready to live your own life as a young couple, independent and looking to a future in which anything seems possible. I was building a life with my best friend on earth, our futures laid out like a blank page in front of us. If we could have skipped ahead and seen some of the things in store for us, we wouldn't have believed it.

For now, we had two delighted sets of parents, and some very happy siblings, too. Knowing how much it would mean to him, Mick had made the old-fashioned gesture of asking my dad's blessing to marry me. Dad didn't even tell Mum, which I thought was pretty impressive. Mick's parents were thrilled too – his dad in particular had taken a liking to me and would tell Mick not to let me get away. My little sister Debbie adored Mick; I mean, everyone did. It was wonderful and annoying in equal measure. I used to joke that my family liked him better than they like me, which falls into the category of 'many a true word was spoken in jest'.

Mick and I started searching for units to rent together, preferably around Hornsby, which was near enough to where we both needed to be. Mick was still at Tech but Mum advised us that if we could find any way to buy a place instead of renting, we should do that. Coming from my Catholic mother, this kind of surprised me because we were not yet married. I had underestimated how much she loved this fiancé of mine and probably wanted to make sure I didn't bugger it up and let him disappear.

She was right, of course, and I'll always be grateful for the advice. For a similar amount as it would have cost us to pay rent, we could repay a mortgage. We just needed a deposit, and to convince a bank that we were good for a loan.

Here's where one of the substantive differences between Mick and I became obvious. He had savings. I had debt – a HECS debt, from my incomplete degree. Although I wouldn't have to pay this off until I reached a certain salary threshold, it was still included in any loan discussion with a bank. Mick had a regular job with a regular salary, alongside his study, while my income was confetti that rained down from all my weird, varied and poorly paid jobs. Getting a loan was hard, mostly because of me, but we eventually talked our way into a mortgage.

We soon realised we couldn't afford a house in the area we'd grown up in, and had to look further afield. Mick talked me into considering the Central Coast, which I thought was too far away from home. I guess I didn't really realise that wherever we settled would *be* home. I certainly didn't know that I would fall in love with the Coast so completely that I would never want to move back to Sydney even if we could have afforded to.

We spent a day up on the coast with a real estate agent who took us to a whole bunch of different properties. None was right. We didn't have a huge amount to spend but I knew that I wanted the kitchen to be open to the living areas. It surprised me how many homes had kitchens tucked away from everything. I already knew I'd be spending a lot of time in that room and it needed to be connected to the living areas of the house. It needed to be a hub. The headquarters. The heart.

Eventually we pulled up on Maple Street in Wyoming, in front of the ugliest place we'd seen all day. The real estate agent actually said to us, 'You won't want this one.' It looked like the back of the house was facing the street. The building was a reddish brick; there was no garden, no front porch, not a single redeeming feature about the place. But something happened when we went through the front door. Something gurgled in my gut and a quick sideways glance at Mick told me that he felt it too. It was perfect. Not perfect-perfect, but perfect for us. It was a mixture of amazing bones and dreadful decorating; a double-brick, concrete-floored, split-level fortress with an interior cobbled together from what looked like a tile, timber and brickyard sale. Someone had painted the whole place pink, including the ceilings. There were exposed brick walls, louvred doors and a tiled benchtop in the kitchen – so many tiles! The backyard was completely concreted, but, my god, there were views across the valley from the balcony outside the wide west-facing windows. There was an awesome huge downstairs rumpus room, and a pool, which we hadn't dared to hope for but really wanted. The kitchen opened on to the living areas, just as I wanted it to. And there was a vibe, a hum that quickened my pulse and told me I was home.

After we looked at this house we sent the real estate agent on his way and drove to the beach. We didn't talk until we were sitting on the sand.

'That's the one, isn't it?'

'That's the one.'

CRAZY LITTLE THING CALLED LOVE

It was 1994. The house was $165,000.

When we moved in, the first thing we did was buy ten-litre cans of ceiling white and paint the whole place. Once the hot pink was gone the house looked twice the size we'd thought it was. We filled it with second-hand furniture we bought from relatives and garage sales. There was no money for renovations beyond painting, so we learned to live with the yellow-and-brown tiled bathroom, the weird gaps in the kitchen cupboards and all the other little quirks the house had. We didn't care. It was ours.

We hadn't been in the house for more than a few weeks when Mick's dad died of a heart attack. He was forty-nine years old and there had been no forewarning. I took the phone call while Mick was out and had to tell him when he got home. My way with words abandoned me and I did an awful job of it. The shock and grief were enormous for us all, but I think especially for Mick's youngest brother, Benny, who was only ten.

For the rest of that year Mick and I were like two ships passing in the night. He was commuting to Sydney for work, and doing his diploma in electrical engineering a couple of nights a week. I was still working in high schools, and driving to Pennant Hills four nights a week to wait tables. Mick was asleep by the time I got home and he left for work before I woke up. We saw each other on weekends and communicated via notes on the kitchen bench the rest of the time. When we were together, we planned for our upcoming wedding.

YOUR TIME STARTS NOW

Lasagne

Whether you're cooking for a crowd, or trying to impress your very favourite person, this recipe – developed with trial and error, love and devotion – is the one you want.

Prep time: 1 hour (15 minutes with pre-made sauces)
Cooking time: 5 hours (one hour with pre-made sauces)
Serves 16

2 quantities Bolognese sauce (see below)
2 quantities bechamel sauce (see below)
3 x 500 g packets instant lasagne sheets
500 g grated tasty cheese

Bolognese sauce

Prep time: 15 minutes
Cook time: 4–5 hours in slow cooker or 2 hours on stovetop
Serves 6–8

1 tsp olive oil
2 brown onions
2 cloves garlic
500 g beef mince
500 g pork mince
2 x 810 g tins crushed tomatoes
1 tablespoon dried oregano leaves
2 tablespoons sugar
1 teaspoon salt

In a large non-stick pan, heat olive oil over a medium heat. Add garlic and onion and stir until soft but not brown. Add mince to the pan and brown. Using a wooden spoon, make sure you get rid of any lumps in the mince.

CRAZY LITTLE THING CALLED LOVE

If you have a slow cooker, put the mince in, along with the tomatoes, oregano, sugar and salt. Simmer uncovered on the high setting for 4-5 hours, stirring occasionally. The sauce initially appears quite runny and not a very rich colour. As it cooks and reduces, it achieves a thick consistency and a beautiful red colour. You will know when it's ready – it becomes very aromatic.

Cooking the Bolognese on the stove top is equally effective but make sure it doesn't burn on the bottom of the pot. Keep it over a very low heat, uncovered, and stir it frequently for around 2 hours.

Béchamel sauce
Prep time: 5 minutes
Cook time: 15 minutes
Makes more than 1 litre

50 g butter
50 g flour
3 ½ cups (875 ml) milk
1 tablespoon Dijon mustard
200 g tasty cheese, grated
Salt and pepper

In a large pot, melt butter and add flour over medium heat. Stir with a wooden spoon until mixture gathers into a dough. Continue to stir for another minute or so (this begins to cook the flour).

Add a little milk – about ¼ cup. This will incorporate fairly quickly into the dough, which will come away from the sides of the pan. Add another ¼ cup milk, and repeat until all the milk has been added. Using a whisk to stir in the milk helps prevent lumps forming in the mixture.

Stir in the mustard, then add the cheese and stir until it melts. Taste, and season with salt and pepper if required.

YOUR TIME STARTS NOW

Preheat oven to 180°C.

In a large baking dish, or two medium baking dishes, ladle Bolognese sauce over the base. There needs to be enough to cover the base but keep it a thin layer (about 5 mm). Over this, lay some lasagne sheets. Depending on the shape of your baking dish, you may need to snap the sharp corners off the sheets so they lay neatly on the sauce.

Ladle more Bolognese sauce over the pasta then ladle cheese sauce on top of that. Carefully spread the cheese sauce to cover the meat.

Scatter a handful of cheese over the layer.

Place another layer of pasta on top and repeat the Bolognese and cheese sauces, and another scattering of cheese.

Place another layer of pasta, then ladle remaining cheese sauce over the top. Generously cover this with the rest of the cheese.

Bake for 45 minutes covered with foil, and a further 15 minutes uncovered or until golden brown and bubbling on top. Insert a skewer at several points to ensure the pasta has cooked through.

CHAPTER 4
WHITE WEDDING

Mick and I were married on 21 January 1995, at Our Lady Queen of Peace in Normanhurst. I wrote my own wedding song and recorded it and all the hymns for the wedding Mass. My bridesmaids wore pink dresses that my mother-in-law-to-be sewed. My dress was a dream; a full skirt of white organza over a hooped petticoat, with an off-the-shoulder bodice covered in heavy guipure lace. I made my own tiara from beads and wire, and my mum did all the church flowers. My wedding car was a pink convertible Cadillac driven by an Elvis impersonator, and our reception was at Asquith Golf Club.

I will never, as long as I live, forget the look on Mick's face as Dad walked me down the aisle. His face was white as a piece of paper, with an about-to-faint sheen. But his eyes, the way he looked at me, the love I felt radiating up the aisle and into my soul – I only hope that my eyes were conveying the exact same thing to him.

Everyone had an absolute blast at the reception and even our Vinnies mates, the Berowra boys, behaved themselves. Until the end of the night. After we'd said goodbye to all the guests and pulled out of the car park, we could see the tribute they had organised – a twenty-one-bum salute. There they were all along the road, pants around their ankles, mooning the car. Except for one guy, Pottsie, who was so pissed he'd only managed to drop his dacks and was just standing there with his willy out and a big grin on his face. Mick and I laughed all the way to the hotel.

We honeymooned in Thailand – the way travel was priced back then, it was cheaper to go to Phuket than to a Queensland resort. Our honeymoon was the start of my love affair with food from other cultures, and my obsession with recreating it in my own kitchen. I was blown away by the flavour, freshness and vibrancy of Thai food. Nowadays, we are spoiled for choice when it comes to creatively named Thai restaurants, but in 1995 it was quite a new cuisine on the scene. Newly married with a mortgage, Mick and I were skating on thin ice financially. We couldn't afford to eat out, so I knew that if I wanted nice food, I'd have to make it myself. And I did want nice food. I relied heavily on a small, narrow cookbook that I found in an op shop. Some of the recipes I couldn't make because of an unavailability of certain ingredients where we lived: galangal, belacan, Thai green chillies – these weren't around on the Central Coast in the 1990s. But I could get the fish sauce, lemongrass, lime leaves I needed, and using ginger instead of galangal and normal birds-eye chillies I was able to put together some curries that came pretty close to what I had eaten on my honeymoon.

As the years went by, and more food shows were on television, and we gained access to the whole world through the internet, cooking the food of other cultures became much more accessible. I'm well aware that nowadays cooking food from a culture not your own can be called out as cultural appropriation. I prefer to call it celebration, and appreciation. I never claim to be the master in a tradition that's not mine, just that I have found a way to cook delicious food

WHITE WEDDING

with the ingredients we have available to us. I am so grateful for the cultural richness of this country and the opportunity that we have to learn about different ways of life through food. Besides, my heritage is Irish and colonial Australian – if I don't take on some other cultural influences I'm at risk of a vitamin deficiency.

Mick and I decided we should probably wait a little while to have a family, at least until we were more financially secure and able to afford living on one income. Great plan, poorly executed. Within a few weeks I was pregnant.

I had always planned to give up my work with Karis, with all the travelling that it entailed, once I was married. The routine during the year prior to the wedding, barely seeing each other between work and study and sleep, wasn't a long-term way to live. I was ready for the next adventure and began looking for work that would keep me closer to home. I would take just about anything until the right job came along.

The first job I landed was in a call centre, selling printed personalised items to businesses – branded pens and coldy holders and so forth. I was put in the cigarette lighter department, cold-calling unimpressed, sometimes furious businesspeople in the middle of their day. I was a terrible salesperson. In fact, in the six weeks that I worked there, I only made one sale, and I am pretty sure that the buyer was stoned. I admitted defeat on the cigarette-lighter-sales front and quit. I don't think any tears were shed on either side.

Not long after that, I received notice that I had landed a job as a senior youth worker for the now-defunct Department of Juvenile Justice. Since my role at Karis had fallen under the banner of youth work, I'd applied for the job thinking it would be a fitting one for me. I would soon learn that 'senior youth worker' in the juvenile justice system really meant 'guard'. This of course happened nearly thirty years ago. I was twenty-four. I haven't worked in the juvenile justice sector for decades, so I can't say for sure if it's faring any better now than then, but by god I hope so.

I was told that I would undergo training before I started the job, but only a couple of days after it was offered to me I got a phone call asking me to cover a 10 p.m. to 6 a.m. shift, starting that night. I was told not to worry about training – I'd be sent along on a course in due time. I was asked to not wear anything provocative.

Kariong Juvenile Detention Centre, near Gosford on the Central Coast, was widely recognised as being a minimum security facility where the boys were pretty much free to roam. To this day I'm not sure how many locals know that there is a maximum security unit on the same property. It was the first purpose-built secure unit for young male offenders who were deemed difficult to manage, and those with a history of escape. It was also used to assess juveniles who'd been charged with serious offences.

That was where I was going to work – a place reserved for the most violent and least manageable young detainees in New South Wales.

My first night I drove down a secluded bush road until I got to a car park outside high fences with razor wire. I entered through a series of locked coded doors. I was shown around by a man who took great delight in shocking me with the stories of the boys who were incarcerated in this place. Boys who had committed some terrible crimes. One was here for setting fire to a homeless man in a park. Another for being an accomplice to killing a youth worker. Another had stabbed someone at a crowded dance party. Three were in for a brutal home invasion where the mother was raped in front of her tied-up husband.

Obviously, these stories were disturbing, and it seemed clear that the gentleman telling them was trying very hard to dissuade me from this job. 'We had a woman do this once,' he said. 'She lasted a day.' I felt a cold horror at some of his tales, but was determined not to show that to this tough guy who thought he could run me off.

I soon found out that I was the only female senior youth worker at the centre. Many of the guys working there were ex-bouncers and ex-cops. Not one of them was thrilled to have a woman alongside them in the job.

My role included escorting the prisoners from one place to another within the facility. Groups to school, groups to work, groups to sport. I set up for meals and packed down afterwards, counting the cutlery and making sure there were no arguments among the boys about what to watch on TV after dinner. I locked the doors on the cells and performed regular checks on the kids throughout the night.

What I learned during this time was that very few of these boys were what I would truly consider bad. I only ever met three who really frightened me, who made me think that perhaps they were irredeemable. Most were just boys who'd been shaped by their circumstances. Destructive boys to be sure, stupid boys, angry boys, silly boys, funny boys. Boys who'd followed other people into terrible situations, and some who'd led other people into terrible situations. Boys who had caused so much harm and some boys who'd caused hardly any harm at all.

There were far too many Indigenous kids in the place, a much greater percentage than there were in the community. I was struck, even back then, at the disparity between the seriousness of the crimes committed by the boys of various other ethnicities, compared with the trivial matters that had seen the Indigenous boys incarcerated. It blew my mind then and even more so now, decades later, when we should be doing so much better.

I was particularly fond of one boy, Jack*. He was irrepressibly good-natured, funny, endearing. His crime was to have conducted a ram-raid on a Payless supermarket with a shopping trolley, during which he stole some tinned sardines. Unfortunately for Jack, he was cheeky, and the bosses didn't like it. So his status as an inmate kept getting escalated and escalated until he ended up in this detention centre for the worst juvenile criminal offenders in the state.

One day Jack was on cleaning duty, vacuuming. I was supervising. He pulled the tube off the vacuum cleaner and started playing didgeridoo. It sounded amazing. I was thoroughly enjoying it until one of my colleagues came in, yelled at him to get back to work, and put him on report.

Jack used to make his cup of tea with seven and one-quarter teaspoons of sugar, the last quarter being measured so carefully it always made me laugh. I wonder where he is now. I hope he's all right.

Nights were the quietest so I was quite happy to do the 10 to 6 shift. There was only one worker per unit during this shift as everyone was locked in their cell. Our job was to peer in through each cell window at regular intervals and keep a log stating that every detainee was still in place. I was shocked to see some of the other guards turn up with their pillow and doona, ready to fill in the whole night's log in the first half an hour and then get a solid night's sleep. I guess part of the reason I was unpopular with my co-workers was that . . . I actually did the bloody work.

The detainees were mostly under eighteen, but a few were older, serving out their sentences in juvy. One of them was a violent, fiercely intelligent, terrifying young man. I came to his door one night during routine checks. Before I could shine my torch in through his window, there was a flare of light and he was staring out of the dark straight at me, a lighter under his chin.

---

* Asterisked names in this chapter are pseudonyms.

WHITE WEDDING

I screamed and jumped back, and he sneered. I told him he was not supposed to have that lighter. But we weren't allowed to enter the cells alone, to protect us from both physical harm and false allegations, so all I could do was to report the incident to the chief. The next day his cell was searched. When I next passed him in the unit he said, very quietly, 'You ratted on me, Miss.'

My blood was rushing in my ears, but I met his eyes and replied, 'You knew I would.'

He cracked a grin. 'Yeah, I did,' he said. 'All good.'

Another night I was told by the chief that one boy was on suicide watch so I must check him every five minutes. The boy wouldn't lie down, he wouldn't sleep. I tried to talk to him through the door but he wouldn't talk, either.

At one point in the night, hunched over, he looked at me strangely. I felt as though something was up and called on a co-worker. Together we entered his room. There was a broken plastic pen on the floor. I picked it up. 'Where did you get this?' He didn't answer. He was holding his jumper over his hands.

'Can you please push your sleeves up?' I asked. He held his arms out to me. He had cut himself with shards from the broken pen. There was blood. I held his hands in mine and tried to comfort him. Medical attention was sought.

My co-worker, on seeing my bloody hands, said, 'I'd wash them good if I were you. That boy has HIV.'

I can't describe the ice-cold shard of terror that went through me. My baby. Dear god, my baby. I scrubbed at my hands with the hottest water I could run, until they were raw. I studied them for days for any cut or nick that could have let the virus in. I was hyper-vigilant and wondered if I should get a blood test; how long the virus would take to show up in a blood test. My knowledge was so limited, my fear enormous.

The boy was transferred out of our unit. Some time later I asked one of the counsellors about his health. I asked if he was doing okay, and if his HIV was under control. The counsellor looked at me quizzically and asked me where I had heard that he had HIV. No inmate, at that time, had it.

Among my colleagues were men who refused to be put on a shift with me because they claimed I'd be unable to back them up if there was a riot. Some of these blokes you could knock over with a stiff breeze but I'm the one who apparently can't hold my own. Luckily at this stage nobody knew that I was pregnant or there would have been a revolt.

By then I'd been asked several times if I'd had my self-defence training with Mitchell*, one of the other senior youth workers. I said no, I haven't had any training. I'm waiting for my training course. And the response was, no, not your training course, your *self-defence* training with Mitchell.

It became quite a frequent question, so when Mitchell approached me and told me it was time for my training session in the gym, I willingly went with him. I soon noticed that he kept moving us right into the corner of the gym, even though there was nobody else in there. Then he showed me how to put handcuffs on, even though we didn't carry handcuffs. He put them on me. He showed me how to hurt a handcuffed prisoner in a way that they couldn't prove. He showed me by doing it to me, and it did hurt.

He showed me how to subdue a prisoner by bending their fingers backwards. He showed me by doing it to me, and it did subdue me. He performed a martial arts move on me that put me on the floor. At this point I started to fear for the baby in me. He put his boot on my hip and was leaning on it with a good deal of weight. I was very close to telling him that I was pregnant and to leave me alone.

I had a small moment of triumph when he asked if I understood everything I'd been shown. I was so shaken; I was bruised. I asked for clarification about the technique of bending back someone's fingers. I bent back his finger, and I hurt him.

A couple of weeks later I was supervising the kids in the gym and the guard I was on duty with said to me, 'If you ever need to mess any of them up, come right up here into this corner. The cameras can't see up here.'

I must be a bit slow on the uptake, because it was only then that I realised my self-defence training session was not department-approved.

One morning I was at a team meeting with all the blokes, and they were passing around pornographic magazines. They were kind of looking sideways at me and laughing, waiting to see if I would react. I didn't. Then one of them started telling a story about how he'd got a blowjob off a girl in return for a lift home and a loaf of bread. I remained blank-faced, unimpressed, unshockable. I then got called out of the room by the chief, who told me I could miss the rest of the meeting. He said, 'You shouldn't have to put up with that shit.' And I agreed with him. But I also thought it wasn't me who should have been removed from that room.

A new guy started. Ross* was a big, burly bloke with the kind of dumb, menacing temperament you come across in men who don't have much to offer in the way of personality or intellect. He hit it off straight away with some of the more obnoxious youth workers. He would stand over me, mock me for being a woman and unequal to the job, generally grunt and strut and showboat. He was an unimaginative bully. He was too moronic to be scary, but he was annoying.

One day he stood in a doorway, preventing me from going through it. I said, 'Excuse me, please.'

He didn't move.

I said, 'Could you get out of my way, please?'

And he said to me, 'What if I don't?'

I said – slowly, so he would understand – 'I will punch you in the nuts.'

He moved, with dumb surprise on his dumb face.

Another time, I asked for his help to unstack the tall pile of tables ready for dinner.

He sneered at me and said, 'Equal work for equal pay, woman.'

I looked at him and said nice and slowly once again, 'I asked you to get them down because you're tall and I am not. I didn't ask you to get them down with your dick.'

I'd never spoken to a colleague in this way before, and I never have since. But sometimes you've just got to meet people where they are. He got the tables down.

A few good guys worked in the unit, who got on with me and seemed to understand that shifts went okay when I was around because I didn't agitate the boys. I spoke to them with respect. Their punishment was being locked away from their people, from their communities, from society. It was not my role to inflict more punishment.

But many of my colleagues felt differently. One morning a guard opened a new packet of biscuits and put them in the kids' tin. Before returning the tin to the cupboard, he shook it so hard he smashed all the biscuits. I asked him, 'Why on earth would you do that?' He said, 'They don't deserve nice biscuits.'

You wonder why these kids end up really hating authority.

Some time after I'd started, we had a staff meeting where the bosses said to us, 'You're forbidden from talking about the personal details of your colleagues around the inmates. They can hold on to any piece of information that you give them and find you when

WHITE WEDDING

they get out to use it against you, or they can pass that information to people outside. It is dangerous to tell them anything.'

Not long after this I had a meeting with these same big bosses to inform them I was pregnant. I told them I still needed to work and that I intended to do so for as long as I physically could. I explained that I wanted the information to be kept confidential for the time being, until I started to show and the subject became unavoidable. The big boss – Feral*, as he was known unaffectionately by staff and detainees – asked me what I would do if the inmates found out before then. I said I would probably feel too vulnerable to continue in my role.

A couple of things happened after this.

The next day, when I turned up to work, one of the young inmates, a gang member who had been convicted of murder and was awaiting extradition to Victoria to face more murder charges, said to me, 'Congratulations, Miss.'

'What for?' I asked.

'I hear you're having a baby.'

I said to him, 'Where did you hear that?'

And he said, 'The boss told us.' Apparently a meeting had been called almost straight after the one the bosses had with me, with a detainee rep from each unit brought into it, each of whom was told to be respectful and careful with me because I was having a baby.

I had mostly borne the insults and inequalities quietly. I knew that any complaint from me would only confirm the beliefs of my colleagues that this was no place for a woman, that I couldn't cut it, that I was too weak or ineffectual for the role. 'If you can't stand the heat, get out of the kitchen' was said to me, apropos of nothing, more than once. So I just knuckled down and did the job to my very best ability. But this, this betrayal of my most important and private information, after I'd specifically asked that it was not shared with anyone, was too bloody far.

I flew up to the office. I was spitting with rage. I addressed Feral, and his smug sidekick whose position I can't remember but he was always hanging around with the boss. I said, 'If you think you got rid of me by doing that, think again. I'll be leaving this place when I'm giving birth and not a minute sooner.'

However, as a casual worker I had no power at all in this situation. I was instantly dropped from forty-plus hours a week to twenty. I was put on four-hour shifts, the dinner shift – the one in which there was most to do and the shortest time to do it in. But I was true to my word – I stayed anyway. Funnily enough the inmates did give me respect. They would catch themselves swearing, and apologise; or not roughhouse too close to me; or pull up a chair for me to sit on if I was standing around. By the time I left even a few of my colleagues had accepted me as well.

Five years after my time there, Kariong Juvenile Justice Centre was brought to the attention of the New South Wales Parliament via a long tabled letter. There were allegations of 'poor administration, lack of transparency, ongoing blatant cronyism, harassment of female staff, and lack of staff discipline'. In all the time I'd worked at Kariong, I was the only female senior youth worker. More must have followed in my footsteps, and it seemed they had fared no better than me. The rot was exposed. I was glad.

On my last day in the unit one of the boys said to me, 'I hope you have a girl, Miss.' When I asked why, he said sadly, 'Cause she can't end up in here.'

And with that I walked out of the razor-wired walls and coded doors for the last time and started getting ready for my new life as a mum.

WHITE WEDDING

Thai green chicken curry

If you find yourself falling in love with a cuisine, do what you can to learn how to make it. Not all ingredients are available everywhere; use what you have at your disposal to make your own version of dishes that bring back beautiful memories.

Prep time: 15 minutes
Cooking time: 15 minutes
Serves 4

½ bunch coriander
1 stalk lemongrass, white part finely chopped
2 small red chillies, seeded and chopped (use Thai green chillies if available)
2 cloves garlic
5 cm piece ginger, chopped
2 tablespoons peanut oil
600 g chicken thigh fillets, sliced
2 kaffir lime leaves, spine of the leaf removed and remainder sliced into fine threads
400 ml can coconut cream
1 small zucchini, sliced into ribbons
50 g green beans, topped, tailed and sliced
1 tablespoon brown sugar
2 teaspoons fish sauce
2 tablespoons lime juice

Wash the coriander thoroughly. Scrape and chop the roots, and chop the stems. Reserve the leaves for serving. Place in the bowl of a mini food processor with lemongrass, chillies, garlic and ginger and grind into a paste.

YOUR TIME STARTS NOW

Put ¼ teaspoon peanut oil in a chef pan over high heat and quickly stir fry ¼ of the chicken until starting to brown. Remove to a bowl and repeat with the remaining chicken and oil.

Add a few drops of oil in the pan and stir fry the curry paste for 2 minutes or until fragrant. Return the chicken to the pan and toss to coat in curry. Add kaffir lime leaves and coconut cream.

Reduce the heat and simmer for 7 to 8 minutes or until chicken is cooked through. Add brown sugar, fish sauce and lime juice. Taste and add more of any of these things as preferred. In the last minute of cooking, add the zucchini and beans.

Serve scattered with coriander leaves.

CHAPTER 5
HOT POTATO

Joseph Brian Goodwin was born three weeks before the Christmas of 1995. I was wholly unprepared for the love that would sweep through my entire being when I met him. For that protective lioness part of me to burst forward. For the joy so soaring it felt almost the same as grief. For the fear that came with the love, fear for his safety, his development, his happiness.

In the days following Joe's birth, Mick was in a kind of daze and he kept pointing at people and saying, 'See her? She was born. Someone gave *birth* to her. And him. And him! Everyone in the world, every person, was *born*!' He couldn't get his head around it. For a while he looked at me like I was a wizard, a miracle worker. It was like he was seeing the world properly for the first time.

Mick was from the outset a fully involved dad, head over heels in love with this new little scrap of a human. If I had been the main breadwinner, he would have stayed home with Joey. But he was, and he went back to work, commuting to Sydney, where he now worked as a helpdesk technician for the Swiss Bank. He had an eight-hour work day but the two-hour commute meant that he left home at 6.45 a.m. and arrived home at 6.45 p.m. Little Joey had colic and spent much of his waking time screaming. I couldn't get him to settle so I couldn't do a thing around the house.

With both our families in Sydney, and few friends living nearby, I felt quite isolated. Mum and Dad were still working, and Debbie had her hands full with her toddler, my beautiful niece Sammie, and her own newborn boy, Luke. I was lucky to have Nan come up and stay in our spare room to help us through the first couple of weeks before returning to her home in Hornsby.

We were a one-car family by this stage. If I needed the car for the day I would have to bundle up the baby and drop Mick to the station. Often this seemed too much of a task, so most days, if I needed to go anywhere, we walked.

Just before Joe was born, we joined a Family Group through our church, Our Lady of the Rosary in Wyoming. I had grown up in a Family Group in Sydney – Family Group was a movement started by a maverick priest, Father Peter McGrath. His belief was that Christianity didn't happen within the walls of a church as much as it did out in the world, in the community, by people getting together and looking after one another. And that's what the Family Group was. Not a religious group, but a social group of families from the parish. The whole idea was to gather once a month and enjoy a game of tennis or a bushwalk or a pot-luck dinner. In this way families got to know each other, and a network was formed that could be relied upon.

I had loved growing up with this network. The families in our group were at my wedding. It was a village, a community where people brought meals to those who'd had surgery or were grieving. They were a shoulder for each other, a support network. I yearned for that here on the Coast, for my little family.

HOT POTATO

When our parish priest announced that he was kicking off a Family Group in Wyoming, we were straight on board. Here was the village we needed, an opportunity to connect with people who lived nearby. It was November of 1995. I was heavily pregnant with Joe at the time, and overjoyed when I was placed in a group with another young woman also about to have her first child. Vickie still is one of my best friends, and the baby she was carrying is, like Joe, now a twenty-eight-year-old man.

I also made friends through the mothers group run by the hospital. We stayed in touch for months after the classes had ended, and one of the group, Louise, has remained a dear friend of mine three decades on. Our sons were born one week apart.

Being in that mothers group gave me some wonderful resources, but it also highlighted that Joe's pain and his crying weren't normal. Eventually I was referred to the early parenting support organisation Tresillian, which had a Family Care Centre not far from our place. They booked me in for a full day so that they could observe Joey and, I think, me. Of course on that day, that one day, the little bugger slept peacefully for hours. I couldn't believe it. While my contrary child was sleeping, the nurse asked me a series of questions, after which she told me that I had scored high on the scale for postnatal depression.

'Let me stop you there,' I said. 'I don't want to hear the word depression. I don't have a thing to be depressed about. I have a beautiful husband and a healthy baby and a house to live in. It would be ridiculous for me to be depressed. Give me the questions again.'

She didn't give me the questions again. She said to me, in the kindest voice, that we didn't have to label anything if I didn't want to, but she would like to check up on me periodically if that was all right.

I had my own ideas and judgements about depression. I had the medical condition all bundled up with pessimism, ingratitude, unwillingness to count blessings. I viewed it as a character flaw, not a common or treatable condition. I would have different versions of this same conversation with other medical providers over the years. I wouldn't acknowledge that term, or allow it to be applied to me, until I was in my forties and the world was going dark around me.

There was so much information and misinformation about caring for babies and raising kids (and if there was a lot then, it must be a billion times worse now with all the sites and influencers and opinions on the internet). But there is one myth in particular that I would like to debunk for anyone who needs to hear it. You *can* get pregnant while you're breastfeeding, it turns out. That's how I ended up with Thomas Roy Goodwin, born just fourteen months after his big brother.

Tom's birth was nightmarish. Just recently in my papers I found a detailed account of it, which I must have written down in an attempt to process what had happened. Rereading it took me straight back to that delivery room. At first it was a normal labour. But suddenly, there were medical staff everywhere. Cold gel, a scope on my belly trying to find life in there. A heartbeat missing for seven minutes. A doctor I had never met shaking her head sadly at the monitor and saying, 'There's no way.' Mick leaning over me, whispering over and over, 'Please God, save our baby, please God, save our baby.'

The midwife put her face very close to mine and said quietly, 'Julie, we have to get this baby out right now. Do you understand me? Right now.' In that moment I wasn't even having a contraction. It was sheer terror and panic that had me push with every fibre in my being. The head finally crowned and the midwife pulled on it as hard as she could. When Tom came out there was no precious skin-to-skin moment, no cutting of the cord for Mick. He disappeared into the waiting hands of strangers while they checked vital signs. I had to ask a few times before I was told that it was a boy, and he was okay.

I was so numb with shock that it was hours before the enormity of what had happened – his little neck, wrapped in the umbilical cord – and what had almost happened hit me and I started to cry. I cried rivers, oceans. Guilt, grief, relief, gratitude, fear, joy all wheeled around in my head like seagulls. He was okay. He was okay. He was okay. It was the only thing that mattered.

Tom was a very chilled-out baby, the opposite of Joe. He slept, he ate, he was happy to wait for things. This remained the case until he hit the famed 'terrible twos'. Recently, Tom's partner, Crystal, asked me at what age he'd outgrown this phase. I told her I'll let her know – he's twenty-seven and we're still waiting. He was, and is, wilful, funny, stubborn, artistic, energetic, loveable and beloved by his doting big brother.

Around this time Mick was offered a new job. Down in Sydney he'd already moved from the Swiss Bank to the IT department of Rothschild, where he had been promoted to hardware team leader. So he wasn't really looking for a new position, but one day he happened to see something in the classifieds of the local paper. It was doing the same work – IT consulting – but it was close by. The job was for a very small firm, which carried some risk, but after much discussion we decided to take the leap.

Life changed immeasurably for the better with Mick now able to be home for much more of every day. Things were good. Some of our friends had moved to the Coast, including Mick's best friends, Adam and Daniel, and their respective wives, Steph and Tash. They both had young kids too, who all played together.

YOUR TIME STARTS NOW

Over many years, Tash would become my best friend. From the time her eldest was born, at around the same time as Tom, she would turn up on my doorstep for a cuppa and a chat, and I was always welcome on hers. Her three children and mine were surrogate cousins to each other. They went to the same primary school and are still friends today.

Best of all, my sister Debbie moved up from Sydney to the very same suburb as me, meaning that now my boys not only had good friends but their cousins nearby as well. Along with Mick's older brother, Paul, and his wife and kids, the Central Coast was starting to become populated with people we knew and loved.

When Tom was nine months old, Mick and I fell pregnant again with number three. Patrick Tony Goodwin was born in August of 1998, fifteen days overdue and still needing to be induced. He was so comfy I think if they hadn't forced him out he'd still be in there and I'd be carrying my stomach around in a wheelbarrow.

Paddy was the most chilled-out baby of all three boys. This was fortunate, considering that when he was born his brothers were two years and nine months, and eighteen months, respectively. Three in nappies, three high chairs, three cots, three little car seats. The soundtrack of our lives was supplied by The Wiggles, back in their early days when it was still the original members and the Big Red Car was a cardboard cut-out.

Three boys under three. It was hectic. But they were so darn cute. They made me laugh with their antics every day. They gave me a headache just about every day too. When we went out I dressed them in matching outfits – call the fashion police on me if you like, but I'd still do it today if they let me. Little denim overalls, or matching Hawaiian shirts, or sailor hats – I was always on the lookout for a bargain. They went through their clothes so quickly, too, the beautiful little grubs.

HOT POTATO

I always marvelled at how different they all were from each other. Joe loved paper craft and was incredibly proficient at the kiddie computer games we would put on for him. He hated loud noises, didn't like his food to touch on the plate, and lined his toys up meticulously every day. He was gentle and quick to laugh.

Tom loved to dress up. He wore a Spider-Man costume throughout a whole summer until it fell apart at the seams. He spent quite a while as a pirate and then as Woody from *Toy Story*. Nothing on earth could coax him out of whatever costume he was wearing. He also loved to draw, and his pictures were detailed and brilliant. And sometimes rude.

Paddy, the relaxed baby, grew into a sport-loving toddler. He was friendly to everyone he met, ready for a chat to a random stranger at the park, and the whole world was a sports field. If it was on the ground, he would kick it. If it was round, he would throw it or hit it with a bat or bounce it.

When I was at uni studying early childhood, we learned about John Locke's theory of *tabula rasa*, which suggests that children are born with their minds a blank slate and they are fully shaped by their environment. The theory basically states that in the nature vs nurture debate, nurture kicks nature's butt. As a mother of three very different little boys who swam out of the same gene pool, and who were raised in the same environment by the same parents, I have this to say about John Locke's theory: what a crock.

Mick's salary barely covered the mortgage, so I took whatever work I could with the babies so little. I cleaned houses with toddlers in tow and took in ironing through a company that would collect business shirts and school uniforms and deliver them to me in a basket, to be collected the next day pressed and on hangers. I worked for Mick's aunty, who had a jewellery and giftware business, gluing crystals onto earrings. I did this at home, late into the night. I had to stop it, though, as I developed a severe allergy to epoxy resin and whenever I used it my head swelled up like a football. I had retired as a clown at kids' parties but I still sang at weddings and the occasional birthday. I had a regular gig at Asquith Golf Club, one Friday night a month, singing mostly jazz standards. I hauled my own sound gear and sang to the backing music I had programmed on floppy disks. I used to joke to Mick that I wanted to be just famous enough to afford my own roadie to carry all the heavy gear.

When it came to the boys and motherhood, I tried to do everything perfectly. I didn't really understand that perfection, especially when it comes to parenting, doesn't exist. I just knew that I loved these boys – oh, how I loved these little boys – and I wanted everything in the world to be right for them. I pegged their wee clothes in size order on the line. I ironed their cot sheets. I soaked their tiny singlets and their cloth nappies in Napisan and hung them in the sun so they would all be perfectly white. None of these things, of course, mattered to them one tiny bit. I wish I had realised. I wish I had spent less time trying – and frequently failing – to make everything clean and tidy and socially acceptable. I wish I had spent more time on the floor with the wooden train set or reading to them or taking them to the park.

There are huge tracts of memory missing from those years. I was exhausted, obviously. But I do remember, always, how I loved my sons. Oh, so fiercely. The funny little things they said and did. How easy it was to make them laugh. The way they played together; the way our whole family played together. Mick taking them to the bike track, to the beach, on little camping adventures. I remember my heart expanding even more as the man I loved, just a boy himself when I met him, became this besotted, devoted dad.

HOT POTATO

It's such a strange thing, to feel grief for people who are still near me, my sons now adult men, who are still part of my everyday life. But those little boys in their matching outfits, those little boys who held my hands and sat on my lap and ran to me when they needed comfort, those little boys aren't here anymore. And I miss them.

Zucchini slice

A versatile recipe and easy for a busy parent, zucchini slice can be thrown together in minutes. It can be frozen, eaten hot or cold, and works as a snack, a meal, and everything in between. The best thing is, your children won't even notice they're eating vegetables.

Prep time: 10 minutes
Cooking time: 35 minutes
Makes 1 slice, 12 pieces

2 zucchini, grated
1 large onion, finely chopped
3 rashers bacon, finely chopped
1 cup tasty cheese, grated
1 cup self-raising flour
½ cup of oil
5 eggs
Salt and pepper

Preheat oven to 170°C. Grease and line a non-stick lamington tin.

Combine zucchini, onion, bacon, flour and cheese in a large bowl. Add oil and lightly beaten eggs, and mix. Season with a little salt and pepper. Pour into lamington tin.

YOUR TIME STARTS NOW

Bake for 35 to 40 minutes until golden and set. Allow to cool slightly before cutting.

Note: the vegetables can be substituted or added to – try corn kernels, grated carrot, shallots, shredded beans, and leave out the bacon for a vegetarian version.

CHAPTER 6

TAKING CARE OF BUSINESS

As the boys grew, and Mick worked his way up in his job, our tight money situation eased a little bit. The mortgage was a lower percentage of our income and we weren't living quite so hand-to-mouth as we had been. There was room for little treats, some new clothes, some nicer ingredients to cook with, the occasional dinner out; there was room to buy wine and beer. In the early days there just hadn't been budget for alcohol. We didn't go out clubbing, or even dining; there was no wriggle room in the grocery bill at all.

But as that eased, I started to drink a bit more than I had in the past. A bit more here, a bit more there. I didn't see it as problematic. I had given up alcohol entirely for the pregnancies and the breastfeeding, and I wasn't gasping for it, missing it, the way some women are when they're pregnant. Having wine in the house was just something I deserved. That was my line on the matter: I was busy, I did so much for everyone, unwinding with a glass or two at night was my right.

Mick was brewing his own beer at the time, in brown longneck bottles that he stored under the house. Occasionally they would explode, scaring the crap out of the dog. Every now and then he produced something drinkable. But Mick has never been a big drinker. He's one of those people who can have one, or two, and then stop. Not me. 'Moderate' and 'sensible' are not words that are often applied to me. Eventually Mick questioned me about the amount I was consuming. He was tentative about the question, and concerned; but I was affronted, and I got mad. Wine wasn't the problem, as far as I was concerned. Wine was the bloody solution. I deserved it and I'd earned it and who was he to take away the one thing I did for myself? That was how I saw it, how I justified it to myself.

When I started concealing how much I was getting through in a week, I told myself it was because Mick was a control freak who just wanted to nag me. The problem was, I knew that this was an outright lie and I couldn't even sell it to myself. Over time, I came to understand that I was in a problematic place and that I would need to do something about it. Of course, understanding there's a problem, and addressing that problem, are two very different things.

One Sunday morning we were in church. The hymn we were singing was 'Come As You Are', which is about being loved and loveable, no matter what you've done wrong. I knew it was written by a nun who'd suffered with alcoholism. And I found that I couldn't sing it, I couldn't breathe. All I could do was feel the words pierce me. All will be well, just come as you are.

After Mass I told Mick that I was going to quit drinking. And I did, completely. For two years.

From the outset, I decided to go to AA to get some support. Because quitting altogether was hard. I viewed it as a habit that I needed to break, which it was. I didn't look for the deeper meanings underneath it; I just wanted an anonymous group of people who had achieved sobriety to tell me I could do it too.

TAKING CARE OF BUSINESS

When I first walked through the doors I was mortified to see two men who I knew, one of them very well – he'd been a friend since I was a teenager. I was welcomed with open arms, but I had not been expecting to have people know me there. I said to my friend, 'How's this meant to be bloody anonymous, then?' He threw back his head and laughed. 'You're right!' he said. In all honesty, I was also glad to see someone I knew, glad to have a friend in this totally alien room.

I attended the group regularly and listened to the stories. I even shared some of mine. But all up it was not a great experience. I know now that finding the right group is pivotal to a good experience in AA, but back then all I knew was that I was among people with stories I could not relate to. Mostly men, and mostly much older than me, they relayed extreme life events: sleeping rough and deep drug addiction, criminal activity and near-death experiences. We were always encouraged to see the similarities with our fellow members, but I couldn't ignore all the gaping differences. After six weeks I stopped attending and managed those two years on my own.

~

Joe started school in 2002, a year after he was old enough to go. Something in my gut made me hold him back. I am not exactly sure what it was; maybe it was an inkling that he was just a little bit different from other kids. Maybe I knew he wasn't ready to spend five days a week in a foreign and what I suspected might be an overwhelming environment. All I knew was that as I sat at the dining table with the enrolment papers in front of me, I was crying like a tap and trying to explain to Mick that I couldn't fill them in. He said quite simply, 'Then don't fill them in. We can enrol him next year.' So the decision was made, and it's one I have never regretted.

Joe had the most divine kindy teacher, Miss Minter, and he loved her so much. One day, towards the end of the year, she asked me in the gentlest way, 'Julie, have you ever wondered if Joe is a little bit different to the other kids?'

It was like, with this question, someone had opened a floodgate. And out of it flowed all the things that Joe did in his own way; the complaints that were made about him by others – his preschool teachers, kids at the park, occasionally family members. He doesn't listen, he speaks in a high-pitched voice, he wants everyone to play by the rules of his game every day. But this one question, asked so kindly by someone who clearly delighted in Joe, finally got me to make an appointment with a paediatrician.

I had no idea what to expect in seeing this specialist. I thought maybe we'd be referred for speech therapy or given some ideas of how to make Joe a better listener. So when the doctor responded, kind of impatiently, to a question of mine, 'Yes, yes, that's the way with all these autistic kids,' I went numb with shock. This diagnosis – and the way it was delivered – came completely out of the blue. Neither Mick nor I had any knowledge at all of the autism spectrum. All I knew about autism were the depictions I'd seen in movies or TV shows – of people with severe behaviours, unable to speak and devoid of affection. I couldn't grasp how this condition could apply to my bright, funny, loving little boy.

We were referred to the READ clinic, a local group of mental health practitioners specialising in children. The most beautiful psychologist worked with Joe and me, observing and testing him, and eventually diagnosing him with Asperger's syndrome, a high-functioning form of autism spectrum disorder – it's not known by that name anymore but that was the diagnosis we were given at the time.

I went into research mode and found out everything there was to know about the autism spectrum and how we could make sure Joe had the best chance for success at school and at life. I didn't want him to feel different, and I didn't want him to define himself by a label or a diagnosis. So I didn't tell him what we'd been told until he finished primary school. That was a mistake. What I didn't realise was that Joe already knew he was different. Once he knew why, and how, it eased his passage through life and I wish with all my heart I had told him as soon as we knew.

That same year, a series of events led us to a decision regarding Mick's career. The company he was working for was relocating to Sydney, so the question became: should he stay with them, or should we make the leap and start our own business? This was something we had discussed in passing over the past couple of years, but it seemed we had reached a watershed moment. Each prospect was problematic in its own way, but in the end we took the scarier path: in November of 2002 we opened up our own IT consultancy, which Mick named Loyal IT Solutions.

It began in our lounge room. Our working capital was a credit card and we shared our one car. Mick went out on the road to visit clients and sort out their IT issues, and I worked at home, taking calls, booking appointments, ordering hardware and invoicing. Paddy hadn't started school and the business was tiny, so work for me was only part-time in those early days.

Even with Joe and Tom at school, there were still hours of the day when all three were at home with me. Those are the hours

I would dread the sound of the phone ringing because it meant I had to grab the cordless handset, run to an empty bedroom, sit against the door, catch my breath, then answer in a bright, cheery tone as though I was at a desk in a quiet office: 'Loyal IT Solutions, this is Julie!' It was always my aim to get through the conversation before some kind of noisy calamity went down in the next room.

Even when all three boys were at school, it was an interesting concept to work from home. I would get up from my desk to go to the bathroom, and on my way I'd pass a bit of laundry on the floor; on my way to the laundry to put it in the wash, I'd trip over a few toys; on my way to the toy box I'd spy dishes in the sink; once the toys were away and the dishes were done, the washing machine would be finished; once the clothes were pegged out . . . the boys would arrive home off the school bus. And the newsletter or the bank rec or the invoicing would still be staring from the computer screen, waiting to be done.

Although IT had never been my career choice, I was so proud of what we were creating. Mick and I carefully nurtured our little business, even in those early days treating it as though it was already a well-established, thriving company. We had beautiful cards and stationery printed. We joined the local chamber of commerce and several networking groups; we planned and worked and marketed, invoiced and reconciled and corresponded late into the night. We set goals and broke them down into quarterly, weekly and daily actions.

It helped that Mick was, and is, a gifted technician and has a natural air of calm and competence about him. Clients warmed to him, trusted him, recommended his services to others. Before too long we were employing staff, and by the time we had two employees our little enterprise had outgrown our house.

TAKING CARE OF BUSINESS

I decided to do a feasibility study on purchasing office space, as opposed to us finding somewhere to rent. I made a bunch of enquiries so that my calculations would be realistic. As part of my research, I even asked the bank how likely it would be that we could swing a loan. So thorough was my feasibility study, with photos, projections, a sale amount and loan repayment information, that really all that was left for Mick to do was to agree. And such was his trust in me that before he even viewed the property I'd set my sights on, he did agree. An offer was accepted and a new adventure begun.

For the next couple of months, while the boys were at school and Mick was seeing clients, I renovated the new office. It needed a new floor and a paint job. What with sawing laminated planks and spraying walls with a spray gun, I probably shortened my life expectancy by a decade, but at the end the place looked fresh, professional and ready for action. It was so exciting to shift all our work-related paraphernalia out of the house. We had our lounge room, our spare room and our front hallway back, instead of boxes of monitors and routers and piles of paperwork. Now, I could really make the distinction between home life and work life, getting dressed and heading in to the office like a normal person.

Mick and I were, between us, still able to parent the boys full-time. I went to work at 7 a.m. while Mick packed them off to school, then I would get home minutes before they got off the bus, barrelling in with bags swinging and bellies rumbling.

In the ensuing years we kept putting a lot of energy into building the business. We engaged a business coach. We held team days and annual conferences. We invested in staff wellbeing and we developed a Code of Honour, which was agreed by all the team as being our core values. Loyalty, respect, team, gratitude, communication, community are some of those core values. Throughout all the challenges that running small businesses brings – staff turnover, cashflow, economic downturns – we operated according to this Code of Honour, and the business thrived. We entered (and quite often won) the local business awards. Our most successful category, for many years until it was discontinued, was Excellence in Business Ethics.

Twenty-one years on, Loyal IT Solutions is still thriving, employing people and supporting families. Mick is still on the tools, out with clients every day.

In the lead-up to our tenth wedding anniversary, Mick and I planned a trip to celebrate. We thought about going back to Thailand where we had honeymooned, but logistically with the boys it was a bit tricky, so we decided instead to go to Hamilton Island. We were leaving on New Year's Day.

On Christmas Day 2004, we headed to Deb's house to celebrate. We turned up at the same time as everyone else – my kids and Deb's four running around the yard in a state of high excitement. I guess all the sudden activity was too much for their dog, a mid-sized sandy-haired boy called Cougar. From inside the house, I heard screaming. Moments later Debbie was ushering Tom through the back door. His shirt was shredded. I could see blood. I could hear the other kids crying. Everything slowed right down and I could hear my voice saying, 'It's all right, it's all right.' I will never forget my sister's face, her wild eyes and the slight shake of her head, as she mouthed the words to me, 'It's not.'

And it was not all right.

Debbie at that time lived only a couple of hundred metres from Hornsby Hospital. We took Tom straight to emergency. The scene at

TAKING CARE OF BUSINESS

Debbie's was surreal; Christmas morning had turned into a horror show. The kids were absolutely shattered. The adults were in shock.

At the hospital Tom's injuries became clear. He had puncture wounds all over his torso, and he needed immediate surgery on the arm that the dog had taken a big chunk of. He had managed to get that arm across his face. If he hadn't, his face might have been torn off, instead of a piece of his arm. His throat might have been opened. I was stunned by how calmly and bravely he handled the whole scenario. At one stage, listening to the doctors talk, he asked in the morbidly curious way of little boys, 'Where is the rest of my arm? Is it in Aunty Debbie's yard or did Cougar eat it?' I can't recall what the answer was, only that the room spun and someone stuck a chair under me as my legs gave out.

The family stayed at Debbie's for the day, and took turns making the trek up to the hospital, bringing gifts so that we could open them together. Joe and Paddy spent some of the day with us, and some back at Aunty Deb's with their cousins as Tom went into, and came out of, surgery. The ward was empty except for us; nothing is scheduled for Christmas Day. I was grateful to my family for making Christmas as good as it could be, but we were all devastated. Deb's kids lost their beloved dog. I lost any hope that I could keep my boys safe in the world.

The very next day, Boxing Day, a tsunami rose up out of the Indian Ocean, one of the deadliest natural disasters in history. Hundreds of thousands of people died in fourteen countries. The scope of the disaster was unfathomable. I tried, I really tried, to put our family's trauma in the context of that terrible global event. I tried to have perspective. The scale of the natural disaster, the sheer breathtaking horror of all those lives lost, had left the whole of humanity reeling. How could I possibly complain about Christmas ruined, about a dog bite, about a family grieving? How could

I even mention it without being the most tone-deaf, inward-looking ingrate that ever lived? What had happened to Tom was nothing in comparison to the tsunami. But it *wasn't* nothing. And our inability to talk about it, to process it by seeking out conversations with our friends or even within our shattered family, meant that it was never properly processed.

Tom, to my admiration and amazement, gradually taught himself to be okay around dogs again. I didn't fare so well. A few months after this incident, exactly two years after I'd given up drinking, I decided that I'd proved my point. If I could give up for two years, I clearly did not have a problem. So I started again. And it was fine, for quite a long time; what most people would describe as normal drinking, within socially acceptable boundaries. But eventually, as trauma remained unresolved and illness unacknowledged, it did come back to bite me.

In 2006, when the boys were in primary school, it became clear that our house on Maple Street was not big enough to contain their growing bodies and activities. The small concrete backyard, which had been great for tricycles and basketball, was less ideal for running and kicking a footy. Tom and Paddy shared a room and we wanted to give them their own space. I'd been lucky enough to have my own room growing up – Mick had had to share – and we knew which we wanted for our boys.

We found a quarter-acre block just up the road in Niagara Park. Two elderly sisters had lived on the property, one in a caravan up the front and one in a tiny cottage up the back. We decided to move our family into the cottage while we built a house at the front of the block.

TAKING CARE OF BUSINESS

The cottage was a funny little affair. It was built, probably in the 1950s, from fibro – asbestos – on the outside. Inside it was lined with old magazines and newspapers, which had been nailed to the struts and painted. I discovered this one day when I leaned a guitar case against the wall and it went straight through, leaving me the surprised reader of a 1956 *Woman's Day* magazine. The floor was damp and smelled like dirt. The windows were made of slats that didn't close, leaving us exposed to razor-sharp wind in winter and Christmas beetles and mosquitoes in summer. The three boys shared a room, Mick and I had a mattress on the floor in the second room, and there was narrow L-shaped living space.

We put everything nice we owned in storage. Nothing but the bare minimum would fit in the cottage – a few towels, a bit of bedding, a couple of toys each for the boys, a handful of kitchen utensils and crockery.

The kitchen was no more than a corridor. I could put my hands out to each side and touch both walls. There was a sink at one end and an outside tap that came in through the window. The benchtop was the size of two chopping boards, and had an oblong hole where the stovetop belonged, but was not. I hammered nails into the wall to hang my utensils. There was no oven – my cooking equipment consisted of an electric frying pan, a sandwich press, a microwave, a toaster and a kettle. But – and here's where it got challenging – I could only run one appliance at a time, or the fuse would blow. This included all the household appliances, not just the kitchen ones – the heater, the iron, the hot-water tank that teetered on the rotting floor of the bathroom. Our family became accustomed to instructions along the lines of 'Turn the heater off, I need to cook dinner' and 'You can iron your shirt when I'm done in the shower.'

Not only was it a logistical nightmare, a daily challenge that led sometimes to frustration and sometimes to hilarity, but it was also an isolating time, not having a kitchen to cater for friends nor a place to sit them if they visited. It was novel, for a while; fun, a bit like camping. The novelty soon wore off, though, as I watched the achingly slow progress of the new house in front of me. But Joe, Tom and Paddy adapted well, knowing that they would soon have their own rooms and play area.

We let the boys write on the walls of our little shack, with two conditions: if they did so when we moved into our new house, they were dead dodos, and they could only write things they were grateful for. We still have a chunk of that wall in our shed. It has gems on it like 'I am grateful for leaves', 'I am thankful for Archie and Buster [our dogs]' and 'I am glad we have a house, even if it's tiny'. I am glad to say they never did write on the walls of the new house.

It was only going to be six months, I thought, to build the new house. I can put up with anything for six months. It wasn't six months, as anyone who has ever built a house will know. But we spent time at the Loyal IT offices, even eating dinner there a couple of nights a week when I wanted us to all fit around one table. I kept the boys as busy outside of school as I could, with art classes and sports training and afternoons at their friends' houses. It was a juggle but between us we made it work.

A few days before our first Christmas in the cottage, Mick's mother called me about who was bringing what to Christmas Eve, when she held her traditional roast dinner. I was surprised but pleased because in the past she had never let anyone bring anything. We brought dishes to Boxing Day and other family occasions, but Christmas Eve was Kath's domain. But something seemed a bit off. She asked me to bring broccoli – strange enough in itself – but also her words were a bit jumbled and she couldn't seem to straighten them out.

TAKING CARE OF BUSINESS

'Hang on a sec, Mum,' I said and put the phone against my chest, moving to the next room where Mick was.

'There's something wrong with your mum,' I said quietly. 'She's having trouble with her words.'

I put him on the phone to her and he chatted to her for a while.

After he'd hung up, he told me, 'She's had the flu. She's just very tired and a bit muddled from it.'

'Mick, I think she may be having a stroke.'

The conversation that followed was more heated than our usual exchanges. He thinks I'm a drama queen. I think he's not enough of a drama queen. He thinks his mother is fine. I think she just asked me to bring *broccoli* to Christmas dinner, *for fuck's sake*, in what way can that possibly be fine?

We agreed to call Mick's sister Liz, a nurse, and let her decide. Within moments of speaking to her mother on the phone an ambulance was called to the house and the waiting game began.

Later that night, we were told by the emergency department that they were unsure what was happening. Mum had a temperature, but it didn't look like a stroke. It was potentially a virus, or it could be that the cancer she'd been jousting with for many years, non-Hodgkin lymphoma, was back and had spread to her brain. They were doing tests and would let us know.

On Christmas morning a phone call came as we were getting out of the car to attend Mass. It was not the cancer. It was a virus. Because of Mum's weakened immune system after a recent stem cell transplant, the same germ that would give you or me a cold sore, had crossed the blood–brain barrier and become herpes encephalitis.

Not the cancer, was what we heard. Not the cancer. *Not the cancer.* We held each other in the car park and cried. Thank god. A Christmas miracle. It's not the cancer. The news couldn't be better. For a few happy days, that's what we believed.

Days became weeks and weeks became months, and Mum never came back to us. The virus (not the cancer) had caused a catastrophic brain injury. Although she became able to walk and talk again, Kath Goodwin had lost her memory. She did not know who we were, or where she was, or where her parents had gone. Not only this, but the severe injury to her hippocampus made her incapable of creating short-term memories. It was terrifying for her, and devastating for us all. She would ask the same few questions over and over, trying to understand her surroundings. We would answer the questions and she would ask them again, in a terrible loop that never ended. Nor could she remember that she had eaten, and somehow her wiring didn't let through the signal that she was full, so she always felt hungry. She didn't know what time of day it was or what she should be doing. She couldn't remember anyone's names, or faces, or who they were to her.

The next few months were a godawful blur. All of us took turns to travel down to Sydney to sit with her at the rehab hospital. We were there for her every waking hour to try and soothe away some of her terror and confusion at simply being in the world. Despite the doctors' hopeless prognosis, I became convinced that we could overcome the odds and bring her back. I read everything I could find on the subject, which was not a lot. Herpes encephalitis only infected one in one million people at that time. (More recent figures estimate one in 500,000.) Whether it was an excess of hope, or an excess of ego, or both, I decided I was going to be the one to overcome the condition with Kath, through sheer stubbornness if that's what it took. I made flash cards and timed for how long she could remember the pictures on them. I recorded the results and desperately scrutinised them for improvements. I made a book for her in which I glued photographs of all the people she loved, labelled with their names and their relationship to her. In it was a

TAKING CARE OF BUSINESS

picture of her home, of the quilts she made, the things she used to do. There was just this hope that the book might bring her some kind of comfort, but there wasn't any evidence that it did.

Any family dealing with such a situation understands how lonely it is, how stressful, how the decisions that need to be made can tear you apart. It's an inward-turning time. Our outside community was forgotten for a little while as we navigated this family tragedy and tried to keep everyone together.

I was so angry. I was furious at the medical practitioners who had, it turned out, taken too long to give her antibiotics. I was angry at the system that made it impossible to get respite or support for our family. I was frustrated by the limited information I could gather on this condition. I was livid with the specialists who kept telling us she would never get any better. I was furious with God, for this travesty that was allowed to happen to such a devout and loving person. I was wild with knowing that once again I could not protect my children from the worst of the world as they grieved the loss of their grandmother while she was still right before their eyes.

She was eventually released from the rehab hospital with no improvement, nor, we were informed, any prospect of it. We tried to keep her comfortable in her own home for a while, but she didn't recognise it. Her need for continuous care became too much for the family and we found a place for her at Bowden Brae, the nursing home I had worked in so many years before.

One evening, in the midst of all this anguish, Paddy swung a golf club and accidentally opened up a third eye in Tom's forehead. There was so much blood. Mick bundled Tom into the car to go and get stitches. I settled Paddy, who was distraught. I went outside and stood in the glow of the setting sun, on the pitiful verandah of our shitty little cottage. The sky was magnificent, spectacular, a Cecil B. DeMille-worthy riot of glorious colour. It offended me to the core of my being. How dare you, God, how dare you put on such a boastful show? My scream came through a jaw so tightly clenched that it barely made any sound at all. Bring it on, I hissed. Bring it on, you bastard, what else have you got? What else have you got?

Anger, grief, despair, worry, sadness, exhaustion, fear; these were like the horses on a carousel. Round and round and up and down they go.

When the cancer came back for her, we did not send it away. For ten years Kath had fought. She had given us the gift of telling us, before the virus had struck, that the stem cell transplant was her last battle, she didn't want any more treatment after that. At least we were spared the guilt of making that decision – she had made it for herself. We made her as comfortable as we could and let that motherfucking lymphoma take its slow, inevitable course.

―

In June of 2008, two whole years after we'd moved into our temporary fibro home, we finally got the keys for our new house. All the delays, and mistakes that needed correcting, and frustrations of the build were forgotten in an instant. Bringing our things out of storage was like a dozen Christmases at once. Some of the toys we had packed away for the boys were far too young for them now. Putting things in cupboards, getting the boys settled in their own rooms, taking a *bath* – oh my word, a hot bath! – these were what we had talked of for so long, and dreamed about. We loved the house we'd built, were so happy, so grateful, so damn comfortable. It was the first time I had ever had brand new appliances and a lovely kitchen to cook in. We got Foxtel for the first time, too. I discovered the Food Channel and I watched it from my kitchen and I cooked, and cooked, and cooked.

TAKING CARE OF BUSINESS

I was in my element – a shiny kitchen with a long stone bench, space for friends and family, a great big table we could all sit at together. It was winter when we moved in, season of slow-cooked casseroles, soup and curry and rich meaty pasta dishes. Roast dinners were back on the menu, much to everyone's delight. I even stepped out of my dinner-making lane and did some baking. I was experimenting with lots of new things, watching travel and cooking shows, revelling in the huge oven and even huger cooktop. Sometimes I boiled the kettle and put the toaster on at the same time just because I could. No fuses blowing in this house!

The boys had done some cooking with me when we lived on Maple Street, but in the cottage we didn't all fit into the kitchen so that had come to a stop. Now there was space again, they started contributing to the family dinners. The way I enticed them to cook was twofold: first, whoever cooked didn't have to wash up or clean the kitchen after dinner; and secondly, they could choose what they wanted to make. This meant I almost always had a volunteer helping me, and as they grew, sometimes taking over the kitchen altogether.

Life was about as good as it could be, Mum Goodwin's illness notwithstanding. It felt like we had reached a destination, like we could really bunker down and enjoy our new house, our new space, and once again have our friends over and reconnect with our community.

That notion, that settled, comfortable feeling, lasted for six months before our lives were thrown into a completely different kind of turmoil.

YOUR TIME STARTS NOW

Slow-roasted pork belly

If you're going to cook this dish, you may as well double the recipe and (maybe) have leftovers for the next day. Make sure you teach everyone in your family how to make the gravy.

Prep and cooking time: 3 hours
Serves 8

2 kg piece of pork belly, bones removed
Salt
Olive oil

Ensure the skin of the meat is very dry. If necessary, leave it uncovered in the fridge for 24 hours before cooking.

Using a Stanley knife or a Mickey knife, score the rind, cutting into the fat but not into the flesh. I like to score the rind about ½ to 1 cm wide. Rub it with a little olive oil and massage salt thoroughly and generously into it.

Preheat the oven to 240°C.

Place the pork in the oven on a rack in a roasting pan, for 30 to 40 minutes or until the skin begins to puff up and look crisp. Occasionally pour some water into the base of the roasting pan if needed, to avoid juices burning.

Turn the oven down to 140°C and continue to roast uncovered for a further 2 to 3 hours.

Remove from the oven and remove the rack from under the pork. Place a second tray on top, weight it with cans, and place in the fridge overnight. (This makes it much easier to carve than when it's hot, and it can be gently reheated before serving. If you don't have time for this step you can just rest for half an hour, carve and serve.)

Use the pan juices to make gravy.

TAKING CARE OF BUSINESS

Simple gravy from pan juices

⅓ cup plain flour

1 litre chicken stock (room temperature, not heated)

Salt and pepper to taste

After the roast has been removed from the pan, place the pan on the stovetop over a medium-low heat. If the roast was very fatty, pour off some but not all of the fat from the pan.

Stir the flour into the pan juices, ensuring there are no lumps. Place the pan over a medium heat and introduce the chicken stock little by little. Bring to the boil, and simmer until the gravy is the thickness you like it to be. Make sure you scrape up all the tasty brown bits from the bottom of the pan.

Taste, and season with salt and pepper. Strain through a wire sieve into a serving jug.

CHAPTER 7
HOT AND COLD

My best friend Tash talked me into applying for *MasterChef*. She'd seen a contestant call on Channel 10 and urged me to apply. I think she was a bit sick of me going on and on about the UK version of the show, which I had been watching avidly. I observed with interest these modest British home cooks arriving in a commercial kitchen, and followed their progress through a series of challenges until the end. A season lasted only a few weeks; the contestants went home at the end of each day. What I really liked was watching as they learned new things, and grew in confidence and ability under the benevolent tutelage of judges John Torode and Gregg Wallace. It did look like a bit of fun and a challenge as well.

I had a look at the application for the Australian show, and it was a huge long process. So I kept putting off filling it in, citing busyness at work. Meanwhile, Tash was telling me that if I didn't apply I wasn't allowed to talk about cooking anymore, which sounded serious. So the day before applications closed, late in 2008, I took half a day off work and waded through the online form. I then promptly forgot about it.

HOT AND COLD

It was early in January 2009 when I got the phone call. There was an audition to be held in January in Sydney; would I be able to attend? I looked at my calendar and saw a very important event set for that same date: Joe's first day of high school.

I was understandably anxious about him going from his tiny primary school, where he was thriving and everyone knew him, to St Peter's Catholic College with over a thousand kids. Maybe on some level it reminded me of my own transition from high school to university. Maybe I was just concerned that my amazing boy, who had overcome his challenges so comprehensively that he was elected his school captain, was going to have to undergo the thing he feared and hated most: change.

I explained to the caller that it was my son's first day of high school and could I please come and audition another day. There was a kind of baffled silence on the phone, before the voice said, 'Uh, no, that's the . . . that's the day.'

So I said I would have to talk it over with my family and get back to them. I was kind of bemused by the call. I thought it was unfortunate timing, that I'd have liked to go and see what it was all about, but that it probably wouldn't happen. I talked to Mick and we agreed we'd leave it up to Joe.

That night I told him about it. I explained that this audition was not a big deal, and that I understood he would probably want me there at the school, to walk him in and help him find out where he needed to be and make sure he was comfortable.

Joe looked me straight in the eye and with a perfectly straight face said, 'Mum, I am begging you, go to the audition.'

So I did. Sometimes I think about that – how life can pivot on these tiniest of moments. We laugh about Joe not wanting me to walk him into school, avoiding me potentially spitting on a tissue and wiping his face before kissing him in front of all his friends and sending him in with a *Toy Story* lunch box. But in all honesty, if that boy had said to me, 'Mum, I'm a bit nervous and I'd like you to be there,' then that's where I would have been. And I would never have taken a backward glance nor given it a second thought. I would have gone about my life and never known about the parallel life I could have lived.

The instructions for the audition were clear. Bring two servings of the same dish, in case you get through to the second round. There would be no heating or cooling facilities, nor access to a kitchen, so the dish needed to be able to be assembled taking that into account.

I don't think I slept properly for weeks, trying to work out what the hell I could prepare. I settled on a trio of mini desserts, which I could keep cool in a little esky and finish off in whichever kind of room I ended up in. I made a mini citrus syrup cake, a mini pav and a mini crème brulée, which I could blow-torch at the audition. I was to be at Darling Harbour at 7 a.m. and I shouldn't expect to be home until late, if I went all right. And I meant to go all right; in for a penny, in for a pound, as they say. No half measures, not for me, not ever.

The morning of the audition there were hundreds of us in a line that stretched from the Darling Harbour Convention Centre all along the waterfront. Everyone was carrying eskies and cooler bags and covered dishes. One guy was riding a unicycle. While we waited, I got a text message from Mick – a picture of Joe in his new uniform. So of course I ruined my makeup and showed his photo to everyone around me, whether they wanted to see it or not. There was a festive air, some of us in the queue (like me) nervous and emotional, some laughing; some there because they were serious cooks and others for a shot at being on the telly.

In the first round we were ushered into various rooms, about twelve at a time. We sat in a circle, introduced ourselves and explained the dish we had brought, and why we liked to cook. There were producers in the room and also a woman who we later found out was the head of the food team on the show, tasting and taking notes.

There was a long, nervous wait while we found out if we were through to the next stage, which we'd been told would be an interview with another group of producers. After several hours I got the nod. I took a deep breath and walked into yet another room for the next round. This turned out to be a kind of panel interview, with some higher-ups in the production company who were making the Australian show, Fremantle Media, and I think some people from Network 10. None of them ate my mini desserts – I decided the food was just there for decoration. They asked me a whole lot of questions, not all to do with cooking. School days, family, work, some general chit-chat.

After this interview I was told I could go home, and that I would get a phone call later that night to let me know if I was through to the next round. That meant cooking for the judges, and it would be on camera. We weren't told anything about who the judges were. I didn't really know what 'on camera' would entail either. The instructions, once again, were clear. This time there would be some refrigeration available, as well as an oven and a cooktop. However, no other equipment would be supplied, nor ingredients. Whatever we wanted, we had to bring. We'd have forty-five minutes to cook in the main room in front of all the other contestants, then five minutes in front of the judges to finish off the dish, or plate up, or whatever we wanted to do to show our skills.

I arrived home at about 9 that night and waited on tenterhooks for the call. It came not too long afterwards. I had made it through, and I was ecstatic. I had to be back at Darling Harbour for 7 the following morning.

I had already decided on my dish, and in the days leading up to the first audition I'd bought its ingredients – worst case, if I didn't get to cook it for the judges, I would cook it for us for dinner. I had decided on roast lamb rump with garlic mash. All my ingredients went into the esky and I packed pretty much every utensil, pot, pan, board, bowl and knife I owned into two giant wheely suitcases. First thing in the morning I loaded up our family van and took off down to Sydney.

All of us who had made it through were taken to a room with two portable kitchens up the front. I wasn't the only one who had packed half their house into suitcases. We were to alternate cooking in one of the kitchens, watched by the judges, who would then taste the results.

When *MasterChef* went to air several months later, the Sydney auditions were shown first. But the judges had actually just come from those in Perth. If you can imagine it, back then Gary Mehigan, Matt Preston and George Calombaris were not yet part of the Australian television landscape, beloved household names, friends we tuned in to six nights a week. To all of us in the room that day, they were just scary-looking dudes. They didn't do much to dispel this impression, either – I think they were meant to be a bit scary. Of course, months and years go by and you realise that they are teddy bears, but at that first introduction I felt anxiety coursing through me like electricity. What they had to say wasn't especially helpful, either.

'We've just come from Perth,' they told us. 'There was a lot of lamb and mash. We don't know what it is with Perth and lamb. So if you're bringing us lamb, it better be the best we've ever tasted.'

It was hours before it was my turn to cook. For that whole time, I was wishing with all my might that the lamb in my esky would turn into a fish or really anything other than lamb. It did not, and eventually it was my turn. Sarah Wilson, the beautiful host of the show, was a kind and encouraging presence, helping us to keep time as we fumbled around trying to get unfamiliar appliances to work.

After my forty-five minutes in the outside kitchen, I wheeled my trolley down the hallway to the room where the three judges were waiting for me. I wondered how nervous a person had to be before they passed out. The trolley shook so hard in my hands that everything was clanking and jangling as I walked through the door and parked at the cooking bench. I had just five minutes to finish my dish, plate it up, and somehow talk myself into a white apron and a spot in the top fifty.

Gary was standing at the bench while I was finishing my sauce. I splashed a little vinegar, for acidity, into the pan, and the vapour must have hit him square in the neck because he coughed, kind of gagging. I felt heat in my face and my stomach disappeared, the way it does when you're on a fast elevator. I might as well have let off tear gas, I thought.

It was the first but certainly not the last time these judges would taste my food with completely inscrutable faces, leaving me wondering whether they found it delicious or disgusting. The tastings never got any easier.

After an excruciating wait, as one by one they tried my lamb and mash, Matt came around the bench and gave me a hug. 'That was fantastic. I've been looking for this – real food that tastes of flavour.'

After also receiving a yes from Gary and George, I was given an apron. I was in the top fifty!

Home life went into a bit of a flurry at the news. I told my family and my closest friends, who were all thrilled with this new adventure. I did what I could to get everything organised for my sudden, potentially week-long absence.

A few days later, I packed my bags and left for a hotel in Sydney for the challenges that would determine who would be in the top twenty. People would be eliminated as we went along, so I could be back home any day. It was an eye-opener, looking around the room where we held our first briefing session. Just me and forty-nine others, from the hundreds who had been in Darling Harbour. And, of course, all the hopefuls who had auditioned around the country. I was a bit shell-shocked, to be honest, but now that I was here I wanted to wring as much as I could out of the experience.

It had put some strain on the business, me having two days off for the first two auditions, so I was concerned that by taking a whole week off I would create real difficulty for the team at work. I hoped, however, that I'd be able to deal with most things over the phone in between us cooking, so we should be okay. So I was a little shocked on the first morning of that week when our phones were taken off us for the day, to be given back only in the evening when we returned to the hotel. It made me quite anxious to be uncontactable – by my work, Mick, and my kids and their schools. But those were the rules, take it or leave it. I took it.

On our first morning we were driven to the Australian Technology Park at Eveleigh in Redfern and given our first challenge: to chop onions. The onions were backed into the makeshift kitchen on a tip truck and poured dramatically onto the floor for us to run around and collect in big silver bowls. George showed us how the judges would like to see them cut – the way chefs do it, halved with the roots left intact then peeled and thinly sliced or finely diced. It wasn't the way I had been chopping onions for the past fourteen or

HOT AND COLD

so years, but my way was not particularly efficient. Anyway, I was there to learn. It's not easy to do something in a competent-looking fashion with cameras everywhere while you're being scrutinised by two blokes – Gary and George – wandering along looking over your shoulder. I managed to not be one of the several cooks who chopped their fingers, and I made it through to the next round. Those who didn't get through went into the first elimination and a handful of them were swiftly, brutally, sent on their way.

The next challenge was to identify seventeen ingredients in a big pot of Bolognese. Gary talked about the unusual spices in there, and my brain fixed on this apparent clue as though it were some kind of life preserver. As a result, I managed to name some of the more obscure ingredients – cinnamon and nutmeg among them – but completely forgot tomatoes, garlic, onions, and basically everything in the most frequently cooked dish in my own kitchen. It would not be the last time in this competition my brain would seize up like poorly tempered chocolate, but it was one of the more mortifying.

After the Bolognese debacle I was put into my first elimination challenge, along with ten others. We were given fifty bucks each and taken to the Sydney Fish Market, where we had to shop for ingredients for two dishes. The $50 also had to pay for a taxi back to the kitchen. The longer it took us to get back to the kitchen, the less time we would have to cook.

We were standing on the pier, cash in hand and hearts racing, when Sarah uttered those words that would become our call to action for the months to come. The words that were, still are, the starter's pistol, an adrenalin trigger, a warning, a threat, an invitation: 'Your time starts . . . now!'

It was absolutely hectic, but I managed to get myself back to the kitchen with some sand whiting and beautiful sea scallops.

Cooking with gas burners in a huge, draughty warehouse is not straightforward. If you've ever tried to barbecue on a windy day you'll know what I mean – the flames just can't get enough heat to the pans. We were all in the same boat, though, all dealing with the same bizarre set of circumstances. Not only were we cooking in this enormous, melodramatic space, we were doing it under the weirdest of conditions – limited ingredients, limited time, with producers interrupting us to ask what we were doing and cameras documenting our every move. In all honesty, I kind of forgot about the cameras, and about the fact that this would be on television eventually. I had tunnel vision on the food; I just wanted to cook. I always thought of this not as a television show, but as a cooking competition.

While we cooked, George and Gary talked to each other off to the side about what each of us was doing. I heard them say something about my dishes being a bit 'domestic-y' and once again my heart skittered and my guts clenched as I second-guessed everything I had decided to make.

Our dishes were tasted one by one, not only by Gary, Matt and George, but also by Greg Doyle, owner and chef at Sydney's prestigious Pier restaurant. The feedback I got was fairly noncommittal, leaving me unsure of how I'd done.

The eleven of us were then asked to stand at the front of the room. Three names were called and the contestants stepped forward, to be told that unfortunately they would not make it any further in the competition.

Matt then said, 'Let's continue with this ugly elimination process. Julie, please step forward.'

Ah god, I thought, I'm done.

'Julie,' he continued, 'Greg's got something to say to you.'

'We felt you were the stand-out chef today,' Greg said. 'Your dishes were well presented, well cooked, lovely flavours. Well done.'

HOT AND COLD

And in that sixty seconds, I had a preview of the coming months. The nerves, the certainty of elimination, the dizzying high of positive feedback. The adrenalin that would surge through my bloodstream like waves on the beach. The inability to breathe or regulate my tears or form coherent thoughts.

I was climbing aboard the wildest rollercoaster of my life.

One afternoon during this week there was a meeting between the producers and those of us remaining contestants; around three-quarters of us. We were told for the first time that if we made it to the top twenty, we would have to live in a house in Sydney to be part of the competition.

I remember feeling numb. I had assumed the show would be like the gentle, civilised UK version, where everyone went home to their families at night and the season was done and dusted in about six weeks. If I had known – and I mean this with all sincerity – if I had known we had to live out of home to compete, I never, ever would have applied. I would have looked wistfully at the contestant call on television and wished that it had come along when our kids were bigger and our business could run without me.

Mick was just as shocked as I was when I was able to call and tell him. We discussed me pulling out altogether. I couldn't see how it could possibly work. After a long conversation, we decided that for now I would keep going and see how far I got. After all, I could be home the next day, eliminated.

'Let's not die wondering,' Mick said. 'Do your best and we'll see what happens.'

YOUR TIME STARTS NOW

The next day we walked through the enormous doors of the Carriageworks warehouse, to see thirty-seven workstations set up in a row. Each workstation had on it a single-burner camp stove, a chopping board, a knife and a timber crate. The very first *MasterChef* mystery box. What we didn't know was that after this cook, the judges would narrow us down to the twenty who would go into the *MasterChef* house and kitchen.

All around me, contestants were freaking out about having to cook with only one burner and one pan. All I could think of was our little cottage: the kitchen that was a corridor with the tap that came in through the window, the tiny benchtop, the hole of a stovetop, and internally I was fist-pumping and fizzing with a sense of destiny. I had been training for this moment! For two whole years I had been getting ready for this very challenge.

Inside the box was a pork chop, a lemon, some bread, parsley, tomatoes, cabbage, an apple, chocolate, sugar, eggs. We had thirty minutes to cook a dish using the ingredients in the box. We didn't have to use them all, but there was no external pantry to choose from. I saw pork, and apple, and cabbage – the makings of a classic pork and apple dish. I think most but not all of us used the pork chop that day.

Only a few minutes in, I placed the pork chop a bit too enthusiastically into my pan. It hit the hot oil and splashed a plume up over my chest. I froze in place for a second while it ran down my front. I thought of the onion challenge, where anyone calling for the nurse had wasted valuable minutes receiving attention. It was a short challenge; I decided to push ahead.

It was only when our time was up that I felt any pain. I remember turning to the woman who had cooked beside me and saying, 'I've burned myself.' She took one look at my chest and called for the nurse. They got my dish tasting out of the way first so that I could be taken to a medical centre. My feedback was lukewarm: the dish was well-cooked but not particularly exciting. The doctor couldn't really do anything for me beyond issuing a bit of burn cream. The oil left ugly splash- and drip-shaped marks on my chest for a few weeks before they faded away.

The next day we spent excruciating hours in a room waiting to be summoned before the judges and told whether or not we had made it into the top twenty. Throughout the week we had been getting to know each other, bit by bit. It was during this time that I had attached myself to Tom Mosby, who was hanging out by himself at the fringes of a lot of very chatty, hyper-excited people. I'm not sure that he wanted company, but I was nervous so I yapped like a chihuahua and eventually must have endeared myself to him, and so began our friendship.

As the day wore on, the producers would come into the room and ask a person or group of people to come and see the judges. Sometimes the whole group would return to the room ecstatic; they had all got through to the top twenty. Sometimes the whole group was devastated; none of them had made it. Occasionally they would ask two people to go in together, and one would be offered a place and the other one would not. It was a hard process and a long day.

I feel as though it was quite late in the day when I was called in, by myself. Through the doors and down the length of the dark warehouse I went. The path was dramatically down-lit with spotlights every few metres. At the end of this were the three judges, perched on stools, with those inscrutable faces I would get to know so well in the coming months.

I had to state my case: why I wanted to be there, and why food was so important to me. 'It's how I show love,' I said. Eventually Matt said that I needed to go home to my family and tell them the bad news. 'I'm out,' I thought. But no – the bad news was that Mick and the boys would have to cope without me for a while because I was through to the top twenty!

I ran back into that room and was swept up into an enormous hug by Tom and a few of the others I had made friends with, all of us jumping for joy. We knew even then that it was the start of something huge.

Roasted lamb rump with garlic and rosemary
Serves 4

3 lamb rumps, around 350 to 400 g each
2 cloves garlic, chopped
½ cup fresh rosemary leaves, finely chopped
½ teaspoon garlic powder
Salt
Freshly ground black pepper
Olive oil

Sauce
½ cup white wine
½ cup chicken stock
1 clove garlic, halved
1 rosemary sprig

Preheat oven to 180°C.

Turn lamb rump upside down on chopping board. Carefully create a split lengthwise, only cutting about two-thirds of the way through the rump.

HOT AND COLD

Combine the garlic and rosemary, and stuff a quarter of the mix into the incision of each rump. Tie with cooking twine to create a neat cylindrical shape.

Combine the garlic powder with plenty of salt and pepper, and scatter on a tray. Roll a lamb rump through the seasoning to coat thoroughly. Repeat with remaining rumps.

Sear the rumps in a frying pan with olive oil, until all sides are golden brown. Transfer to a baking tray (or use the frying pan if it has an ovenproof handle) and bake at 180°C for around 10 minutes. Test by piercing with a skewer. Pink juices indicate a medium roast, bright red indicates a little more cooking time required.

Rest the meat for 10 minutes before serving.

Meanwhile, deglaze the pan with white wine. Add garlic, rosemary and chicken stock. Simmer until reduced to about two-thirds of a cup, and thickened. Serve with the lamb.

CHAPTER 8
THIS IS ME

I headed home with only two weeks to prepare to go into the *MasterChef* house. There was so much to be done: I had multiple roles in the business that needed to be procedurised and handed over. Not to mention family logistics – who would take the boys to sport and art; who would cook dinner; who would take care of the house? Mick and I had always shared these jobs, and to take one half of our team out of the picture was definitely going to leave a gaping hole in our family life. The boys were in Years 5, 6 and 7. They still needed their mum. They needed help with homework, and hugs, and the right uniform on the right day, and matching socks. They needed hot dinners.

Mum and Dad committed to coming up the coast every week to help around the house. Debbie came to work at Loyal IT to do some of the jobs I had been doing. Our friends and our Family Group arranged for meals to be dropped over and to have the boys for dinner. Others helped with taking the boys to their after-school activities. A whole community machine sprang into action to support my family while I was absent.

Nevertheless, I can tell you that there was an enormous amount of mum guilt in the decision to take this opportunity. Enormous.

Moving into the *MasterChef* house with nineteen strangers was quite the experience. The house was a five-storey waterfront mansion on Darling Point, a wealthy suburb on a peninsula overlooking Sydney Harbour. The entry was at street level and the front of the building ran down a cliff face from there. Upon arrival, our bags were searched and our phones removed. I knew my phone would be taken away but was surprised when my laptop, keys and even my wallet were removed from my bags. When I asked why they needed my wallet, I was told *I* wouldn't be needing it. I think it was to remove the possibility of us busting out for a wild weekend or something.

In the house there was a lift, a lap pool, and a huge master bedroom with a spa bath in the middle of it. There was a bidet in the upstairs bathroom. All the surfaces were hard and the house echoed. If you sneezed on the top floor someone would bless you from the bottom floor. We were told that we were not allowed out at all, and that the foyer and front door would be alarmed at night. (They weren't, I tested that early on in the piece.) Treadmills and a ping-pong table were eventually installed in the garage so that we could exercise without going out of the house.

We settled in, as much as we could. We all shared rooms; some rooms had only two beds while a big living area downstairs was set up with bunk beds. This was the party room. The master bedroom with the bathtub became a bit of a bachelor pad, with four of the guys sharing it. I was in a three-bed room for a while, which I moved out of as numbers began to ease.

We were allowed two fifteen-minute phone calls home per week. These were initially supervised but later we were allowed to take the calls in private. This was nowhere near enough contact for me and my boys. Most nights I was back from filming well after they were in bed, so sometimes a couple of weeks would go by without me being able to speak to them. It caused us a lot of heartache. One day I was talking to Paddy. He was ten, he'd had a hard day at school and he was crying. I was crying too.

'I wish I could be there to give you a hug, Paddy,' I told him.

'It's my dream for you to give me a hug,' he said, 'and it's your dream to win *MasterChef*. So make your dream come true, then come home and make my dream come true.'

Looking back at the cooking challenges in series 1, I am struck by the differences in the rules between then and now. As is frequently noted, the standard of cooking has gone up and up over the years. There are lots of reasons for this; one is that we were initially set up for maximum drama rather than cooking the best food. Each time we were sent into the pantry we were given not only a time limit but also an ingredient limit. Most days, it was two minutes in the pantry and ten ingredients. We couldn't return to the pantry if we forgot something – it was just tough luck. In recent seasons, contestants can return to the pantry as many times as they like, and take as many ingredients as they wish.

As a small business owner, I know that one of the keys to success is knowing your target market. In our IT business, our clients were small to medium businesses, with a certain number of employees and a certain set of business goals and requirements. It was our mission to understand the needs of our clients and assist them to reach their business goals. In *MasterChef*, my target market was almost exclusively Gary, Matt and George. I tried to get to know them, and what they were looking for, as best I could under the circumstances. Contestants were kept completely separate from the judges when we weren't actually in the kitchen. But it was in the kitchen that I needed to find out what they liked.

THIS IS ME

At the beginning, when the judges were tasting our dishes, the guys up the back of the kitchen couldn't hear the feedback Matt, Gary and George were giving the contestant at the front of the room. I asked for some amplification so we didn't miss any important tidbits of information, and a speaker was provided so we could hear every critique. I learned that George didn't like too much chilli, and he hated it if you took the cute little tops off your beans. Gary loved sweet things, saucy things and crunchy things. Matt loved to get the story behind the dish. I took these and other little gems and served my very niche target market as best I could.

At the beginning of each day, we stood at the front of the imposing *MasterChef* kitchen, facing the judges, waiting to hear what the day's challenge would be. I can still feel the tension in my body, my shoulders hunched and my jaw clenched, hands and knees shaking. I was in this heightened state for much of the time, in and out of challenges. I never once slept through the night; I awoke with my heart thundering, shaking off the remnants of some cooking-disaster-related nightmare. Fight, flight or freeze; this adrenalin-fuelled state became my norm. Sometimes I froze. Sometimes I fought. But I never fled.

For our first invention test, the theme was Italian food and we were given a whole rabbit to cook with. Two panicked minutes in the pantry and ten ingredients later, I was at my bench looking at a protein I had never eaten, let alone cooked, and at my sorry array of ingredients, none of which was remotely Italian. The dish I cooked was abysmal. I believe that Matt's commentary was along the lines of him being sad for the mother of my rabbit, knowing that her baby had died for this plate of food. It was brutal but justified, and I found myself in the first pressure test of the season.

Back then, for pressure tests we were supplied with a black t-shirt and pants to go with our black aprons. Over the next few months I became accustomed to this outfit, as my *MasterChef* road went up over high hills and down into deep valleys, over and over and over.

The first pressure test of the first season of *MasterChef Australia* now seems almost ridiculously simple: an apple tarte tatin. I was not much of a dessert cook – my cooking had grown mainly from my desire to feed my family and to entertain my friends. We didn't eat weeknight desserts at home, and when I had friends over I usually tasked them with bringing the sweets. So a dessert was not my ideal scenario. But in a pressure test we were given a recipe, and all the ingredients were already at the bench. This was so different to the other challenges, where we didn't have any recipe at all and no access to them, and we had to gather our own ingredients within the cooking time. With a recipe – as I saw it, a full set of instructions – in front of me, I was able to make a tasty tart and survive the day. It served as a warning, though: I would have to cook things well outside my comfort zone – like desserts – in this competition. Little did I know then, how often my entire fate would rest on a sweet dish I had never encountered before.

~

I had been gone from home for about three weeks when my nan turned ninety. After a lot of to-ing and fro-ing between the producers and my family, I was allowed to attend the birthday party in her nursing home. That weekend I was driven from the *MasterChef* house to Pennant Hills and given a couple of hours to see everyone and wish Nan a happy birthday. I was so very grateful to be allowed to do this.

At one point Mick asked me to come out to the van to look at some clothes he'd brought, to see if I wanted to take any back to the house with me. When he opened the back door, all the seats were folded down and there was a mattress and blankets and pillows laid out. I laughed so hard I could hardly breathe. A few minutes later we were back inside, having birthday cake and hoping nobody noticed a bit of dishevelment.

We contestants kind of settled into the routine of our new lives, if you could call it a routine. We knew that episodes filmed for a Sunday night would consist of a mystery box then an invention test, which was followed by a celebrity chef challenge and a pressure test to eliminate someone. We knew that team challenges were followed by a team vote. Team challenges in season 1 were their own kind of torture. The elected captains took turns choosing their team members. This gave me flashbacks to primary school, where I was always chosen near to last for team sports, my fellow students being awake to the lack of coordination and skill I would bring to the game. I was slightly surprised to find the same thing happening in this cookery arena. I was pretty sure I could cook better than I could hit a softball, but nobody else seemed to have figured that out yet.

The big difference between season 1 and every season that came after it was how the team wins and losses were handled. Back then, the winning team would be sent to a reward lunch in an iconic Sydney restaurant, while the losing team had to vote for somebody to go home. This system had a really unfortunate side effect – it created alliances and tensions between us. Contestants were always courting the majority so that if their team lost, they would be popular enough to remain in the game. It was a bit like *Survivor* – you needed to be in a strong alliance if you were going to survive the 'tribal' or team vote. This left me feeling quite vulnerable; I felt that if I wasn't seen as being valuable enough to be chosen early in a team pick, I might be in trouble if our team lost. Thankfully I was only on the losing side of a team challenge once throughout the whole competition, so I didn't have to get involved in those manoeuvrings very often.

I did, however, enjoy some wonderful lunches and glimpses into some of the top kitchens in the city. The most memorable kitchen was Peter Gilmore's Quay restaurant, on Sydney Harbour. After an amazing lunch of food I didn't even know existed, he took us into his enormous kitchen. I was stunned: there was gentle music playing, and an army of chefs working quietly at their stations, performing the exacting tasks required to produce Quay's outstanding cuisine. It was such a far cry from the kitchen at the Black Stump, with smoke billowing, pans crashing and swear words flying.

There were often cameras at the house, capturing us getting ready to leave for the day, or waiting at night to see who would come home from an elimination. Every time we were up for elimination we had to pack our bags with all of our belongings – if we were out, we didn't get to come back to the house to say goodbye to our friends. My minor rebellion against this rule was never to remove my photos from the wall. I started with a couple of them but as Mick and my friends sent me pictures from home they were added to my collection until images of home and people close to me covered the whole wall. My rationale was that if I didn't take them with me, I would have to come back to them, and that would keep me safe. It was one of the superstitions I developed along the way. I also wore lucky socks that Tom Mosby had given to me.

I was so grateful to have Tom in the house. We had a lot in common: we were both in decades-long, committed relationships; we shared many of the same life values and a had a similar sense of humour. We hatched wildly improbable escape plans, shared stories about home, fought over the crosswords in the paper, and we had each other's back. More than once you could find us in the kitchen of the house, singing Kenny Rogers songs into broom handles at the end of a long, stressful day.

The group of contestants was always collected early in the morning from the house and driven to the kitchens in readiness for filming. But there were no amenities for us there, and just about everything was filmed as the producers and director worked out the shots they'd need, which meant a lot of downtime. We spent many hours sitting on the gravel driveway outside the studio waiting for our challenges to begin. With no phones, computers, coffee machines or even chairs to distract us, there was literally nothing to do but talk about food, complain about the conditions, and crack each other up with stupid stories. On rainy days we'd be allowed up to the mezzanine level of the *MasterChef* kitchen, where there was a collection of couches we could use. Us being up there made it hard for Production, though, as they had to try to set up challenges with us essentially in the same room. Nowadays there's a green room for contestants which is actually very comfortable.

We filmed our interviews at night and on Saturdays, when we had to describe – in the present tense and in the first person – what had happened during each challenge. This is how the show is narrated – by the contestants. We were instructed on how to do this: we were to describe what we had been doing during the cook in the present tense. For example, 'So I'm cracking my eggs and whisking them as quickly as I can . . .' or 'I'm almost finished cooking the chicken when I realise I have set my tea towel on fire.' Some of us took to this more naturally than others; it's a weird way to speak. During the cook, the producers would take notes on what we were doing at any given time, to help us to remember when we were in the interview room.

On Sundays we were sent out to various restaurants and cafés around Sydney to do work experience in their kitchens and learn about cooking in commercial environments. From fine dining restaurants to local cafés and pubs, we were given a taste of real kitchen life. In these places, we weren't television contestants, we were an extra pair of hands, and we were put to work. The experiences ranged widely. In one café that seated a couple of hundred people for breakfast, I learned the simplest, most effective way to poach eggs, which I still use to this day. In one very posh, highly regarded restaurant, I was immediately confronted with a familiar old-school attitude. 'We have two four-letter words that we use all the time in this kitchen,' said the head chef, looking closely at me as he enunciated clearly: '*Salt*, and *cunt*. If you can't hack it, you can fuck off.' Ah, but I had met men like this before, little men with big mouths. I'd stared them down in the juvenile detention centre, I had put them in their place at the Black Stump, and I wasn't going to give this guy the satisfaction of a reaction. I didn't flinch, I looked at him levelly and said, 'Where would you like me to start?'

My favourite story from these work experience days was from Poh and Andre. Poh was as renowned as I was for being a messy cook; and also like me, she'd had some disasters in among her high points. She was creative, effervescent and enormous fun to be around. Andre was kind of like her annoying brother, or maybe Poh was the annoying sister. Andre had stated all along that he wanted to open an Italian restaurant, and that his passion was Italian food. He never wavered from this, and many years later is one of the best restaurateurs in South Australia. But for now, they were a happily squabbling pair of reality TV show contestants, lost in Sydney. One Sunday they had completed their shift in a kitchen a couple of suburbs from the house, and jumped into a taxi to return. They handed the driver the cabcharge card they'd been given, but then realised they had no idea of the address and no way to call anyone as our phones had been confiscated. The cabbie ended up driving randomly around Darling Point until Poh and Andre saw a familiar-looking street and could navigate from there. This certainly highlighted a few of the logistical loopholes in our situation.

Life in the house was hectic, especially at the beginning. We were twenty strangers vying for kitchen and bathroom time; people who snored and ones who partied; some who didn't clean up their own dishes or change the toilet roll. One day there was blowout over an empty toilet roll that somehow had ended up in the bowl and clogged things for a bit. There were accusations and finger-pointing and, really, far more fuss made than there should have been. I stayed out of it; I had already fulfilled my lifetime quota of toilet-roll conversations before I'd got to this house.

At home, Mick and I had a rhythm about us, a routine, almost a dance; we shared our space with a minimum of fuss, mostly in peace and harmony. The boys obviously created their own brand of havoc, as kids do, but it was a cakewalk compared with the competing needs of these twenty adults in one house.

As contestants were eliminated, though, and the numbers dwindled, logistics became slightly more manageable and we found a more harmonious way to live together.

About six weeks into the competition, we were allowed to go home for the Easter long weekend. All of us were utterly overjoyed when we were told. The first episode of the show was due to begin two weeks after Easter, so that long weekend the promo ads were running, which was making it easier for my boys. Instead of me simply being gone, they could properly understand now that I was gone for a reason – and one they could get excited about. That Easter was so special. We stuck to each other like glue. I cooked our traditional Easter roast – pork with crackling, and lamb and potatoes and gravy and all the sides. I had to do this; even when we lived in the cottage with no oven at all, I borrowed my friend's kitchen to cook the Easter roast. It's a non-negotiable part of our family life and it was my absolute joy to be doing this for them, in my house, my own kitchen, no giant clock hanging over my head.

Saying goodbye on the Monday night was incredibly hard – we knew that we wouldn't get to see each other for a while, or talk to each other very often at all.

When the show came on air a couple of weeks later, the boys at least felt like they got to *see* me, even if they couldn't talk to me. And of course the show became a frequent topic of conversation among their friends, which I think eased the difficulty of me being away from them a little bit.

I had one of my best and one of my worst days in the kitchen all in the same week. It was filmed over two days but went to air on one Sunday night episode.

The mystery box was revealed to be a cupcake challenge. More than one contestant expressed the opinion that this was my challenge to lose. I wondered if this was because I was a mum, or because I was fat. Either way, these opinions were incorrect because baking was not my bag, and except for a few months in my new house, I hadn't made any kind of cake in an oven for a couple of years. So, cupcakes weren't one of my strengths, but we had a basic recipe and I'd made enough of them in the past to give it a good go.

Our brief was to make a signature cupcake, and we had a huge array of ingredients to choose from, which was a nice change from the usually limited pantry. I decided to keep mine straightforward and to make the most lemony cupcakes I could. I used the yellow and green layers from licorice allsorts to carve little lemon segments and leaves to decorate the cakes, and I called them Lemon Divas. When I was asked why, I said because they're pretty to look at but they pack a punch.

One of my single favourite moments of the competition was when George, after the clock had stopped but before the official tasting, came by to sample our cakes. He cut one into quarters and popped a quarter into his mouth as he went by. Now George never ate very much of anyone's dish, he only kind of nibbled at things and tasted enough to get the idea. So when he turned back and grabbed the rest of the cake I was jumping around on the inside. He likes it! He likes it!!!

I did win the cupcake challenge, confirming the beliefs of the other contestants even though they were baseless. I received the advantage for the invention test, which was to select the main ingredient that everyone had to cook with, and also to have extra time to choose ingredients. We used to call it 'the curse of the mystery box', because almost without exception whoever had this advantage mucked up the next challenge. I thought I would buck this trend. I did not.

As the mystery box was unveiled the following day, so was the celebrity chef and judge for that episode, and it was none other than the long-time host of the UK series, John Torode. Bear in mind that in the months leading up to my application for the Australian inaugural series, I had been binge-watching the UK version of *MasterChef* in my new house, so when its esteemed judge walked into the kitchen in Sydney, my belly did some weird flip thing and my brain hung the 'out to lunch' sign in the window while it went on a fangirl spree.

The theme was British, my chosen ingredient was a leg of lamb, and I was a disaster. I'd taken on too many tasks, and ran out of time; my veggies were still in the oven rather than on the plate, my sauce was on the stove, and the butchery on my lamb, which I had intended to roll and stuff, was disastrous. In between the end of cooking and the tasting I pleaded with the producers not to make me serve my dish to John. They insisted that I had to. It was mortifying, but he was kind, telling me I was a good cook having a bad hair day. If only he knew. Every day is a bad hair day for me, but I almost always cook better than I had for him. Back into the 'chef outfit of doom', as I dubbed it, and into another pressure test.

It was after this debacle that it really dawned on me that if I didn't get a handle on my ridiculous nerves, I would be out on my ear before too long. I embarked on a mission to gain control over my exploding brain. I read some books about it, and I started to do breathing exercises and other cognitive behaviour practices to help me to focus and stay on task even when things went wrong. As the weeks went by, I became better able to settle into the unpredictable nature of this experience and more calmly face whatever came my way. But these practices didn't always work, and they weren't a cure-all. There would still be a rocky path ahead for me in this kitchen.

In the real world, it was coming up to Mother's Day. I asked very nicely if there was a chance we could skip Sunday work experience to spend the day with our families. The answer at first was just no. Only a couple of us in the house were mothers, so the reasoning was that it would be unfair to everybody else to let us have a special day. I campaigned a little, pointing out that *all* of us would love a day off and to be allowed out and about for a few hours. We were all on board with this idea and, about two days before Mother's Day, we were told that we would in fact be allowed out for the whole day. We were under strict instructions to return by 9 p.m. I asked our house coordinator how early I could leave. She said she didn't care, as long as I didn't wake everybody up.

THIS IS ME

I made the call to Mick. He was beside himself. He had previously declared that it would be easier if I were in prison because he would at least get conjugal visits. ('Easier for who?' I'd asked.) Anyway, when I told him I could leave as early as I wanted, he said with not a hint of a joke, 'I'll be there at 1 a.m.'

I wasn't sure that 'leaving early' meant 'leaving in the middle of the night', but I figured it's better to ask forgiveness than permission. Which is how I found myself, as a thirty-eight-year-old mother of three, sneaking out of the house with my shoes in one hand and my bag in the other, relieved that the front door was not in fact alarmed. Mick was out the front with the engine running, and we cacked ourselves all the way home to the Central Coast, where I got to wake up in my own bed for Mother's Day.

After the most beautiful few hours with my boys and my dogs and my couch and my kitchen, we piled into the van and drove back to the house in Darling Point. It was a few minutes to 9. We were all holding on to each other; we were all crying. I looked at those heavy timber doors, and I could not make my feet move towards them. I made a decision.

'Take me home,' I said to Mick.

He looked shocked.

'Let's just go. I can't go back in there. Please take me home.'

This is what I identify now as another of those pivotal, life-changing moments. If Mick had done what I'd asked, I would have gone back to the Central Coast and been so happy to be back with my family.

But he didn't. This man, who was missing me so much, and was suffering without me in every area of his life, held my face and said, 'Babe. You'll be home soon enough. But first, go back in there and finish what you started.'

So I did.

YOUR TIME STARTS NOW

Lemon Diva cupcakes

They look pretty, but they pack a punch. Popular with children and *MasterChef* judges.

Prep and cooking time: 20 minutes
Makes 12

Cupcakes
100 g unsalted butter, softened
¾ cup (165 g) caster sugar
½ tsp vanilla extract
2 eggs
1⅓ cups (200 g) self-raising flour
½ cup (125 ml) milk
zest of 3 lemons

Icing
125 g unsalted butter, softened
2 cups icing sugar mixture
2 tablespoons lemon juice
1 drop yellow food colouring, if desired
licorice allsorts

Preheat the oven to 180°C (160°C fan-forced).

Line a 12-hole cupcake pan with paper cases.

Using electric beaters, beat the butter, sugar and vanilla extract until light and creamy. Mix through the lemon zest.

Add the eggs, one at a time, beating well after each egg. Gently fold through the flour and milk in two alternate batches.

Divide the mixture evenly among the paper cases. Bake for about 12 minutes, or until golden brown and springy when touched. Remove from oven and transfer to a wire rack to cool completely before decorating.

THIS IS ME

To make the icing, use an electric beater to beat the butter until light and creamy. Add the icing sugar a little at a time, beating constantly. Add half the lemon juice and beat until well combined. Add remaining lemon juice a little at a time until the desired consistency is reached.

Pipe onto the cooled cupcakes. Decorate with a small lemon shape cut from a yellow piece of licorice allsort.

CHAPTER 9

UNDER PRESSURE

The weeks went by, and I held my own. Sometimes I skated through the middle, neither the best nor the worst on the day. Other times I lost my shit completely, ended up in a pressure test, and managed to pull it back on black apron day. Looking back, I wouldn't have it any other way. Every pressure test was another chance to cook in that kitchen, to strengthen my skills and my resolve, to build my fitness for the unique nature of this competition. By the time I reached finals week I had been in more eliminations than anyone else, and had managed to beat at least one person every time. Which was, at the end of the day, all I needed to do.

I was still running on adrenalin. My heart never fully slowed down, nor did my brain. Sleep was broken and my guts were constantly in a state. Routine of any kind was non-existent.

The weeks went by and, one by one, our fellow contestants were sent home. Some eliminations were harder to bear than others. Sometimes as we sat on that couch at the end of the day, waiting to see who would come down the stairs or the elevator, I would be wishing so very hard that it would be my mates who had prevailed.

UNDER PRESSURE

Of course, sometimes it was not, and the world inside the Darling Point mansion would become smaller in more ways than one.

Contact with my family still consisted only of our twice-weekly phone calls and the letters and cards we sent back and forth to each other.

While I was away, Mick had been struggling. Looking after the business, caring for the boys, sharing the care for his mum with his siblings, just missing me – all of it was taking a toll. He didn't tell me that he had been losing weight and seeing a doctor for anxiety, but my friends in their letters described how hard he was working and how sad he was. I didn't know what to do. He assured me that he wanted me to stay and keep competing.

I have all the letters that Mick and I wrote each other during this time. My beautiful husband, who had for years been dreadful at expressing his feelings, found the language of his heart. His letters were many and long. They swung from love and pride, encouragement and strength, to frustration at the limited contact, grief, loneliness. My letters to him spoke of fear and excitement, of anxiety and isolation, of being away from my tribe and surrounded by strangers and competitors. And love – we both wrote about love. The things we loved about each other. What we missed the most. What we looked forward to; what the future might hold, and how it didn't actually matter as long as we were together. The journal he kept while I was away counted down the days from the start and the days until the end. He never wavered in his belief that I would win.

He started to include in his letters bits and pieces from our past. Notes we'd left each other on the kitchen bench from when we first moved in together. A card I'd made him for his twenty-first birthday. Photos of us as teenagers. Tickets to concerts we'd been to. The minute details of a shared life – things I never knew he had kept. Evidence of two people utterly intertwined and dependent on one another. All this went up on the photo wall next to my bed, and I could feel our whole shared past radiating out from that wall as I slept and woke, slept and woke in this house that was not my home.

Every week the boys would write a newsletter for me. Each contained a photo of them, their highlight of the week and their favourite dinner, news from school and a joke. This is how I learned about new footy boots, sleepovers, who was helping with the cooking; stories about the dogs and homework and random little pieces of their day.

Although Mick and the boys wrote and sent these newsletters regularly, mail was only passed on to us sporadically. I could go a couple of weeks without any, then receive a huge bundle from not only my household, but my friends and parents and extended family as well. One lunchtime, I was showing one of the producers my letter from the boys and she burst into tears.

'What's wrong?' I asked, surprised.

'I just sometimes forget that you guys have lives outside of here,' she said. Which was, I thought, incredibly honest.

At home, I was a list-maker, a diary-keeper, a planner. I had all the details covered and knew what each day had in store. Some might say unspontaneous and a control freak, others might say organised and efficient. A diagnosis of such traits might mention perfectionism or the unrelenting standards schema, but that would come later. The point is, I always liked to know what was ahead. *MasterChef*, by the very nature of the competition, didn't allow this. In fact, we were kept deliberately in the dark so our reactions on camera would be authentic. We often didn't know what time we had to be awake the next morning until we were about to go to bed. We were never told what the following day would bring, which led to a lot of speculation and some truly creative, hilarious, and way-off theories. In order to survive I had to let go of my need for control, and embrace whatever the day brought. And it brought a wide variety of experiences. In the space of only a few weeks we had cooked for celebrities, competed in hectic team challenges, eaten in beautiful restaurants, and cooked with ingredients we'd never seen before.

And yet I was still knocked sideways by the sight of Adriano Zumbo walking through the doors with that bloody croquembouche. After the most hectic cook so far in the competition, the four of us in that challenge were elated. We had all managed to make a croquembouche! Poh's was a work of art – she'd somehow gone from staring into the oven in a kind of trance to producing something you'd see in a French bridal magazine. Mine was, of course, stumpy; Chris's was pallid; and Tom's had a bit of a lean, which became more pronounced as time wore on.

Over the next couple of hours, the four of us experienced those *MasterChef* mood swings that anyone who has been on the show knows so well. We were sitting in a room waiting to take our 'tower of terror' to Gary, George, Matt and Adriano to be judged. Our mood ebbed with our adrenalin levels as it sank in that one of us would be leaving. We had all managed to make a croquembouche, for god's sake. The unfairness of it rankled. Tears were shed. Elimination never stopped being a brutal process.

The quality of my choux pastry and crème patissière saved me, despite the stumpiness of my croquembouche. Tom, my trusted friend, my roomy, my karaoke partner and provider of lucky socks, was eliminated. I was heartbroken.

It was around this time that Mick's mum started to decline rapidly. The lymphoma was accelerating and she was placed into palliative care and given only weeks to live. Mick told me this on the phone during one of our scheduled calls. I told him that I was packing my bags, that I wanted to be at home for him and for my boys. He sounded so exhausted, so beaten down, but he said to me, 'Jules, you can't quit. This whole community has rallied around us. Our family has put their lives on hold for us. Everybody is pitching in so that you can be there. If you're eliminated, I will welcome you home with open arms. But you can't quit.'

I spoke to the producers and told them what was going on at home. I told them I was worried about my family and I thought I should be with them. A decision was reached that I would be given a phone call each day, if filming allowed, to touch base with home and make sure everyone was all right. This was a kindness for which I will forever be grateful.

Mick and I came to an arrangement. I would ask him each time I spoke to him if he needed me to come home. He promised to be honest and say yes, if he did need me to. And I promised that if that happened, there would be no second-guessing and no looking back – I would come.

Every time we spoke from then on, I asked, 'Do you need me to come home?'

And every time, Mick replied, 'Ask me again tomorrow.' And so it went.

The competition rolled on. We cooked for a posh cocktail party, we attended masterclasses, we catered a wedding on a boat on Sydney Harbour. The wedding was huge: we weren't just catering the event, the night before we had to bake the wedding cake. Poh, the accomplished artist of the group, stayed up all night to decorate the cake with a filigree of hand-piped black lace to

UNDER PRESSURE

match the bride's wedding gown trim. It seemed to me so unfair, given her effort, that after the wedding dinner she was put up for elimination and ultimately sent home.

One of the things I loved about our season was that quite often in team challenges the punters got to decide who won. They either voted, or they paid for their food, and whichever team made the most money was the winner. I liked it when the public got to choose as I felt that I could make food to please ordinary people more successfully than I could make food that pleased the judges. These days, the punters eat and the judges judge – I haven't seen a popularly voted challenge in years.

By now, seven of us were left in the competition. Five were in the kitchen – Chris, Andre, Sam Ciaravolo, a young call centre manager, Justine Schofield, a feisty and wonderful cook of French cuisine, and me. Julia Jenkins, previously a marketing specialist, and Lucas Parsons, a professional golfer before he'd turned to cooking, would be coming back to compete in finals week. Julia and Lucas had both cooked for immunity against a celebrity chef – Julia against Pete Evans, and Lucas against Ben O'Donoghue – and respectively won. The prize for beating a chef in series 1 was that you made it straight to finals week – but the twist was, you had to leave the *MasterChef* kitchen in the meantime. Julia and Lucas were free to go and work in commercial kitchens, or study, or practise at home, or do whatever they wanted to hone their skills ready for battle when they returned. I actually think this was a dreadful disadvantage, especially for Julia, who 'won' the prize quite early in the competition. Cooking in the *MasterChef* kitchen is different to any other kitchen in the world, and the best training for doing so is, in my opinion, to be in that unique kitchen. I think the producers came to the same conclusion because this was never again offered as a prize.

To our astonishment, some weeks before this, those of us who remained were told we needed our passports. So we were obviously going to go overseas at some stage, if we weren't eliminated in the meantime. That's all we were told – we needed passports.

Mine had long expired, and due to me never officially having changed my name when Mum remarried, it became a bit of a palaver to get a new one. Despite the fact that I'd had a driver's licence, a marriage certificate and a previous passport with the maiden name I had used since I was six years old, I had to get a heap of paperwork done to change my birth name to my step-dad's name, even though I was now using my married name. Bureaucracy at its finest. I was unable to assist in my own cause, because I didn't know anything about the trip I wanted a passport for. I was taken by production to the passport office in Sydney to get it sorted in person. I was told to tell them it was urgent.

'Where are you travelling?' asked the lady at the desk.

'I don't know.'

'When is the trip and how long is it for?'

'I'm really sorry, I don't know.' Good grief. I tried to explain that I was in a very weird situation. I tried to do it in a way that didn't mention *MasterChef*, which I was not allowed to do, as it would provide a possible spoiler for who was still in the series at that point. Eventually, the producer who had taken me to the office asked me to go to the other side of the room so that they could speak out of my earshot.

After the series was finished, I was told that this roadblock had caused quite the panic. A lot of conversations needed to be had and papers signed before I was issued a passport, just in the nick of time for the big announcement: we were going to Hong Kong!

I had never been to Hong Kong, or anywhere in Asia for that matter, and to say I was excited was an understatement. Of course I knew it wouldn't be a resort-style holiday, but I was thrilled to be going somewhere new.

So, as the final weeks of the competition began, Chris, Sam, Andre, Justine and I arrived at the Langham Hotel, along with around forty crew. It was enormous. The five of us were put into a suite, where the boys shared one half of the space and Justine and I had a room together. We were, as always, kept very separate from the judges, Sarah Wilson, and the crew.

That night we were taken on a walk through the amazing wet markets to get a feel for the city's food culture. The streets were lined with vendors selling their wares in a vibrant array. Exotic fresh fruit and vegetables lined up alongside whole barbecued ducks and slabs of juicy glazed pork hung from hooks, and tubs and tubs of live fish, strange clams and unidentifiable pulsating anemones. I had never seen anything like it.

We filmed long hours each day. I had one of those weeks where I hit all the highs as well as all the lows. After a dumpling challenge, won by Sam, we travelled to a fishing village where we had to 'catch' our own fish out of a big tub, and cook it outdoors on a pier. The recipe was a steamed rainbow fish, and we were given a demo by a skilled Cantonese chef of how to humanely kill the fish, fillet and steam it, and make all the beautiful garnishes to go with it.

The fish were huge, probably fifty centimetres long. It took me forever to catch mine – he was feisty as hell. Maybe he saw the steamer basket with his name on it. I eventually got him onto my cooking bench, ready to conk him on the head and knock him out, and he flipped his big tail, sweeping all my bowls onto the floor.

'Sorry, mate,' I said as I got a better grip and did the dirty deed. It was pretty gruesome, wrangling a live fish on TV – I've never seen another challenge where contestants have had to dispatch their own ingredients, and I am glad of it. Everyone else was already filleting; I was a hare-brained mess, but once I got underway I powered through and delivered the dish of the day.

Having won this challenge, I was given the opportunity to cook against a chef for the chance of going straight through to finals week. I was taken to the Hong Kong Jockey Club, an exclusive, expensive racing club.

I stood out on the balcony in the soupy humidity. I was sick as a dog that morning; it was appropriate that I was at a racetrack because I had a severe case of the trots. I let the production team know that if I said I needed a bathroom break, I was not mucking around and they'd better clear a pathway. Fortunately, someone found some kind of drug I could take and that problem was solved.

We got down to the brass tacks of the challenge. Donovan Cooke was the chef; I was to cook his signature pigeon and truffle dish against his young protégé. I didn't win, but I learned so much valuable stuff in that challenge. Donovan showed me how to layer thinly sliced truffle under the skin of a pigeon without tearing even a tiny hole; I learned how to use a sous-vide machine for the perfect cook on the breast, and how to make the tiniest amount of rich jus using the rest of his little bones. Donovan also gave me plenty of tips on how to streamline my processes and keep a bit more organised than I usually was.

The next day we cooked a mystery box outside our hotel, each of us with different ingredients. Chris won that challenge, which gave him immunity the following day from the Hong Kong Super Challenge. With hindsight, I am so glad I got to compete on this day, as it was possibly the most memorable of the whole competition.

UNDER PRESSURE

Justine and I were competing against Andre and Sam. We started at The Peak, a mountain top overlooking Victoria Harbour and Kowloon Peninsula. We were outside in the driving rain with the three judges. Matt was gesticulating dramatically and shouting into the wind about dragons and pirates and trade routes. We had three and a half hours to buy all our ingredients from the markets, find our way back to the hotel kitchen, and cook three dishes – razor scallops, suckling pig and a toffee apple dessert. We were given HK$1000 and a laminated map.

We ran around like headless chickens, trying to bridge the language gap with bewildered taxi drivers and bemused store owners. Eventually Jussy and I got everything we needed and set off sprinting for the ferry. We managed to leap aboard just as the gate was closed. We'd beaten the boys.

I don't know what it was about tearing around Hong Kong with a pig in a bag, us wringing wet and mostly lost, which made us laugh, but we did, helplessly, for the whole ferry trip back – we laughed like we'd lost our minds.

The laughter didn't last, though – we lost the challenge. That meant Jus and I had to go head to head in a pressure test. We cooked a sweet and sour duck with noodles, in the kitchens of Langham Place. Mine was deemed the better dish. Beating someone in a challenge like this was always bittersweet, especially if it's someone you're close to. Justine was by this stage a dear friend, someone who had shared so many wild experiences with me, a person whose team I loved to be on. She was also an accomplished cook, a huge personality, and as I told her more than once, the daughter I never had. Jussy went home, and Matt told me they were going to start calling me The Eliminator.

I was the only cook who competed in every challenge in Hong Kong. Some days I was still filming my interviews at 2 a.m., then was up again at 6. It was an exhilarating but exhausting week, and by the end of it the nerves of both crew and contestants had been rubbed raw.

I'm not sure if it was the sheer exhaustion of the week, or if I had gained all I wanted to from this experience, or if I just wasn't getting great vibes from Andre, Sam and Chris, who had morphed into a bit of a boys' club at that stage, but this was the point where I lost my mojo. I was 7000 kilometres from home. My family needed me. What the hell was I doing in Hong Kong, and even on *MasterChef*? It was time for me to go. I was happy to have made it to the top four, I could be proud of that and go back to my life with my head held high.

I was well aware of what was happening in my brain. I had watched it happen to some of the other contestants – that soft letting go, a willingness to exit this television world and re-enter the real one. When I saw one of the others enter this phase, I'd be sure that they would be the next to go. I didn't talk about this with anyone; I just thought it was an interesting observation. And now it was happening to me. I wasn't going to *quit*, but I was at peace with the idea of going home.

We flew back to Sydney and resumed the competition. For the next episode, we were taken to Garden Island, where the HMAS *Kanimbla* was docked, and up on the deck were Gary, George and Matt. Before the challenge was announced, a little boat came into view, heading straight for the ship. I couldn't quite tell who was on it at first, but as it drew closer I recognised my beautiful friends Poh, Tom and Justine.

And just like that, my mojo was back! Top seven? Forget it. Actually top nine, since Lucas and Julia would be rejoining us in finals week. Bugger that for a joke. My friends were back and my joy was instantly restored. The competitive lion inside me, who had laid down for a little rest, sprang back into action with a roar. Yeee-haw! Game on, bitches!

Amid the many wonderful experiences I had as a part of this inaugural series of the show, the greatest honour was to cook for the legendary Margaret Fulton. She arrived in the kitchen the following week, along with Armando Percuoco, pioneer of Italian dining in Australia; Jacques Reymond, iconic and hatted French chef; and Cheong Liew, recognised as being one of the fathers of modern Australian cuisine. This was a group with a mind-blowing two hundred years-plus experience and influence in Australian food between them.

Of the four, I was most familiar with Margaret Fulton. Her cookbooks were in just about every kitchen in the country; her first, *The Margaret Fulton Cookbook*, has sold a million and a half copies. She was eighty-three when we met her, and in her long career had demystified the cuisines of other nations, from those in Europe to Asia, and taken us on a journey, bridging gaps between cultures and making exotic or unknown dishes and ingredients achievable to meat-and-three-veg Australians. She was a beloved household name, she was and is one of my culinary heroes, and I could not have been more thrilled to see her walk through the doors.

When she spoke to us, she was so straightforward. Cook nice food. When you cook nice food, everyone loves you. Little children, even the dog loves you if you give it something nice to eat. Margaret was sprightly and sassy and smiley and warm. She reminded me of my nan. It made me more determined than ever to cook well for her and somehow by doing so, reach Nan, who I missed so much.

And I did cook nice food, for her and for those other esteemed guest judges. We served these culinary legends, and their host Matt, a formal dinner, taking a course each. I made a spiced layer cake with orange syrup, white chocolate and yoghurt ganache, almond crumble and fresh orange segments. In presenting my dish I got to talk about home, my beloved Central Coast, orchard country with orange trees in every backyard. Margaret loved it and I scored second highest after Justine, who wowed her own culinary hero, Jacques Reymond, with an exquisite duck dish.

The following year, Margaret Fulton wrote the foreword for my first cookbook. I have written seven cookbooks now, and no others have a foreword. I could never work out how to follow up a Margaret Fulton foreword, and decided that you can't. Her words are inspiring, kind, loving, lovely. Like her.

Not long after the Margaret challenge (as I thought of it), I was asked to come off set by a producer to take a phone call. I was instantly frightened – this could only be bad news. They never, ever interrupted filming. There were too many people involved, too many moving parts. I expected it to be Mick with news of his mum. I expected to be taken back to the house to pack my bags.

It wasn't Mick on the phone, it was my mum. She told me as gently as she could that Nan was very sick; that she was not expected to live much longer. Maybe weeks.

I couldn't quite grasp what was being said to me – at Nan's ninetieth birthday only a couple of months before, she had been so sharp and witty, alert and happy. When what was being said to me finally got through, I told Mum I'd be there as fast as I could be. I would leave right now.

'Julie, I want you to listen to me,' she said. 'If you're still there when the time comes, I will call you, and I'll ask you to leave. But for now you have to keep going.'

I objected and I cried. But Mum was firm. 'Nan would never forgive herself if you left because of her. She's the queen of the nursing home right now. Every morning the staff come and sit on the edge of her bed and they rehash last night's episode. She's so proud of you. Just keep going, and I'll call you when we need you.'

I took myself into the bathroom, sat on the loo and cried like my heart was breaking. Because it was. I felt so stuck, so deeply selfish for staying with this – this television program instead of being with my family. For leaving my husband to deal with our sons and their grief. For leaving my parents and my little sister to be with Nan. I look back on it now with bewilderment: I can't figure out what was happening inside me to even consider not walking out the door. All I can think of is that we had already been through so much, being apart for months now – that I had to hang in for the last few weeks to somehow make the whole thing worthwhile.

I eventually calmed down enough to come out of the bathroom. Standing at the door was a cameraman, and a story producer with a clipboard. I'd forgotten that we wore microphones every hour of every day; not only would they have heard my side of the phone call with my mother, they would have borne witness to my howling in the toilet as well.

'What are you so upset about, Julie?' the story producer asked. I'd always been very amenable to answering questions while I cooked and been really open about what was going wrong with my dishes. It's television, I get it, their job is to capture the drama and make a great show out of it. So I think it was a surprise to her when I looked straight down the barrel of the camera, shook my head and said, 'Not today.'

I would say to anyone who watches reality TV shows that sometimes, when a contestant is crying or distressed about something, it's very possibly not because of what's happening on the screen.

YOUR TIME STARTS NOW

You never know what's going on behind the scenes, what people are carrying around from their real life while they perform on camera.

―∽

White chocolate yoghurt ganache

This is a twist on your usual super-sweet ganache, the yoghurt giving a sour tang that makes it pair beautifully with spiced layer cake and fresh oranges. I have it on very good authority that Margaret Fulton loved it.

Prep time: 5 minutes
Cooking time: 5 mins

125 g white chocolate
½ cup (140 g) plain yoghurt

Melt the chocolate in a bowl over a pan of simmering water. Once melted, allow to cool slightly. Stir in the yoghurt and chill until serving time.

CHAPTER 10

THE FINAL COUNTDOWN

We were hurtling towards finals week when there was a 'Christmas in July' challenge which saw Jussy and I paired up as a team again. This time, though, we won, with a whole salmon as the centrepiece of our menu. We had to decide which one of us would cook against the chef for a chance to head straight to finals week. We had both already had the opportunity once each, me against Donovan Cooke and Jussy against Matt Moran, so we each wanted the other to take it. In the end we flipped a coin, and I was to cook against meat maestro Adrian Richardson.

The idea of beating Adrian and dodging the last few bullets before finals week was compelling, not to mention the opportunity to spend a few days at home. Under Adrian's patient instruction I learned how to bone out a saddle of lamb, and turn it into an elegant dish with a potato galette and a little sphere of baby spinach. I burned myself pretty badly during this challenge, grabbing the handle of a frypan that had just come out of the oven, but I didn't have time to stop. I got the dish finished, and I was so proud of it, but Adrian's was of course perfect. It didn't win me a ticket straight to finals week, but it did give me a welcome shot of confidence and some new skills as well.

Tom was back in the competition for only one day before he was eliminated again. I was gutted. Sam left after the Christmas in July challenge landed him in a pressure test. Andre was next in one of the elimination challenges that I always thought was harsh – a taste test.

Lucas and Julia returned to the kitchen after their time away, and there we were for finals week: Poh, Justine, Chris, Julia, Lucas and me. One of us would be eliminated each day, until the remaining two would go head-to-head in the grand finale.

The first elimination of that week was a pie challenge, with famed chef and restaurateur Luke Mangan. We had to cook two pies – a savoury and a sweet. We had two hours to produce them and the condition was that they both had to include pastry. I set about making a chicken and mushroom pie for my savoury, and a passionfruit and white chocolate tart for my sweet.

We were all pretty frantic in the kitchen. Pastry needs time to rest and, after it cooks, time to cool before you can take it out of the tin. My sweet pie shell hadn't had enough time to cool, and when I turned it out the sides collapsed. Once again my language had to be beeped out for viewing. I could see my exit from the competition right in front of me. And, I felt, it would be so easy simply to stop, throw in the towel, and go home. But my chicken pie was great, and by the time we had to stop cooking I'd managed to get my sweet tart on a plate. Because of its crumbled edges, I called it a Passionfruit Puddle Pie. I thought this was a stroke of marketing genius, but it was probably the most stupid thing I have ever done. Because it became the name for all the scandalous conspiracy theories that flowed about me from that episode on.

THE FINAL COUNTDOWN

I recall looking around at some of the other contestants who had not turned their pies out of the tin, and kicking myself. Why hadn't I thought of that? I could have served my sweet pie with its walls nicely buttressed by the tin, and Puddle Pie-gate (as it was later dubbed in certain newspapers) could have been avoided.

I had been back at home for a few days when this episode was broadcast. I was excited to watch finals week with Mick and the boys. But I will never forget the cold feeling of dread that settled over me as we watched the pie challenge unfold. I was stunned by the omission of every positive comment that was made about my dish. The edit did not show Luke Mangan asking me for my passionfruit crème patissière recipe, then saying he would happily serve it in his restaurant. It did not show him picking up the whole plate to keep eating it. It did not show George acknowledging that the pastry was well cooked, or any of the other positive reviews. My sweet-pie cook was aired as an unmitigated disaster.

In the world of television, this is called 'jeopardy'. It's a mechanism to ensure that the result is a mystery to viewers. On *MasterChef*, in my experience every dish, almost without exception, is rated with pluses and minuses. But of course how it is portrayed to viewers is a matter for the editing suite.

I've always kind of raised an eyebrow at reality TV contestants who claim to have been edited unfairly. Certainly, personality traits can be exaggerated by only showing certain sides of us and playing down or entirely omitting others. But nobody's personality is ever truly contrived. They can't show you saying bitchy things if you don't say bitchy things. They can't make other contestants act sad when you leave if you've been an arsehole to everyone. If it doesn't happen on camera it can't happen on TV – but if it does happen on camera, it's fair game for inclusion.

On the show, the same goes for the food. The cameras can't create a disaster out of a perfectly executed dish, and they can't create a perfect dish out of a disaster. I was perhaps a bit too willing to wear all my fuck-ups on my sleeve, to point them out and talk about them, making it easy to tell that story. And I had plenty of fuck-ups. But I also made plenty of really good food; tasty dishes that received comments that sometimes made it to air and sometimes didn't. In finals week, a lot of them didn't.

As Mick and I watched these last few episodes, I saw this jeopardy play out again and again and it was immediately obvious why: the show's creators wanted suspense. They did not want my winning to be seen, in that final week, as the likely outcome. With each episode my dread grew because I knew what it would mean. Since leaving the relatively safe, technology-free cocoon of the *MasterChef* house, I had gone online. I had read the forums, seen the opinions, felt the anger of super-invested viewers. I should not have done this: the commentary was vicious. It was like being repeatedly kicked in the stomach. I acknowledge that a bit of jeopardy made for edge-of-your-seat viewing. But it also created a storm of controversy, a howling from a portion of the public about the competition being rigged, unfair, skewed in my favour. The fallout was intense, and it was only just beginning.

To the outrage of many viewers, Lucas went home after the pie challenge. Julia left the next night after a Malaysian-themed challenge. I've always believed their so-called advantage, of being sent away from the competition and out of the *MasterChef* environment, contributed to them being the first two sent home in finals week.

With four of us left, on day four of that week we had to make a multi-layered chocolate mousse cake with a variety of decorations and flourishes. I chose a good day to have my shit together, and ended up being the only one of us to complete the dish. Justine was eliminated for the second time. She was gutted, of course. So was I. This place, this competition, was such a unique experience. It welded us together in a way that can't be replicated in a normal environment. Our hearts, bodies, skills and dreams were all constantly on display, constantly on the line. Failure here felt like so much more than just a bad plate of food; it felt like letting everybody down – not just judges, or ourselves, but everyone we had left at home while we vanished from our lives to pursue this elusive goal. Watching this episode back, I want so much to reach into the TV screen and say to Justine, 'It's okay, beautiful girl, you're going to be a star. You'll be on telly every day, have your own little family, go from strength to strength and be loved all around the country. You will do so well out of this.'

But of course, at the time, none of us knew what was coming. We didn't know at all.

The last challenge before the finale was on: Chris, Poh and I were to cook a three-course meal for Donna Hay, and pitch to her our idea for a cookbook. The food we cooked was supposed to be representative of what we would publish in our cookbook. I made a rolled stuffed chicken thigh, a roasted lamb loin and a flourless chocolate cake. In my usual style I had set myself too many things to do, and didn't get all my garnishes on my plates. But the food I served was good, properly cooked and tasty. Donna loved my idea for a cookbook, too. I described it right down to its title – *Our Family Table* – and the blank chapter in the back so whoever owned the book could add their own cherished recipes.

At the end of this challenge, it was Poh and I who were left standing.

Because I'm not mean, I won't say what I wish was aired in that episode. Suffice to say, the result was not as surprising to the people there that night as it may have been to the viewers.

Upon finding out that I had made it through to the finale, I felt a wave of emotion that is impossible to describe. The time away from my boys – more than four months, by that stage; missing my friends and my community; most importantly of all, being absent from Nan and my mother-in-law in their final weeks – maybe I *could* make it worthwhile. Maybe it could mean something, maybe it wasn't all a big mistake.

It was around this time that we were told there would not be any more phone calls home, that we needed to focus on the days ahead without any distraction. This sent me into a bit of a tailspin. I had to know that Mick was okay with it; I had to know that news from home could still reach me if Nan or Mum went downhill. I was assured that I would be told if anything like that happened. Poh and I wondered, we hoped and wished, that perhaps they were cutting off contact because they were going to bring our families down for the finale. We had everything crossed.

I had spent the whole competition wishing for one of those challenges you sometimes see on reality cooking shows, where the contestants arrive and their family members are sitting in the restaurant, or are the guest judges, or just there in some capacity. It hadn't happened, but maybe this was it. Maybe they were on their way. I could hardly contain myself.

All the eliminated contestants were brought back for a final, hilarious masterclass before the end game. Gary and George were made to compete against each other, cooking a mystery box of ingredients that Poh and I had selected. They hammed it up, pretending to be super nervous as they presented their dishes to us. At one stage, George threw flour on his face and said, 'Look! I'm Julie!'

The finale of series one of *MasterChef* Australia went to air on Sunday, 19 July 2009. The episode lasted ninety minutes. It took

THE FINAL COUNTDOWN

three days to film – one challenge per day – and was all over seventeen days before it went to air.

I was so thankful to be going into the ending of this epic experience with my funny, generous friend Poh by my side. We laughed together, supported each other, were happy for each other in those last weeks. And in the final days, we had conversations about being the winner or the loser and being comfortable either way. We wished each other luck and we meant it.

It was strange, being in the enormous *MasterChef* house, just the two of us with the house coordinator. It was such a far cry from when there were twenty of us trying to carve out a little piece of space for ourselves and navigate the logistics of living with a bunch of slightly crazed reality TV show contestants. The house was as big and echoey as ever, but much, much quieter. The view was, as always, spectacular. I looked at the sky at the same time every night, and so did Mick, and we communicated silently via the moon or the stars or the clouds.

Those three days of filming for the finale had a surreal quality to them. I remember having the sensation of being underwater; I didn't feel like I could hear or see quite properly. My movements seemed slow and unconnected to my brain. I wondered if I was losing my marbles right at the final stretch, but Poh told me she felt weird too, so I guess it was just the immense stress of nearing the end of this months-long out-of-body experience.

The first of three rounds was a taste test, of Gary's bourguignon. I walked into the kitchen with a faint hope of seeing my boys there, but not today. All the past contestants were, however, cheering us on from the balcony.

After this round I had correctly named one more ingredient than Poh, which put me on twelve points and Poh on eleven.

The second day of filming, and again the boys weren't there. Poh and I had hopes that maybe our families would appear for the final challenge. For this second challenge, we had to cook a chicken dish. A whole chicken had been the core ingredient for the very first cook in the *MasterChef* kitchen, and the judges wanted to see how far we had come since then. In this round they had brought in Curtis Stone to be a guest judge.

I was so grateful for the people I'd met and the things I'd learned along the way; I was spoiled for choice in terms of what to put on the plate. I'd learned to stuff the skin of a pigeon and make a velvet celeriac puree from Donovan Cooke; I'd learned how to roast chicken on the crown from a masterclass with George; I had learned about butchery and making a neat little spinach ball from Adrian Richardson. I'd learned the proper way to make sauce from Gary. I incorporated all of these techniques and ingredients into my chicken dish. It was a far cry from my first plate of food in this kitchen. Poh also made a beautiful dish, elevating Hainanese chicken rice to restaurant level with beautiful condiments and a pandan dessert. Yes, she made a dessert; completely off her own bat she decided to put a second dish up. She's a mad, glorious genius and this is one of the reasons I love her.

I pulled one more point ahead after this round, scoring seven out of ten from Curtis, but a more generous nine from each of George, Gary and Matt.

One more challenge to go, one more day left. I had everything crossed that tomorrow would be the day my family came to the kitchen.

When we got back to the house that evening, a strange thing had happened – all the furniture was gone. My bed was still in my room, and Poh's bed was still in hers, but every other stick of furniture had disappeared. The stuff that had been on my now absent bedside table was in a neat pile on the floor. There was no lounge, no dining table, not a chair left. Apparently the

THE FINAL COUNTDOWN

furniture had had to be returned to the rental company. We wandered around calling, 'Hellooooooooooooooo??!! We're still heeeeeeeeere!!!!' We laughed in disbelief. Our house coordinator had bought a bunch of lovely cheese, crackers and fruit, and our last meal in that house was a picnic on the lounge-room floor. It was, in fact, the perfect ending to our stay there – unexpected and bizarre right to the end.

On the last day, Poh and I were taken in two separate vans to the *MasterChef* kitchen and we sat outside, apart, until they were ready for us inside. I am not sure how long we were out there for, but it seemed like a long time. The young lad who was my driver asked if I would like some music on while we waited and I said yes, why not. He put on some opera. I sat in the back of that van and summoned all the calming techniques I had practised for the past few months. I breathed as slowly as I could. The sky outside was vivid blue and I just breathed it in, that blue sky, and breathed it out, and let the opera wash over me and around and through me. I pictured my hands as steady and sure. I pictured my face as calm and determined. I pictured my heart beating slowly and regularly. I pictured myself as confident and competent.

Poh and I walked into the kitchen hand in hand, hoping to see our families (nope) and ready for our last hurrah in this kitchen. Our final challenge was, of course, a pressure test. I was fit for this kind of challenge, having been in so many of them, but inevitably it was a dessert, and a tricky one at that: the chocolate assiette, from the menu at Matt Moran's Aria restaurant in Sydney. It was an impossibly elegant creation and required a number of different techniques and elements: chocolate pastry, the filling, a chocolate pipe, a sauce and a separate glaze, chocolate sorbet and a macaron, with crumbs. Making the pipe involved tempering chocolate. This sounds like the kind of thing that might be talked up on TV as being harder than it is, but don't be fooled. Tempering chocolate can work perfectly, or it can fail miserably, and there is hardly a second or a degree or a drop of moisture between those two possible outcomes. It is a bastard of a thing to do and ever since then I gladly leave it to the chocolate gurus and pastry professionals.

We had two and a half hours to cook. It was Gary who said, for the last time, 'Your time starts . . . now!'

Poh and I were cooking face-to-face at our benches. All the past contestants on the balcony were calling down to us, encouragement (mostly), and advice. There was a heart-stopping moment when Curtis and Matt came to the bench and tasted my sorbet. Off-air, before we had started cooking, Matt Moran had told us we might struggle to get the right consistency with the domestic ice cream machines we had to use, and he was right. My sorbet was grainy. In one of many, many scenes that didn't make it to air, they tasted Poh's as well, and advised us both to remake our sorbets. I took the advice and started mine again, with more success the second time.

As usual, there was barely enough time to complete the tasks before us, and at the ten-second countdown I was still putting my sorbet onto the plate – but I got it done. At literally the last second. When time was up, Poh and I hugged, exhausted. I remember saying, 'It's over, it's over!'

After presenting our dishes to the judges for the last time, we stood on the floor of the kitchen that had become our whole world over the past months. Almost all the chefs who had participated in the show had come in through the doors, an overwhelming parade of talent and skill. All the contestants whom we had lived and worked with for the past four-plus months were gathered to the side. Sarah, Gary, George, Matt and Curtis stood at the head of the room, resplendent in their evening wear.

THE FINAL COUNTDOWN

While we waited for the final scores to be delivered, I said to Poh, 'I wish our families were here,' and she said, 'I know, Jules. Same.'

I had no idea how the final scoring would play out. Being a couple of points in front meant nothing if an element of my dish didn't compete with the same element on Poh's dish. Anything could happen. Curtis Stone was the first to score us, followed by Matt, George then Gary. After Poh's scores were read out, giving her a total of seventy-five points, it was my turn. Curtis scored me a nine out of ten. I was stunned. When Matt revealed his score, nine, a tiny part of my brain piped up and said, 'I think you might have this.' I told that part to pipe back down. Ain't over till it's over.

Then I got a nine from George.

'Julie, you need a three from Gary,' said Sarah.

'God, the suspense is killing me,' said Poh. You can see why I love her.

Gary couldn't say his score as I think he had something in his eye. He held up his card. It was a nine.

I was declared the winner. Australia's first MasterChef, they called me. The contestants gathered around in a happy mob, hugging and cheering.

Then Sarah started talking. I couldn't quite process what she was saying. Something about there being someone here to see me. I barely dared to believe her as I spun around to see Mick, Joe, Tom and Paddy – my humans – all come running through the doors. Poh was saying to me, 'Jules, it's what you wanted!'

Mick was wild-eyed and white, looking as if he'd wandered into the path of a semi. We hugged and we cried. 'These are my boys!' I introduced them to the judges. My boys; the ones I never stopped talking about. The ones I cooked for. The ones who'd supported me to be here, even though it hurt. The boys who are my heart and my soul and my life. 'These are my boys!' Our tears weren't the only ones in the room; a few of the visiting chefs and judges seemed to suddenly develop eye issues. There were more tears, and cheers, and love in the kitchen as Poh's family were also ushered in.

Mick tells the story of waiting outside the studio doors for about forty-five minutes. It was raining and there were crew holding umbrellas over them, and Poh's family. They could hear silences and bursts of cheering, without knowing what was happening. Then suddenly the executive producer of the show said to them, 'She's won! Go in and congratulate her!' and kind of pushed him and the boys through the doors into a space he had never been in before. Later, I asked Mick, 'Did you see the giant camera on the jib? The one I was telling you about? How cool is it?'

'I didn't see anything,' he told me. 'I just looked for you. I just wanted to get to you.'

When the noise died down and I was standing in front of the judges, holding my family as close to me as I could, Sarah asked Joe, 'Are you proud of your mum?'

Joe replied, 'Of course I am.'

'Are you surprised that she won?' she said.

Joe answered casually: 'Not really!'

Amid laughter, hugs, confetti cannons, tears and cheering, Mick and I found our way back to each other. He bent down to kiss me on the face, a moment captured by the camera and shown just before the credits rolled.

He said, his throat thick with tears, 'Ah, what's happened?'

And I said, 'I dunno.'

I don't think I've spoken truer words.

THE FINAL COUNTDOWN

How to temper chocolate

My first recommendation for tempering chocolate is this: don't.

If, however, you find yourself cooking a Matt Moran chocolate dessert in the finale of season 1 of *MasterChef*, follow these steps to the letter.

Preheat oven to 160°C.

Place 200 g of dark chocolate pieces in a glass bowl over a pot of barely simmering water. Using a candy thermometer, stir the chocolate with a spatula until it reaches 55°C. Remove from the heat, add 50 g more chocolate, and continue to stir until the temperature drops to 27°C. Place the bowl into the oven for five seconds – yep, five seconds!!! Hopefully the temperature of the chocolate will then be 30°C.

It is now tempered and ready to use as you wish. *If* it has worked, of course, which for a chocolate amateur, nine times out of ten it won't.

Or you could go to Matt's Sydney restaurant Aria, order the chocolate assiette dessert, and save yourself the trouble.

CHAPTER 11
CHANGES

After the finale, our family spent the night in a Sydney hotel as there were meetings lined up for the next day. I was desperate to get home, but most importantly, I was with my beautiful family. I couldn't get over any of it; it didn't seem real.

One of the meetings the next day was with the *Australian Women's Weekly*. I was offered a position as a columnist. *AWW*, or Ay Dub Dub as it is affectionately known, was at the time the largest-selling women's title in Australia and I was absolutely knocked sideways by the offer. The women on the food team, titans of the industry, would go on to train me in the discipline of recipe writing, and this served me well not only as their columnist but also in the writing of my own cookbook.

That was the other meeting that morning – with my new publisher. Part of the winner's prize on *MasterChef* was to have a cookbook published, and Random House had won the contract to do this. I had a laundry list of wishes for the book – fabric binding, hard cover, beautiful paper, a ribbon bookmark, a folder in the back to slip in handwritten recipes. Something else I wanted

CHANGES

very much was the blank chapter I had described to Donna Hay, in which the owner of the book could write their own family's favourite recipes.

I remember being told that I was probably aiming a little high for a first book; it would likely be a simpler affair, and we could add in all the bells and whistles some time down the line, in a future book. I was still overwhelmed and thrilled to have a publishing deal at all.

There was a gap of seventeen days between the filming of the finale and it going to air. Those days had a surreal quality about them, a feeling of suspended animation. My boys had been sternly cautioned by the production team not to tell anyone the outcome of the show, and they took their responsibility seriously. I was advised to keep a low profile, which was not hard: I was still in a state of something like shock. In all honesty, the whole thing didn't feel real to me until I watched it on television myself.

One day during this strange limbo I ducked down to the local shops. It was my first time out in public in our neighbourhood since I'd left the *MasterChef* house. I'd only been out for a few minutes when a lady came up to me, hugged me and said, 'Oh Julie, never mind. You did so well and got so far! We're all very proud of you.'

I realised that she must have assumed, seeing me out and about, that I'd been eliminated from the competition. I didn't know what to say beyond an awkward, 'Oh, haha, thanks!'

I scurried home and kept my head down from then until after the finale went to air.

It was during this time that I began to get a sense of how popular the show had become. The number of articles in the paper blew my mind, the radio chatter, the messages of support up on school signs around the Coast. It was also during this time, while we watched the last two weeks of the series as a family, that I started to feel that sense of dread about how the finale was going to be portrayed. About how *I* was going to be portrayed.

The night of the cookbook episode, when only Poh, Chris and I were left, came around. We pitched our ideas to Donna Hay; I outlined my desire for a blank chapter so whoever owned the book could make it a part of their own family's heritage. I later learned that after this episode went to air, Random House started to receive phone calls from the public and from booksellers wanting to know when my book would be out and how to order it. The next time I went into the office for a meeting, which was just after the finale had been aired, there were piles of beautiful, high-quality cookbooks for me to look at so I could decide what kind of format I would like. They were hardcovers; they all had lush paper and ribbon bookmarks. My book was going to come to life just the way I had dreamed it.

I am fortunate to have remained friends with the *MasterChef* publicists from that time, Steve Murphy from Fremantle Media and Kirsty Wilson from Channel 10. They liaised with the media, organised interviews and created PR opportunities in order to try to make *MasterChef* the most talked about, and ultimately the most viewed, program on TV. We had a chat only recently about how those days in the lead-up to the finale unfolded. Their memories are of an electric time; of promoting a show that was taking everyone by surprise. By the time the last few weeks of episodes were being broadcast, Kirsty was receiving calls from newspapers asking for enough material for a twenty-four-page spread – absolutely unheard of for a television show.

Since we contestants were still in a cone of silence, there wasn't enough interview material to feed the media beast. So, in the absence of actual interviews with actual contestants, journalists began to turn to the internet for their stories. Viewers' opinions were picked up from online forums and published in the print media. It's Steve's theory that this may have been the first time in Australia we saw social media becoming newsworthy in its own right, when comments made online became their own story. It's hard to imagine now, in the time since a US presidency was practically run via Twitter, that social media fifteen years ago carried nothing like the same weight it does today.

The day the finale was going to air there were huge spreads in all the papers speculating on the outcome. More random viewers had their online opinions published. Renowned chefs and restaurateurs were interviewed, and their opinions were published too. All but one of the latter said either that Poh would win, or I would win but didn't deserve to. The most scathing column was written by a well-known restaurant critic, who blasted me, my abilities and the production itself. This critic had very strong opinions as to who the better cooks were in the competition (a hint: I was not one). I found it curious that a restaurant critic could have such firmly held views about food they had never tasted. Were all of this critic's reviews based on such untested assumptions? They questioned the integrity of the production; I questioned the integrity of their journalism.

As well as claiming there was 'something fishy going on' and that my now-infamous Passionfruit Puddle Pie was 'a joke', this columnist added, 'By no means is she the best chef, the most creative cook, or even the person with the most interesting vision for a cookbook. She's toiled for years to raise her children and now feels it's time to do something for herself in life. Plenty of us can relate to that. But does that make her "Australia's best amateur chef"? Hardly.'

Oof.

I'm better at letting criticism roll off me these days; sometimes it still stings, but I've grown a thicker hide. Back then, I was a normal person living a normal life. I had never invited conflict nor sought arguments – let alone publicly. The biggest controversy I'd been involved in was asking my kids' primary-school teachers to give the boys less homework so they had time to play outside.

To be the subject of such scorn, such vitriolic accusations, such *hatred*, was devastating. Everything was up for public comment: my weight, my cooking, the fact I sweat and cry, my fashion sense, my commitment as a mother – all of these were fair game. The observation that I'd abandoned my kids to go on TV was brought into the narrative. I was labelled, among other things, a cheat. To be called fat, ugly, a bad mother, a terrible cook, a hot mess – these slings and arrows were nothing I hadn't already shot at myself at one time or another. But a *cheat*? I'd never worn that label, not even on my worst day.

In the days leading up to the finale going to air, I was trying to work out a way to undo the harm I felt I had done; to wind back the clock and go with Joe to his first day of high school; to turn to a different page in this choose-your-own adventure.

I begged my kids not to listen to the people who were writing and saying nasty or untrue things. I told them, and tried to believe myself, 'The people who know us, know better; and those who don't, don't matter.' There were moments around this time and afterwards when I thought that the only way to escape the furore would be to relocate somewhere overseas.

It's part of the human condition to notice and take to heart negative feedback and experiences far more than positive ones. Neuroscientists theorise that our negative bias is a result of the gradual evolution of our brains, which are still keeping us safe from life-threatening dangers such as sabre-toothed tigers. You know the feeling – your boss can say a hundred nice things but then suggest one improvement you could make, and that's all

CHANGES

you can think about. That's what it was like when I was at the receiving end of all this loud criticism: it was hard to hear or see anything else. Kindness can get overlooked when there's nasty stuff coming at you hard.

But there *was* kindness. I had so many beautiful messages as well, and they were a balm on my aching heart. I received dozens of letters in the mail, some only addressed to 'Julie, *MasterChef*'. Somehow the postal service got them to my letterbox. It must be how Santa feels when his letters get delivered to the North Pole without a proper street address. There were letters from kids who had taken up cooking having watched the series; letters from mums who'd been inspired by *MasterChef* to start their own businesses; cards from people who'd reconnected with far-flung family members because of *MasterChef*, texting each other every night while they watched. It was a privilege to be the recipient of these stories and the kind words that came with them.

On the night the finale was being broadcast I invited a few of my closest friends and my extended family over to watch. I had been forbidden to tell anyone the result, and I hadn't. Mick and the boys obviously knew, and those closest to me had a reasonable idea, but I never said a word.

Watching the last episode, safely in my own home and surrounded by people I loved, was the first time I really allowed my win to sink in. *MasterChef*'s first season was over, and I had won. As the scores were read out on the screen, the yelling and cheering in my house near lifted the roof off. Mick and I held on to each other like the world would end if we let go. And perhaps it would have.

Very early the next morning Mick drove me down to the Channel 10 studios in Pyrmont, where I met Poh and we settled in for that huge day of back-to-back interviews. First of all we sat in a small room for several hours doing chat after chat on breakfast radio. At one point, during a short break, Kirsty Wilson walked into the room clutching a piece of paper. Her expression was stunned, her face white, a sheen of tears in her eyes.

'Are you all right?' Poh asked.

'Four million,' she said.

'Huh?'

'The ratings. Four million. Over four million. It's broken the record.'

It's hard to describe the mood, the vibe, at Channel 10 that day. After our radio interviews Poh and I were walked through the open-plan offices to leave for the airport. As the team noticed us coming through, they stood up from their desks and clapped and cheered. Even though we were just little cogs in this vast *MasterChef* machine, in that moment we felt like rock stars.

After flying to Melbourne to do a couple more days of publicity (including *The Project*'s very first episode), I arrived home to a house full of flowers. Arrangements had come from everywhere. The front hall was filled with boxes sent by Sheldon & Hammond, a wholesaler of beautiful kitchenwares. The phone was ringing constantly. No matter what the papers had printed, there was love to spare here, from all over the place. It was overwhelming, heady, other-worldly. I was home. I was blessed.

Five days after the finale went to air, in the cyclonic aftermath of this reality television show, Nan passed away.

Five weeks after that, Mick's mother died as well.

It was a time of enormous emotion – elation, fear, safety, danger, confusion, excitement, uncertainty, confidence, bewilderment, joy. Love. Grief. It seems to me, as I look back on it now, that the grief had to be folded into little squares, like a hanky, and tucked into a pocket. It could only be brought out behind the closed doors of my house, or in the hotel rooms I stayed in as I bounced around the country taking up all of these incredible opportunities that came my way. Maybe, with the wisdom of hindsight and knowing everything that was yet to come, I was too efficient with this grief; maybe I folded it a bit too tightly and kept up that cheerful public face a little too well.

I have been asked so many times, 'How did your boys deal with the fame?'

I answer jokingly, but it is in fact true: they didn't seem to notice a lot of it. It kind of flowed over and around them. They would occasionally let me know that the teachers were sussing out their lunchboxes, or that kids at school were looking for invitations to dinner. But on the whole, they just got on with life. In the early days, when shopping was a slow process because of all the people who wanted to chat, they would stand patiently by, occasionally offering to take a picture if one was requested.

I was really proud of them, all three of them. They didn't get caught up in the frenzy; they were just happy to have me back home. It was only a few weeks until they were saying, 'Hey, Mum, remember at the swimming carnival . . .' and I would have to remind them that I hadn't been there. The four and a half months I was away were so intense, long and lonely; we'd all felt the hole in our lives while we were apart. But once I was home, it was amazing how quickly we re-formed our circle. The hole filled and the loneliness was a distant memory. We turned inwards for a time, as much as our new normal allowed, while we reconnected, and then as we tried to process the loss of two of the most important women in our lives.

Another question I am asked regularly is 'Did *MasterChef* change your life?' The answer is that in one way it changed everything, and in another way nothing. It changed what I do for a living, the things I could offer my family, my life's trajectory. It didn't change what I love the most, where I live, who my friends are, my favourite things to do. I guess I could say that it added a great many new things, but it didn't alter the heart of my existence. It didn't take anything away. In retrospect I might say that it added a little too much, and I didn't have the wisdom or the skills to limit what came in through the door.

People used to ask me if I'd do it again and I'd laugh and say, 'Not in a million years.' Little did I know.

~

A couple of months after the finale, Mick and I took the boys to Hong Kong, using some of the prize money for the trip. I wanted to experience Hong Kong as a tourist instead of a freaked-out reality TV show contestant, and I wanted Mick and the boys to see where I had been and to get a feel for the places they had watched on television. It was the boys' first time outside of Australia.

We went to the top of The Peak and they stood where Gary, George and Matt had stood, pretending to send me off on my big challenge. 'This is dragon's breath,' roared Joe, waving his arms around. We stayed in the same hotel, the Langham Place, in Mong Kok, and visited the wet markets.

I said to the boys before we left home, 'I want you to step outside your comfort zones a bit and try some different things in this new country. If you're only going to eat what we eat at home, we may as well stay at home.'

Parents with a child on the spectrum will understand that this is not an ordinary request. For Joe, it was the laying down of an epic challenge. Yet I was blown away by all three boys and their willingness to try all the weird and wonderful food on offer. You could have knocked me over with a feather when Joe selected snails from the breakfast buffet (he didn't like them, but he did try them!) and when Tom ordered frogs' legs from a street hawker. Challenge accepted, and nailed.

On one special evening, we were guests of the manager of Langham Place and his wife in the private dining room of the Ming Court, where we were served a multi-course fine-dining Cantonese feast. Smoke poured from under huge shining cloches, fragrant steam wafted around the room; my wide-eyed boys were being taken on a culinary journey the likes of which they had never experienced. The theatre and the unfamiliarity of the dishes, all in our own private dining room, created a food experience that none of us has ever forgotten.

It was a wonderful, eye-opening trip and it gave the boys the travel bug. Now, as adults, they save up and go to new places with their friends and partners – and us too, of course.

During this time, I was writing my first cookbook. I used the training that I had been given at the *Australian Women's Weekly* to write the recipes I wanted to include.

I quizzed everyone I knew about their favourite recollections of food; who cooked for them, and what the occasions were; what the rules were in their house around meals when they were growing up; what the rules are for their own families; their cooking disasters; which recipes they would be willing to share.

The result was the most extraordinary outpouring of stories. Joyful, melancholic, hilarious, nostalgic – all the contributions had one thing in common: food was at their centre. Which is the way with food really, if you think about it. It's at the heart of every important occasion that marks our lives: weddings, baptisms, birthday parties, funerals. It binds our friendships and defines our differing cultures. For the lucky ones, it's the centrepiece of the day and the opportunity to connect with other people.

We have a few physiological needs for our basic survival: air, water, food, sleep, safety, clothing and reproduction being the bare minimum. They sit at the base of Maslow's hierarchy of needs. Some of those are essential to survival, such as breathing. Others, like clothing, shelter and food, have been raised to art forms. Food is not just fuel for our bodies but sustenance for our spirits, our relationships, our sense of wellbeing. For those of us who provide the food, it becomes part of our esteem needs, and for those of us who strive to excel, it becomes a part of our self-actualisation. So it is for me, and for many of the people I interviewed for my first book.

These stories, and the recipes that came with them, as well as plenty of my own, became the basis of *Our Family Table*. Mick's grandmother, Imelda Henebery, was a beautiful and prolific baker, and many of her family-famous biscuits, cakes and slices are in those pages. My favourite story, the one that I think sums everything up, came from Mick's late Aunty Carmel. She told of how when she moved out of home to another state, she unpacked her bags to find two giant tins of her favourite biscuits – hazelnut choc chip cookies. 'A wave of homesickness washed over me,' she said. 'Not because I would miss my favourite foods (which I would), but because of what those tins represented – home, warmth, and the person who knew what my favourite bikkies were: my mum.'

My nan was far less inclined to write her recipes down, so many of my favourites from her had to be worked out by trial and error. It was a lesson to me in the importance of recording things accurately, so that they are not lost when our loved one is lost. It's why I have that blank chapter in my cookbooks; it's an encouragement, a reminder: what we don't record might never be recovered.

Our Family Table was published nine months after the finale, and I received a phone call from Random House when it arrived from the printers. Mick took a day off work (unheard of!) and drove me to Sydney to see it for the first time. I was determined to behave in a professional manner – I was an author, after all, and this was a moment all authors experienced in a calm and measured manner, I was sure. Then the book was placed in my hands. Hard-covered and cloth-bound, with a thick blue ribbon bookmark, it was hefty with the weight of all the stories that had been gifted to me. It carried pictures of Nan, Mum, my family and friends, my history. It was exactly how I had dreamed it would be. It was beautiful. I couldn't help it, I cried.

The book was released into stores in time for Mother's Day 2010. It coincided with the beginning of series 2 of *MasterChef*, so it was all tangled up with and benefitted from the hype for the show. I embarked on a tour around the country, attending speaking events in libraries and book signings in enormous shopping centres and small book stores. It was intense; in some places a signing queue had been forming for hours. In Canberra, Emma, my publicist, and I missed our flight and had to drive back to Sydney. There were people in Canberra who had been waiting patiently for hours to get a book signed, and we couldn't just walk away.

Perhaps the most unbelievable tour stop was the Dymocks in Westfield, Penrith. I arrived there in time for a 6 p.m. signing and was told that people had started lining up from 3 o'clock. We had passed the line on our way into the store – it went out of the doors of Westfield and down the street. At some stage Dymocks ran out of copies and had staff run up to Big W to buy more. They kept the bookstore open past the 9 p.m. closing of the whole shopping centre, as we hadn't yet reached the end of the queue.

As people brought their freshly purchased books for me to sign, they shared their own stories. Their struggles with food intolerances or illness; their losses; their ideas for new recipes or new enterprises. I heard their uncertainty about taking the leap into a different career, or their pride for having done so. They spoke of the things they loved to cook or the things they wanted to learn, the people they cooked for or the person who cooked for them. I was shown photos, and given cards and drawings and jam and teacups. Because of this book, because of this television show, I was having stories and other meaningful items bestowed upon me. I pinched myself regularly; it was humbling and ego-inflating all at once. I have often reflected on how grateful I am that this particular thing happened to me when I was in my thirties. If it had happened when I was younger I might have believed all the hype and got an insufferably fat head.

Always keeping me grounded were my boys. I would get a text saying, 'Ma, can you please drop my PE uniform to school? I forgot it,' and I would have to reply, 'I can't, sorry, I am in a different state to you.' This still happens – I got a text recently while I was in New Zealand presenting at the Food Show: 'What's for dinner?'

'Whatever you like. I am in a different country to you,' was my reply. It's nice to still be needed.

I was back on set in the *MasterChef* kitchen – I think it was for the launch event of season 2 – when Nikki, my publisher, called me. 'Are you sitting down?' she asked. I said yes, even though I wasn't. 'It's number one,' she said.

This might shock you, but I cried. *Our Family Table* was a bestseller. It sat at number one for ten weeks. It was the bestselling book by an Australian author in 2010 – not bestselling cookbook, but book. It's uncomfortable to even write this; it feels like bragging. But I want to try to convey just how surreal my life had become. Winning *MasterChef*; being a magazine columnist; being a bestselling author. An award-winning author, after the book won the ABIA (Australian Book Industry Award) for best illustrated book

2010. The little kid who'd never won a single trophy for sport or dance or anything, finally at age thirty-nine had something for the mantlepiece.

By this time, I had also been made resident cook on Channel 9's morning show, *Today*. Every Tuesday I had four minutes to demonstrate a dish on live TV. Sometimes there would be a special request from the producers as to what I should cook, but mostly I made suggestions and they were approved.

The hosts of the show at that time were Karl Stefanovic and Lisa Wilkinson. They would join me in my little kitchen as I cooked and explained how to make easy meals for families. Lisa would ask questions that the audience might like to know the answers to, and Karl would eat my prepared ingredients during the ad break. I learned pretty quickly that if my dish had any kind of cheese, or nuts, or really anything tasty to nibble on, I would have to prepare a second quantity of it so I could swap out the one Karl had snacked on just before we went live.

Early on in this job, I got a phone call asking me if I could make sausage rolls because Karl wanted a sausage roll on a roll. On a *bread* roll. I'd never heard of it. But anyway, I said I couldn't make sausage rolls because there was no oven. It was explained to me that I should bring some already-cooked sausage rolls and produce them from under the bench as though I had baked them in an oven that sat invisibly out of shot. I said I couldn't do that – cold sausage rolls look gross. So an oven was installed in the studio kitchen and everyone was happy, especially Karl.

Each week I bought my own ingredients and I would prepare the recipe at each of its different stages – there's only so much you can actually do live in four minutes. So if I wanted to demo lasagne, which I did one week, I brought the raw ingredients, plus the sauces ready to go, plus a pre-cooked lasagne that showcased the final result. I remember lasagne day well, as I was demonstrating bechamel sauce and how the milk should be added a little at a time or the sauce becomes lumpy. I was facing Lisa, about to explain this to her, when Karl, trying to be helpful, poured the whole jug of milk into the pot, turning my bechamel into a lumpy mess. Sometimes learning comes from what *not* to do. It did on that day, anyway.

Live television is completely different to shows that are filmed and edited months in advance. There's no redoing mistakes or disasters. It is what it is: if the pan isn't hot enough, or something gets dropped or knocked over, or you set fire to the tea towel, the people watching at home see it all. One day, I was making mock cream for cream horns, the speciality my mum creates for family parties. I was whipping butter with a hand-held electric mixer fitted with a balloon whisk. As I whipped, one of the wires of the balloon whisk came loose and flicked a big glob of butter into the air. It landed in Karl's eye. 'It's in my freaking eye,' he said in disbelief, live on air. I stopped the mixer and didn't know what to do. 'The mixer has broken,' I said, a bit helplessly. Karl took the electric beater from me, put it back in the bowl and turned it on. Butter flew everywhere as I begged him to stop. He wouldn't stop – he was having a ball. Butter landed on the lens of the camera filming the carnage. It sprayed up the front of Karl's suit, and my blouse, and all over the cameraman. Lisa and Georgie Gardner were hiding under the bench and behind the wall, trying to pick pieces of butter out of their hair. It was glorious chaos. We cut to an ad break.

No cream horns were made that day. Years later, somebody sent me a link to an episode of a UK television show called 'When TV Goes Horribly Wrong', and there we all were in our butter-covered glory.

CHANGES

Six months after I got the gig on the *Today* show, Channel 9 broadcast the first episode of my very own show, *Home Cooked!* It aired on Nine on a Saturday afternoon, never at quite the same time each week as it dodged footy games and other sports events. The format of the show was simple: I would cook my signature family-friendly dishes, and each episode I would be joined by a celebrity. I experienced many pinch-me moments during this show as I cooked with the likes of broadcaster Amanda Keller, singers Kate Ceberano and Ricki-Lee Coulter, cricketer Steve Waugh and actor Gyton Grantley.

That year I got an invitation to the Logies nominee announcements. I assumed the *Today* show was up for a nomination. When I got to the event a journalist approached me with a microphone and asked, 'How do you feel about being nominated for a Logie?'

I laughed and said, 'No, no, I'm here with the *Today* show.' I couldn't find the team before the formalities started, though, so I was sitting on my own when the announcement was made, and it turned out that *I* had been nominated for a silver Logie – for Best New Talent. Nobody had told me. Or maybe they had but I hadn't absorbed the information. It was for *Home Cooked!* Although the show itself had only aired for a few months, it was enough to get me nominated. Also in my category were Poh and Chrissie Swan, who went on to take out just about every gong that year, including Best New Talent. My colleagues from the *Today* show weren't even at the nomination event!

I was the resident cook on the *Today* show for more than four years. Every week I shopped and prepped, ready to be picked up in the very early hours of Tuesday morning and taken to the Channel 9 studios in Sydney's Willoughby. There, after getting my hair and makeup done, I would unload my ingredients onto my bench, which was a portable boat of a thing with wheels and a gas cooktop. It sat outside the studio, in a huge, draughty warehouse filled with old props and equipment. Most weeks I would say hi to Kerri-Anne as she arrived to get ready for her show at 9 a.m.

When it was time, my bench would be wheeled into the studio by the guys on the crew, ducking cables and cameras until it was manoeuvred into place. Just before the show went to an ad break, the big camera on the jib would sweep past me in the kitchen, stirring or chopping, and I would wave at the audience at home. When the ads were done Karl and Lisa would be in the kitchen with me, and it was time to cook.

I loved this job; it was exciting. My colleagues were beautiful, supportive and interested. I met some amazing people backstage, guests on the show, and even better were the times I got to cook with them in my segment. Live TV was nerve-wracking, of course, but the more I did it the more comfortable I got. I cooked for pop legend Cyndi Lauper one day, and on another day Kermit the Frog – my early childhood hero. This remains one of the greatest highlights of my post-*MasterChef* career.

I was asked by the *Today* producers, after the season 2 *MasterChef* finale, if I could please recreate Peter Gilmore's iconic dessert, the snow egg, for my segment the next day. The answer, which I delivered as gently as I could, was no. I could not produce an intricate dessert that required specialised equipment and took four hours to make, in my four-minute segment. I did deep-fry a Mars bar once, at Karl's request. But my favourite segments were when I demonstrated nourishing, easy, affordable mid-week meals. My passion, my mission really, was to provide achievable, accessible recipes. Food that people at home would have the ingredients for, or be able to get easily. My favourite things were, and are, those dishes that make dinner-time interesting and fun. Or at least, if not fun, not too burdensome or stressful.

CHANGES

Then came a phone call one afternoon, from the new executive producer, a man I had not met. 'We won't need you back' was how he put it.

'You mean next week?' I asked, confused.

'At all,' he replied. 'Ever. We're changing up the segments. Don't take it personally.'

Don't take it *personally*? Unsure of how else to take it, I tried to stem my damn tears – why do I have to cry when I least want to? I asked this man some questions, seeking to understand, but no real answers came. Devastated, I let my colleagues know. Karl, Lisa, Georgie and Richard Wilkins all responded to me with kindness and encouragement. I had no way to contact any of the people from hair and makeup, the backstage team or floor crew; no way to say thanks and goodbye other than to ask that my best wishes be passed on.

In all my time on the *Today* show I had never submitted a receipt in order to be reimbursed for ingredients. I had my own space in the props area for the equipment, utensils, appliances and crockery I'd brought in from home over the past four years. I considered it my workplace, and the people around me my colleagues. This weekly job was an anchor in the maelstrom of ever-changing commitments that made up the rest of my life. I gave it my best and I'd made it my home.

I had to make an appointment to go back to Channel 9 to collect my things from the props department. I was escorted by security – it was humiliating. I'd never been fired before; I was just gutted. But that, I was learning, is how it rolls, how this television business goes.

How to write a recipe

Or perhaps it should be, how and *why* to write a recipe.

Why? Because if you don't, and you die, nobody will know how to cook the things you cooked; the flavours that brought them comfort or joy when you cooked them. The food they will remember you for, that they will yearn for, that they would give anything to have you make for them once more.

I know this because my nan didn't write much down, and I had to rebuild the things she cooked from scratch; and I will never really be sure if I'm doing them right.

That's why. And here's *how*, according to the iconic women in the Australian food scene who taught me.

First, under the recipe's title, add a description of the recipe, or a little story about it, a memory that connects the reader to the food you're going to explain.

Also add how many people the recipe serves, how long it takes to prepare, and how long to cook. Add its resting time, chilling time, setting time – as required.

The list of ingredients comes next and should be in the order of use. After the name of the ingredient, if anything needs to be done to it that can be described in a word or two, add that here. For example, 'Two potatoes, peeled and sliced 5 mm thick'; 'One brown onion, peeled and halved'.

Ingredients should be described in measurements: 'Half a teaspoon of salt', rather than 'A good pinch of salt' – everyone's idea of a pinch is different.

Next comes the method. If an oven needs preheating, write this down first so that the oven is hot by the time the rest of the food preparation is completed.

Work through the steps of the method in order. Sentences should be constructed in this order: the equipment, the heat, the ingredient. For example: 'Place a large, non-stick pan over high heat and add butter. When butter is foaming, place salmon, skin-side down . . .' etc.

CHANGES

Be sure to describe not just the temperature and the time but also the colour, sound, smell or behaviour of the ingredient – ovens, stoves and pans vary in how they cook ingredients. For example: 'When the cake springs back when lightly touched and is coming away from the sides of the tin, it is ready.'

Recipe testing – cooking a dish to record the recipe – is different to cooking it just to eat it. You have to pay attention to times and temperatures. Every time you add a bit more salt, or a dash more stock, or set the timer for a few more minutes, you have to make a note of it so it can be incorporated into the ingredients or the method. It can be tiresome, but it is worth it.

Please, do all this. Please write your important personal recipes down.

CHAPTER 12

DANCE MONKEY

In the months after *MasterChef*, my calendar was jam-packed and there was no typical day: I could be anywhere, doing a wild variety of things. I might be heading to Sydney for a photo shoot for my *AWW* column. I might be flying to Melbourne to meet with cookware retailers. I might be taking a tinny across Brisbane Water from Gosford to Palm Beach to the set of *Home Cooked!*, or I might be appearing on other shows – *Getaway*, or *Domestic Blitz*, or *Family Feud*, or *Australia's Funniest Home Videos* birthday special. Some days I'd be recipe testing for a cookbook or the magazine. Some days it would be a speaking engagement or filming a television commercial for a product I was endorsing. Other days I'd be doing cooking demos in shopping centres, or food festivals, or retirement villages.

Each time I called Mick on the phone I'd make a joke of how random and unexpected life had become. 'Hi, it's your wife the cookbook author here,' I would say. Or, 'Hi, it's your wife the laundry detergent ambassador.' Once, when I was at a photo shoot for a fashion label, I was able to say, 'Hi, it's your wife the swimsuit model here,' and we're still laughing about that one. It seemed so long ago that I'd been a house cleaner, a waitress, a youth worker.

I couldn't have juggled any of this without the team who managed me – who still manage me. My days and hours were arranged with military precision, my appointments and appearances and transport all organised for me and put into my Outlook calendar according to a strict protocol to make sure nothing was missed. Deadlines, charity events, personal appointments, appearances, interviews and meetings were all colour-coded so I could see what my week comprised of. If there wasn't enough green (family time) then I knew I had to address the imbalance. Self-care was not a category. I didn't know what that was, let alone give it priority.

I came to my management team via Fremantle Media. When we signed our contract for *MasterChef*, we also signed on with their management company for a term of one year. I was so comfortable and happy with this team that I am still with them all this time later. Lisa Sullivan and Caitlin Sullivan from One Management did, and do, much more than just organise appointments. They filter hundreds of requests – probably thousands by now. Back then they helped me to navigate a world I didn't even know existed – a world of appearances and endorsements and events. They helped me to choose the jobs I should take and those I should leave. They always placed my personal values over monetary value. I was never pressured into taking a job, no matter how high-paying, if it wasn't right for me. That meant turning down some pretty lucrative offers; but if I don't use a product, or love it, or feel excitement for its possibilities or what it does, then I can't endorse it.

I'm sure there are managers out there who would push their clients to accept some deals that may not sit well with their clients, but my team has always been on my side and gone in to bat for me. I've said no to processed food products I wouldn't use in a million years; I've said no to diet companies because I will not join the ranks of people telling us how we should look; I even said no to a huge advertiser, a skincare company that wanted me to pretend I had acne prior to using their product. I suffered with a few things as a teenager but by a stroke of luck acne was not one of them. It may have been an amazing product, but I wouldn't know: I had never used it.

Things in the advertising world nowadays have changed a lot since 2009. Back then the deals were lucrative and long term. Product managers would engage a brand ambassador for years at a time. Now, with social media at the forefront, deals are smaller, and shorter term: instead of a multi-year partnership, you might be offered a three-month contract that involves creating some online content for a brand and posting it to Instagram or TikTok. These pieces of content are filmed mostly on personal phones and posted to personal accounts. In those early years, the idea of making advertising using an iPhone would have been laughable, unheard of. The ads we shot were huge productions.

Once, my whole family was asked to be in a Glad ad with me. Glad produces baking paper and food storage products – cling wrap and snap-lock bags, among other things. Glad wanted to film the ad at our house, which was fine with us. Mick and I were away the night before, at a show in Sydney, and the boys were on a sleepover. Mick and I had to be home by 7 a.m. to let the film crew inside to set up.

I'll never forget driving around the corner into our street – and hitting the brakes. We sat in the middle of the road like stunned mullets and surveyed the scene. Our quiet little street was full of trucks, and equipment, and people unloading stuff into our driveway. There was a full catering truck with a coolroom set up out the front of our neighbours' house, and the caterers had put trestle tables on their front lawn to serve the crew breakfast and lunch. I was slightly panicked, imagining what the neighbours might say when they woke up and looked out the window.

The back of our house was tented for lighting purposes, our dining furniture and our family room furniture swapped around, our front room set up as a control room with monitors and lots of people with clipboards. There were lights on stands and cameras and crew everywhere. Upstairs in the bedrooms the wardrobe people had prepared outfits for us, and the hair and makeup lady was set up at the kitchen table. It sounds chaotic but was actually a well-oiled machine.

Through the two-day shoot the boys were great, taking orders from the director far more willingly than they ever took orders from me. At the end of the first day, we were shipped off to a hotel for the night and a security guard was parked in the driveway. At the end of the second day, everything was put back into order and everyone disappeared without a trace, leaving me with the faint feeling of it all having happened in my imagination.

Compare that to creating content these days. I whack on a bit of lippy, prop my phone up on a pile of cookbooks and switch on a ring light I bought for $12 at Kmart. Job done.

My role as a mother was changing in these years. It changes for all mothers, of course, as their kids get older, but this transition happened a little more quickly than I expected. I was home more than I was away, but I was away enough. The boys had become pretty self-sufficient while I was on *MasterChef*, and after the show they and Mick still had to do without me a fair bit, while I juggled all these opportunities and commitments. I still cooked every night I could – sitting around the dinner table with my family remained the most important and best part of my day. That has never changed and is still true now, even though the boys are all grown up.

Making time together, although trickier than it had been before *MasterChef*, was a priority. One activity we did together for quite a few years was cook at Coast Shelter, the local homeless shelter. Mick had started volunteering in the kitchen in Gosford once a month from around 2008, when it was still located in Donnison Street in Gosford. He continued this for around twelve years, until COVID temporarily closed the community centre. The boys and I eventually got involved as well. Once a month we prepped and cooked in the restaurant. Clients arrived between 11 a.m. and 1 p.m. to have a hot meal or a cuppa. The ingredients we used to cook the meals were mainly rescued from local businesses or donated by the public. There was usually a reasonable pantry, although sometimes stocks got low and had to be supplemented.

Mick started his Coast Shelter volunteering when the boys were young. When they were old enough, they joined in. When they got older still and were busy on the weekend, other people would come and volunteer with us – school kids doing their Duke of Edinburgh awards, clients of Loyal IT, friends. It was important to Mick and me that the boys understood that not everyone is given the same opportunities in life. And that people who are struggling are no different to us, it's just that different things have happened to them. Some of the Coast Shelter clients were regulars, others came when they needed to. More than once we served meals to families from the same school the boys went to. It brought home to us that you just never know what anyone's situation is. You often don't really know what's happening even in the house next door – how close your neighbours or families at your kids' school or your work colleagues are to being evicted or having their home repossessed. How just one medical event could be the end of a job. How a whole family can be a pay cycle away from being without a roof over their head. How a mechanical failure could mean the choice between getting the car fixed and being able to get to work, or having enough money for school excursions and shoes and three meals a day.

At Coast Shelter, and everywhere we go, Mick is the gatherer of stories. He has a natural curiosity about people, and what I think is a rare attribute in adults – an utter lack of judgement. If we go on a holiday, he knows where everyone else is from and where they are headed before I've even figured out where the bathroom is. He knows who is moving in and out of all the houses in our street. And at Coast Shelter he knows at least the broad brushstrokes of the lives of the regular clients. He asks after their pets or their job-hunting or their fishing expeditions. He asks without pity, without giving advice and with genuine interest, a real desire to engage and learn.

The regular clients of Coast Shelter have stories that are wide-ranging and complex. Some of them choose to sleep rough; one man owns a house but finds himself unable to enter it, and sleeps underneath it on the ground. One woman lives out of her car, while another rides the trains all day. One regular literally has to choose between paying the rent and buying groceries. She chooses to pay the rent and leans on charity to be able to eat. One guy used to work the mines in Western Australia. He owned three houses and worked six days a week, letting loose with a few drinks on the seventh day. Eventually the booze got hold of him and he lost everything: his job, his houses, his teeth. His family.

There, but for the grace of God, go I.

Some of these people, my fellow Coasties, have substance abuse issues; some have children; some are impeccably groomed; some have their whole lives packed into plastic bags. Some are survivors of domestic violence. Some are emerging from incarceration. Some – many – have mental health issues. All have trauma, of one kind or another. All need not only nourishment but a bit of human contact, a sense of community. They need – we all need – moments of belonging, of being a family around a table. They come to the shelter not just for a plate of food but for a bit of banter, a laugh, a hot meal, a shower, a load of laundry and maybe some fruit and bread to pack up and take away for later.

For all our differences, we humans, we are really all the same.

This desire for our boys to experience the breadth of the world, and its inequities, led us to India in 2010. The kids were still young: Joe was in Year 8, Tom in Year 7 and Paddy in sixth grade. The opportunity arose through a charity called 40K, which I was introduced to by my sister. It was started by two university students, who had an initial goal of building a school in a remote community outside Bangalore (or Bengaluru as it's known now). They achieved this goal – and they have set and are achieving even more ambitious goals now. They planned a celebration for the opening, and we were invited to attend.

Part of the trip was a visit to the community in which the school was built. It was in some granite quarries. Families lived in A-frame huts with dirt floors. As soon as the children were old enough to swing a hammer, they were put to work in one of the quarries. When we were there, an older guy, in his sixties, was still swinging a hammer and breaking rock. He was near blind, as many of the workers were, from looking at white granite in the glaring sun all day. This was life in that village, and this is what the children who lived there had to look forward to.

At the official school opening, children talked to us of their dreams of being airline pilots and doctors; of travelling and writing.

There was a lot of celebrating in that village, for the chances these kids were being given.

As we travelled north, through Agra and Jaipur and Delhi, we witnessed a country of extremes – the Taj Mahal in stark contrast to families living on roundabouts, traffic flowing around babies sleeping in cribs made of cloth tied between two sticks. It was an overload of sights, sounds and smells; the boys clung tight to us. We were amazed and distressed and shocked and awed by it all. Occasionally I questioned the wisdom of us taking the kids there; it was a lot. To this day they remember it, and they maintain that they're glad that we went. Their worldview was altered forever.

In 2012, Lisa, my manager, called. I was at home, relaxing in the backyard actually, on a sunny afternoon. 'They're making a *MasterChef All-Stars* series and they want you to be in it.'

I don't remember what my exact response was, but I know that it involved hysterical laughter that became hysterical tears, and me saying something like, 'Why the bloody hell would I want to do that?'

The emotional fallout from 2009 was still so fresh. I had not yet – maybe still haven't – healed from the shock of the online backlash, the scathing commentary of strangers. Why on earth would I want to go back on television, into that arena, to contest a title I'd already won? Not only that, but I was still experiencing imposter syndrome after that 2009 win. Actually, I had been experiencing it for years – I remember having three little babies and thinking, who on *earth* left me in charge of small people? What possible qualifications could I have for this job? Who thought I would be able to grow a human from a wet bundle to a functioning adult? I hoped nobody would notice how little I knew, and take those babies away from me to give them to someone competent.

It was the same after winning *MasterChef*. There was an expectation that I would have expertise in all different areas of cooking. I became used to people assuming I would know how to roast a pheasant or make Roman gnocchi or decorate a wedding cake, or any number of other things I didn't know how to do. I was always honest when these situations arose, but felt terrible guilt for not knowing *everything*. I would study and practise to make sure my knowledge and skills were growing constantly, to try to keep up with these expectations – both external and internal. This sounds like hard work, but actually the work itself was a pleasure, a joy, an adventure; it felt like what I was meant to do. Food and cooking were, are, my obsession, and being able to immerse myself in them for a living was a dream come true. But the more you learn, the more you realise how much you don't know. It's impossible to know everything, of course, but that good old imposter syndrome kept me on my toes, trying to be all food things to all food people – an impossible task, a fool's errand.

So the idea of putting myself out there for *MasterChef* again was, at first, quite terrifying and not something I immediately wanted to embrace. But once I had calmed down enough to listen to Lisa properly, I saw that *All-Stars* wouldn't be a regular season of *MasterChef*. I learned that the contestants who'd been picked – four people from each of the first three seasons – would compete in teams, and the proceeds would go to our chosen charities. The series would air mostly during the summer Olympics from July 2012.

Mick and I had met in the St Vincent de Paul youth group, and with my involvement in one kind of charity work or another, I've always had a strong sense that winning *MasterChef* happened in part to give me some leverage to do more of this kind of work in the community. I feel a responsibility to make good use of my unexpected public profile. I don't mean this to sound holier-than-thou, or like I'm doing anything differently to other people; contributing in this way just feels . . . kind of vocational, I suppose. Like some people feel called to be surf lifesavers or horse riders or artists, I feel called to community service. Maybe it's because I still remember feeling the warmth, all those years ago, when two guys in cardigans gave me batteries for my mechanical toy puppy.

So I threw my hat in the *MasterChef* ring again. My chosen charity was Oxfam's Grow! campaign, which was about food security, particularly in developing countries. I ended up placing fifth in the competition, and through the money-earning challenges along the way won $15,000 for Oxfam's campaign.

For this reason alone, but also others, I was glad I went back on the show. It had a completely different vibe this time round. *All-Stars* was more light-hearted, more fun. Gary, George and Matt were able to engage with us contestants far more than they had in season 1. It was lovely to get to know them on more of a personal level than we had previously. I noticed that contestant welfare had moved up in priority as well: we had a green room and some home comforts – couches, a kettle, a sandwich press. The twelve of us were still living together in the same giant house in Darling Point, which at first was so strange, but we were allowed to have our phones at the house and we were allowed to go home on the weekend. These things made the world of difference and in a way helped me to recover from some of the stress and anxiety of the first series.

The best part about *MasterChef All-Stars* was getting to know the other contestants. I already knew my team, obviously, but was able to befriend contestants from Series 2 and 3, who until then I knew only from watching them on the television. It was great fun and cemented the sense that has endured ever since – that we're part of a kind of family. A strange sort of a family, to be sure, but we all have something quite unique in common that you'd be hard-pressed to replicate in any other situation.

~

The roller-coaster my life had become continued. As well as all the different work opportunities that were coming along for me, my whole family was enjoying the aftermath of *MasterChef*. Apart from those beautiful family holidays we were able to take to Hong Kong and India, we also took the boys to Italy, where we travelled for three weeks all the way from Milan in the north to Sicily in the south.

There, we took cooking classes as we travelled, all of us together. It was in Italy that I first really understood how important food is as a conduit into the heart of a culture. We did all the tourist things, of course; saw historic landmarks like the Trevi Fountain and the Leaning Tower of Pisa, rode Venice's gondolas and toured the Colosseum in Rome. But it was in the homes of ordinary Italian people that we learned the most about their way of life.

In Bologna we met Carlos, an elderly gentleman who took us to the markets, before we cooked with his helper, Luciana, in his home. We went from stall to stall and then from shop to shop, sourcing the best ingredients. We visited three different delis because one had the best prosciutto, another had the best mozzarella, and the third had the best mortadella. In each place we shopped, Carlos chatted at length with the providore; we sampled cheeses and meats. The whole process took hours. And in those hours I learned something I hadn't fully grasped before: that shopping for ingredients is not the annoying bit you have to do before you cook, it is *part* of the cooking. Maybe the most important part. After this trip I learned to slow down, to go to the places that have the best tomatoes or the best meat; to not rush, whenever possible, the gathering of groceries. Life naturally intervenes in these plans and good old smash-and-grab shopping is still on my agenda, but it's not my main modus operandi anymore.

Sitting around the table with Luciana, we made tortellini. From the hand-making of the pasta without any kind of kneading or rolling machine, we sat fashioning tortellini to go into a beef broth – a celebration dish, a family dish. Luciana became a bit teary as she showed my boys how to expertly fold the small parcels. Even though she had little English, and I had little Italian, she expressed to me that this reminded her of happy occasions with her own family; that it felt like holidays to her. We bonded over the understanding of how special it is to have your family around you while you are doing something as simple as preparing a meal.

Italy was pure, unadulterated magic. We hired a car to drive the jagged cliffs of the Amalfi Coast; we saw glass being blown in Murano, visited markets and roamed the cobbled streets with their music and shopfronts like film sets. We nailed the gelato challenge – to eat gelato every day. We got lost on a group tour, visited Pompeii and stood in the Sistine Chapel.

I actually got into trouble in the Sistine Chapel. The visit there was part of a very long tour of the Vatican, and the boys were tired and getting a bit bored with it, to be honest. When we entered the chapel we were warned against making any noise; there were guards around who glared at anyone who spoke too loudly or took flash photos. Joe sidled up to me and whispered out of the side of his mouth, 'Are there fifteen more of these?'

Sixteenth chapel. When the penny dropped I accidentally let out a hoot of laughter that bounced around the acoustic space and earned me a deathly glare and shake of the head by a moustachioed guard.

When the boys discuss what *MasterChef* did for our family, they are mostly recalling the good times. I think we managed to protect them from the worst of the media stuff and the online stuff, although inevitably some of it seeped through.

One day I was in Melbourne for a photo shoot. I'd left home early that morning and was halfway through hair and makeup when Mick rang to tell me that there was a newspaper article saying that our marriage had broken down. He'd found out about it via a phone call that morning from our local radio team, Rod and The Flack at Star FM. Mick, to my surprise, had become a bit of a radio regular while I was on *MasterChef*. Rod and the Flack had found his number and called him every now and then to discuss an episode they'd watched and try to get a bit of insider gossip. On this particular morning, they were concerned. 'Mate, are you guys all right?' they asked Mick. 'The paper says you're splitting up.'

Mick, who was just waking up, said, 'Uh, she was okay when she left this morning . . .'

Mick thought it was kind of funny, but I didn't. The shock I felt was physical – it was like a hard blow to my stomach. I got on to my management team, who tracked down the article. It had been written by a woman who had interviewed me and asked what it had been like on *MasterChef*. I told her the truth – that it was the hardest thing we'd ever done. That being apart from my family was awful but it shored us up like nothing else could have; Mick and I were stronger than ever and understood how much a part of each other's days we were.

Somehow, that had become the headline 'How *MasterChef* Scrambled My Marriage'. In the article, the journalist wrote,

'*MasterChef* winner Julie Goodwin says her time on the hit TV show put strain on her marriage and family.' Which I never said.

Even Mick lost his sense of humour about it when the boys came home from school, bewildered and upset. 'Everyone at school says we're breaking up. Are we breaking up?' asked Paddy.

And so my kids learned the hard way that some newspapers and trashy magazines, and online news outlets, make things up. They can conjure up a story in its entirety with no facts behind it at all, and publish it. And unless a person has enormous resources, they can't challenge these media outlets. We had to remind the boys, like a mantra, 'People who know us, know better. And people who don't, don't matter.'

The negatives were far outweighed by the positives, though, and the boys remember the positives in their own way. Joe is especially grateful for the opportunities he's had over the years to witness, and participate in, television being made – both ads and live shows. He credits meeting Ben, a producer on *MasterChef* series 14, with encouraging him into his current career in television. I am grateful to Ben but also think Joe needs to give himself some credit for attaining his university degree and winning multiple awards for his short films; plus his several years of hard graft before he got his opportunity in TV. He is absolutely loving life.

The thing Tom is most grateful for is the travel, especially our trip to Hong Kong. He often likes to say that it's where Dad bought him his first beer. We didn't realise the corner stores sold alcohol, so one afternoon we let the boys choose a drink each from the fridge. After a couple of sips Tom said his tasted weird. Upon reading the small print we discovered it was a fruit-flavoured shandy – half soft drink and half beer. He was twelve years old.

Paddy, our little sports fanatic, has been able to meet some of his sporting heroes. On his twelfth birthday, we kept him out of school for the day and went down to Concord Oval in Sydney to watch the Wests Tigers train. We're a mad Tigers family; it's generational on both sides, and Paddy loves them. (I mean, it's a tough gig being a Tigers supporter at the moment, and for the past few moments, but we diehards hang on. Our day is coming; until then our favourite year is 2005.)

At Concord we were able to attend a closed training session, the only people there who weren't connected to the club in some way. After training the whole team signed Paddy's jersey – while he was wearing it – and he got to chat to some of his league heroes. He didn't do a whole lot of chatting – he was pretty starstruck. We stopped for Chinese food on the way home and he told us it was the best day of his life.

These are the moments, the opportunities, the gifts, that came with winning *MasterChef*. These are the memories our family returns to and laughs about and truly, truly appreciates.

In 2013 Mick and I were approached by ChildFund. The charity had noticed that we'd been on its books for over thirteen years, and asked me to be an ambassador as well as to go to Uganda to see firsthand how donated money is used. We'd never been tremendously involved as sponsors – we sent the money, but with the business and everything else going on we hadn't been very good at writing letters to the kids ourselves. We knew how the children were doing, though, from the annual updates and handwritten notes we got from them. I was always blown away by how much was achieved with the small amount we sent. What for us would have paid for a nice breakfast out could kit one of the kids with all the clothes and shoes they needed for the school year. But as we learned on this trip, that was only a part of it.

The trip was astonishing. I'd never realised quite how child sponsorship worked; I thought that the sponsorship money benefitted one child in a family. But although each sponsored child is taken care of, the money also goes to assist communities in a holistic way. We saw schools that had been built with money donated to ChildFund, access to clean water that had been organised, skills workshops for teenagers, and self-managed lending programs so that the women in a community could start their own small enterprises.

One day we travelled for several hours to a town called Mbale, for its quarterly nutrition day. Among dancing, singing and celebration, this day involved measuring and recording the weight, height, girth and arm circumference of the children to make sure they were not displaying any signs of malnutrition. There were educators there, Ugandan women showing the mothers how to make sure their children were getting enough protein, carbohydrates and leafy greens.

Mick and I were welcomed with incredible warmth and hospitality at each stop on the way to Mbale. It was beautiful but also almost embarrassing – as though we were being given credit for all the people in the world who sent sponsorship money to Uganda. We were met with dances, songs, handmade gifts; we were met with fierce embraces and tears. It was overwhelming and humbling – a reminder of how different peoples' circumstances are. But even more than that, it was another affirmation of how *alike* we are. What our very core is. What we want for the people we love; our children, our parents, our siblings and friends.

Our best day was meeting Hamad, our ten-year-old sponsor child, a beautiful little boy who was holding a bunch of flowers, which he handed to me. It was clear that he was overcome; he didn't make eye contact. I wanted to gather him in a giant hug but sensed that this would be too much, so I shook his hand and we headed indoors for a more formal welcome. Hamad was sitting between

Mick and me, still looking a bit lost. 'Are you okay?' I whispered to him. He said yes.

'Are you a bit nervous?'

He said, 'Yes.'

'I am too,' I said. 'So we'll get through today together, and we'll have a good day, okay?' Again, he said yes.

And we did have the best day. There was a huge cheer from the kids when we produced a soccer ball – such a small thing to us but these children had been kicking around a plastic bag stuffed with other plastic bags. There was an even bigger cheer from the adults when another as-yet-uninflated ball and a pump were revealed, for when the first one wore out.

We spent a couple of hours just with Hamad and his siblings. We played soccer and had cold drinks and talked and laughed on this sweltering day. Hamad wanted to be a doctor. One of his brothers also wanted to be a doctor, another wanted to be an engineer and his sister a fashion designer. These kids, they were so full of ambition and hope.

Later that day I was invited to cook with the women in the urban slum where Hamad lived. In a courtyard between the tiny mud houses we prepared the food in the traditional way, kneeling on the ground. This, I was told through translators, was a gesture of respect to the food; standing was disrespectful, as was sitting all the way down. The food, mainly rice and starchy vegetables with some delicious sauce, was wrapped in leaves and cooked in big kettle-drum–style stoves over a long period of time. When it was ready, it was indicated to me that I was to serve my husband as tradition dictated – on my knees.

Well, I was here for the cultural experience so that's what I would do. Mick was sitting on a chair near the other men. I made him a plate and, with my inner feminist roaring obscenities at me, knelt in front of him and handed him his plate. With a twinkle in his eye he gave me a kiss and thanked me. 'Don't get bloody used to it,' I muttered. The women and men around us didn't need a translator to know what had passed between us. They roared with laughter.

My enduring memories of Uganda are of joy. Dancing and drums, vibrant colour and delighted laughter. Children with hope for the future and communities filled with pride. There is so much more to do, more villages and communities still without school buildings and fresh water and reliable food sources. This trip, for Mick and me, was a testament to the human spirit, and a realisation of what incredible outcomes can come from small donations.

Throughout these post-*MasterChef* years, I was still involved in Loyal IT, but only marginally. I organised the conferences, team days and the client Christmas hampers. The fun stuff, in other words. Pretty much everything I was doing was fun, if intense. My third cookbook, *Gather*, was published. I was invited to be the demonstrating cook on the *Murray Princess*, a paddle steamer on the Murray River, a peaceful and beautiful trip and one I took for several consecutive years.

I was still writing for the *Australian Women's Weekly*, travelling to Sydney most months to photograph the food, and for the portrait shot of me in 'my' kitchen. I used to laugh that people would think I redecorated my kitchen every month, as its backdrop changed in each issue to a different colour, with different props and furniture.

I loved these days with my *AWW* colleagues. As with the *Today* show, it was nice to have a regular set of people who I worked with;

it gave me a sense of belonging to an organisation. The *AWW* job required me to submit seven recipes per month, to a prescribed theme. If it was Easter, for example, I might be asked to prepare Easter baking recipes or an easy Easter lunch feast. Other themes were food that catered for a certain budget or amount of ingredients; or seasonal recipes – summer fruits, winter stews – or meals to entertain large groups.

I'd send the recipes off, and on photo day in the studio I'd sit in hair and makeup while the cooks from the magazine would make the dishes from my recipes. There was always a food stylist on hand, who'd hire beautiful plates and linen and utensils to tie in with the colour scheme and mood for that month's column. There was usually a wall behind me, and this would be painted to match the theme as well. A rack of outfits would be brought along to see which fitted me and matched the style of the shoot.

The photographer directed the shoot, deciding where the dishes of food should be placed on the table, where and how I should position myself. I had a great deal of admiration for the thorough and considered way each of these people went about their jobs, for their attention to detail and commitment to making everything beautiful. It was an insight into yet another world I had never really thought about until I was thrust into it myself. I learned so much about how to style a table, how to make the setting attractive, how to take my time and consider a scene in detail, from every angle. There was such a mindfulness about the whole process. It was a far cry from my everyday rush to get food on to the table, my mind always bolting ahead to the next place I needed to be and not necessarily appreciating where my feet were.

I have often read about 'trickery' in food photography; that food is painted to make it look better in photographs, or is not really food at all. I have to say that in almost ten years at *AWW*, and after writing seven cookbooks and attending the photo shoots for those, I have never seen this happen. That's not to say it doesn't happen, but not on the *AWW*, nor with my publishers. I just don't think it's common practice in Australia. Of course, the food is cooked and arranged to look its absolute best – and these guys did a much better job of that than I could ever do – but it was authentic. Usually, after the dish was photographed, we'd all gather around and eat it. I think I gained about five kilos while my first cookbook was being shot.

Around five years after I won *MasterChef*, I started to feel an urge to settle down a little bit. Besides the *AWW*, I didn't have a regular job; my work was all over the place – trips and demos and speaking engagements, events and shows and appearances. As exciting as it had been in the beginning, it was becoming tiring and, as the years wore on, less and less lucrative. The big endorsement deals had disappeared as my relevance waned and social media began to take over from traditional advertising. The time felt right to start a new chapter, to create my own business and my own opportunities instead of relying on the jobs that popped up randomly here and there.

I knew exactly what I wanted to do.

YOUR TIME STARTS NOW

Handmade gnocchi with burned butter and sage

Patrizia, a beautiful cook from Florence in Italy, taught me how to make feather-light gnocchi, the first gnocchi in my life that finally helped me understand what all the fuss was about. The secret was in her touch, kneading and rolling the dough as if it were as fragile as a newly hatched chick.

Prep time: 20 minutes
Cooking time: 20 minutes
Serves 4

1 kg Sebago potatoes
1 egg
½ cup plain flour
50 g butter
½ bunch sage (about 24 small leaves)
Half a lemon, zested and juiced
¼ teaspoon sea salt flakes
¼ teaspoon ground white pepper
40 g parmesan cheese

Peel the potatoes and cut them in half if they are large. Try to have them all a similar size so they will cook at the same time.

Place in a large pot of salted water and bring to the boil. Boil for 10 to 15 minutes, depending on the size of the potatoes, or until a skewer easily goes into them.

Drain the potatoes. Make sure they are very dry. Put them through a potato ricer or a mesh sieve. It is important that they are mashed very finely.

Scatter the flour over the potatoes, add the egg, and stir with a wooden spoon until the mixture comes together in a dough.

Flour a work surface and turn out the dough. If it is very sticky, add a little more flour. Gently knead the dough for only as long as is necessary to bring it together in a smooth mass. Roll it into a large sausage and cut it into eight pieces. Roll one piece into a sausage about the thickness of your thumb and cut into 2 cm lengths. Roll into a ball and then gently roll the ball down the tines of a fork.

Place the gnocchi onto a heavily floured tray. Repeat this process with the remaining pieces of dough.

Bring a large pot of well-salted water to a rolling boil. Drop the gnocchi in. In a couple of minutes, they will start to bob to the surface. Once they are floating, they are cooked. Lift very gently out of the water with a wooden spoon and drain.

In a fry pan over medium heat, place the butter and cook until it starts to froth. Add the sage leaves. Cook until the white milk solids from the butter start to turn golden and the sage becomes crisp.

Once the butter is a nut-brown colour, turn the heat off and add the lemon zest, juice, salt and pepper to the pan. Tip the cooked gnocchi into the sauce and toss through until well-coated.

Serve into warmed bowls and grate parmesan directly over the top.

CHAPTER 13

A WHOLE NEW WORLD

I had decided to explore the idea of running some cooking classes. Now that I wasn't cooking on the television anymore, I liked the idea of sharing recipes in person, and creating the kinds of experiences Mick and I had in other parts of the world.

Mick and I went to classes everywhere we travelled: me because I am obsessed with cooking, and Mick because he is perpetually interested in learning things and even if cooking isn't his passion, he does enjoy eating. And, luckily, hanging out with me. One of the classes we attended was in Paris.

It was a dream of a trip. I had done an ad campaign for an airline, and part of my fee was two business-class tickets to anywhere in the world. Can you imagine? We chose Paris. Mum and Dad came and stayed at our house and looked after the boys, and Mick and I spent the most glorious few days in this magical city.

My favourite place to eat in Paris was Polidor, an historic little restaurant where Ernest Hemingway and James Joyce used to hang out. It was the meeting place of artists and students, politicians and intellectuals. I could easily imagine revolutionaries making their plans to storm the Bastille in this steamy, tile-floored, aromatic venue. The food was simple provincial French fare – hot and inexpensive and delicious. I think we often associate French food with fine dining, tinkly piano music, rarefied air, stereotypical poshness. But for me, the best of this cuisine lies in its regional dishes, made from humble ingredients into comforting, warming food. Bourguignon – slow-cooked beef in red wine; or bouillabaisse – seafood in a rich tomato stew; or blanquette, which is essentially any light meat in a velvety white sauce. This is where the heart of French food is, for me; and Polidor was where we found it.

One day while we were in Paris, I set off by myself to E. Dehillerin, the specialist cookware store, much lauded in foodie circles and once frequented by the divine Julia Child. It was founded in 1820, an ancient shop of many levels, its timber shelves groaning with every cooking implement you can imagine and a great many you probably can't. I really wanted to buy a copper pot. I'm not even sure why; I just had it in my head that that's what I needed to buy in this store, in this city.

After looking around the shop for what seemed like an hour but probably wasn't, I couldn't find exactly what I was looking for and the place was so crowded, higgledy-piggledy and chaotic that I couldn't find an assistant to help me either. I left the store and stood out the front feeling so deflated and frustrated I was near tears – this had been top of my to-do list for this trip. So I took a deep breath and went back in. I finally found both an assistant and the courage to try to communicate with him in my halting high-school French. He helped me to find the pot I was looking for; actually, a much smaller one than I was looking for, as they were eye-wateringly expensive. The second time I left the store I was walking on air. Not only did I have the most beautiful, heavy, gleaming copper pot, but I had trodden the same boards as one of my culinary heroes.

The class that Mick and I attended was a croissant- and baguette-making workshop. We stood around a bench in a pâtisserie kitchen while the chef-instructor showed us how to fold and roll, cut and shape the most delicate pastries. We learned about baguettes, the strict rules that govern them in France: ingredients, weight, size all have to be within a government-set standard.

While I loved this class, I was a bit startled by its abrupt end – we didn't sit with a cuppa and chat after we'd finished baking, and eat what we'd created. Our pastries were bagged up as soon as they were cool enough and we were back out on the street. I knew then that if I ever held my own cooking classes, I would do things a little bit differently. The point of cooking, surely, is eating – and the best way to eat is communally. Any cooking class of mine would culminate in enjoying the food we'd made, and the talking, laughter and community that always takes place at a shared table.

By the time I'd decided to launch some cookery classes, Loyal IT had outgrown our first offices, so Mick and I started to look for a building into which we could relocate and have space to expand. I wanted a place in which we could not only run the business with more room, but also where I could test my recipes, store my cooking gear, and create food photos for my website. My space needed to be a bit separate from the IT business, obviously; you can't have some madwoman sizzling and bubbling and steaming away while you're trying to solve people's technological issues.

We found a building that, on first inspection, seemed like a hard no. It was a former lawnmower shop that sold and repaired mowers, whipper snippers and all kinds of garden equipment. It stank, as you would expect, of petrol and grease, which had soaked into the hardwood floors upstairs. It was dark and dirty and not overly charismatic.

Downstairs was a cavernous concrete-floored area with three giant roller doors. Many years prior, before the lawnmower shop had taken it over, it had been a motorbike dealership. There were rectangular pits in the floor where bikes were serviced. I am told, by people who remember, that it was a bit of a biker hang-out as well.

Now, it was being used as storage. Full of the carcasses of unrevivable ride-on mowers, tools, cardboard boxes of random stuff, it also stank of petrol and grease and damp and something undefinable. Maybe something dead. The raw brick walls of this downstairs area were painted a dirty white, with bright blue columns the colour they used to paint railway stations. Across the roof were huge, roughly painted red steel beams. Besides the beams and the pits in the floor, the only other architectural feature was a load-bearing wall about two-thirds of the way up the room. There was one small office right up the back, a bare earth underfloor space, and a single toilet screened in with a couple of sheets of fibro. It was not salubrious.

But . . . but. It was sturdy and strong; it had sat squat on this block of land just outside Gosford CBD for a generation, and it had seen all sorts of things. It had stories to tell. It had *potential*. It whispered to me about the things we could do; it was not just an out-of-the-way corner of my husband's IT business, but my very own place. A big place, safe and warm and beautiful. A place that looked as though it had been built to withstand a tornado. A place where we could really make magic happen.

In July of 2013, we put in an offer on the building and it was accepted. The magic, with all the frustration and excitement that rides shotgun with any transformation, began.

We worked on the upstairs first, to get the Loyal IT guys into their new offices and out of the old building. Month by month the lawnmower repair shop metamorphosed into a sleek business space, with high ceilings and glass offices and a big, bright, open-plan work area and kitchen. In the conference room we buffed and polished the beautiful hardwood floors, grease stains and all, in a nod to the building's history.

While Loyal IT's home was taking shape, I was dreaming up my cooking school. The initial plan of inviting in a few people to stand around a bench to watch me cook, then to sit down to eat, had to grow: the room was too big for such a modest venture. The building required more. And so the idea grew . . . and grew . . . and grew.

I tried to come up with the right name for it, something edgy or memorable or indefinably cool. Sadly, I do not possess the quality of coolness, so nothing really seemed to fit. I just wanted people to come to my place, the way they came to my house. And that's where the name came from. Where are we going? To Julie's Place.

My business plan was good enough to get a loan for the renovation and fit-out of the downstairs of our beautiful brick fortress. I had the walls acid-washed, leaving bits and pieces of the white paint while removing the blue altogether. The service pits were filled in and the concrete floors were polished. The roller doors were replaced with glass doors and windows; we added a second office, three brand-new bathrooms, one with a shower, and a storage room. My favourite part was the enormous pantry, which ran the whole length of the kitchen.

At the front of the space we put in a beautiful arched brick wall to hold the ovens, and an island bench for the cooktop and sink. Behind the brick wall was where we washed up, and where all the crockery was stored. There were miles of shelves; finally I had a home for my hundreds of cookbooks, which I arranged according to the colour of their spines.

Getting the place painted turned out to be outside of the budget, so I did that myself, with the help of some friends. It was a massive job: the ceilings were painted black to make the enormous space closer and more intimate; the walls were painted a warm shade of white. Cutting black cornices into white walls took literally weeks of standing on a ladder trying to keep my hand steady. I was ecstatic when it was done. The bathrooms were painted in a brushed bronze metallic paint. The lounge area was furnished with soft brown leather couches, a 1970s television, and, in pride of place, my nan's pianola with all the paper rolls for it on shelving either side.

In the main part of the kitchen there were six stainless steel benches with cooktops, each large enough to comfortably accommodate four people. The benches locked into place, but were on wheels so they could be moved around into different configurations. There was even enough space in the storeroom to put them away completely, to create a huge restaurant floor or party room.

I equipped the kitchen with absolutely everything I could think of that might be needed to teach cookery. I had seven of everything – one for each bench and one for the front. In the enormous pantry I had floor-to-ceiling shelves of utensils, appliances, pots and pans and gadgets. Opposite those were floor-to-ceiling shelves of bins filled with flour, sugar and racks of spices, oils, vinegars and all the things needed for the alchemy of cooking. It was glorious.

If you have ever built a house, or done a big renovation, or even started a business, you will know this to be true: it always costs more than you think. The very best-laid plans can come unstuck, and the simplest of things overlooked in a quote – like, for instance, needing insulation in a ceiling that had not previously existed – can send the budget into chaos. I poured just about all our resources into this cooking school. And when they were done, I borrowed and poured in some more. Mick, always the more prudent of the two of us, put his absolute faith in my ability to make it work. To make it viable.

I justified it to myself by believing with all my heart that this was the next step, the right thing to do – it was me taking power over my life. I was removing uncertainty; I would no longer be at the whim of brands wanting a spokesperson, or festivals wanting a presenter. I'd be driving my own bus. Running my own show. Providing for my family, while conducting my own orchestra. And for a time it seemed as though it was working.

While the renovations were taking place, I planned all the different cooking classes I would run. There are areas of cooking that aren't my forte; I looked for people to step in for those. You can't teach something you're not proficient at, but you can find the teachers.

My beautiful friend and cake decorator Julie Wilson was the first person I turned to when I wanted some help with ideas for the school. She was wildly enthusiastic and her generosity of spirit and excitement for the whole project were so infectious. We spent hours poring over beautiful books and talking about the classes we could run, how to market them, who to invite.

We were only a few months into trading, her decorating classes always selling out, when she became unwell: a little bit confused, a bit dehydrated, nothing too serious, we thought. But a trip to hospital told us otherwise. A tiny mole under her arm had become a malignant melanoma. The cancer had spread throughout her body and into her brain. Seven weeks and two brain surgeries after her diagnosis, she was gone. It was a shattering blow for all of us, most especially her family: her husband, Terry, and her young adult children, who were in the throes of having families of their own.

Edna White, my beloved Nan, and me.

Six months old. The bow is sticky-taped to my head.

Three years old. Whoever is off-camera was obviously cracking me up.

Four years old and in my happy place.

My beautiful little sister, Deb, and me.

Me with Mum, Nan and Deb, on a road trip in Nan's brown EH Holden Special. I'm holding my teddy bear, Joey, after whom I named my first child.

Year 7 at Hornsby Girls High School.

I wasn't what you would call a cool kid.

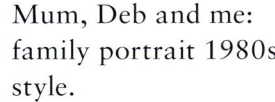

Dad, Mum, Deb, Nan, and me aged thirteen.

My fifteenth birthday, with the fanciest cake you could buy, a Sara Lee Black Forest gateau.

Mum, Deb and me: family portrait 1980s style.

Dad and Mum, Nan, me and Mick celebrate Nan's birthday. I'm nineteen in this picture.

Camp cooking in Toowoon Bay with Mick in 1990. It was the first trip of many.

Singing with the band in the Emmaus Productions days in the early nineties.

One of my clowning gigs in the early nineties was for so many kids that I roped Debbie in to help! Here I am holding Alexander Monkey, who survives and pops out to say hi to this day.

Right: Nan with me at my engagement party in 1993. She was so happy – she loved Mick as much as the rest of my family did.

Bottom left: Around twenty-one years old.

Bottom right: One of my gigs was at Westleigh shopping centre, wandering around singing carols. Mick accompanied me on guitar, c. 1993.

21 January 1995, with my new husband.

Below: Mum, Dad, Nan, me, Mick, Mick's mum, grandpa and grandma.

Tony Hunt, my dad from age six, much-loved Pop to my kids and great-pop to Delilah.

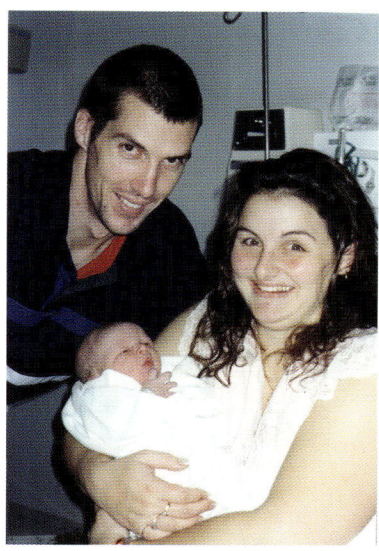

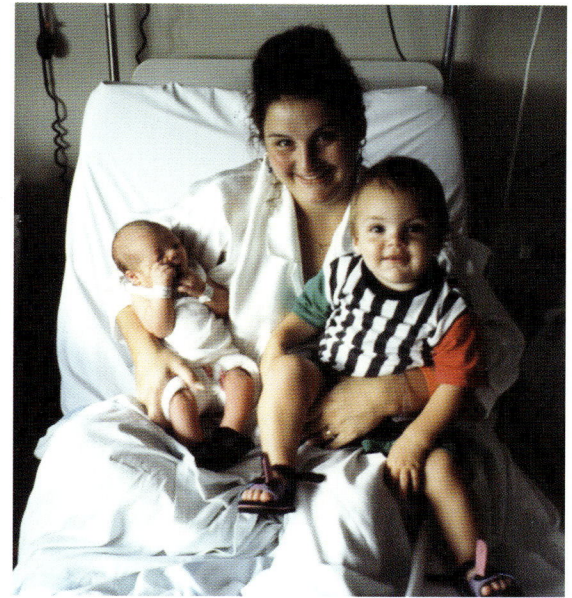

Looking a bit shell-shocked here after Tommy's very traumatic birth.

Joe, at fourteen months old, becomes a big brother.

It's an old and careworn picture but it's my favourite. My three little boys, brothers off to the beach.

Debbie and me with Nan and our families. *From left:* Paddy, Mick, me with Joe and Tom, Nan, my niece Sammie, Deb, my nephew Luke and niece Lauren, and Deb's partner, Kieron. Deb's littlest, Jess, would come along not long after this was taken.

Look at my boys. Just look at them. Aren't they gorgeous? I wish they would still put on matching shirts for family portraits.

Out of the cottage and into our new house at last!

I sang at Asquith Golf Club once a month for a few years when the boys were little, hauling my own sound gear and programming my own backing music.

Host Sarah Wilson with Gary, George and Matt – not just judges but our mentors and tormentors as well! All of them really special people who were a huge part of creating the juggernaut that *MasterChef* became. (Richard Dobson/Newspix)

Top 20, with a white apron and ready to go into the kitchen.
(© Network 10)

Each week the boys sent me a newsletter with all the most important things that had happened to them in the past few days. They were a comfort and a heartache all at once.

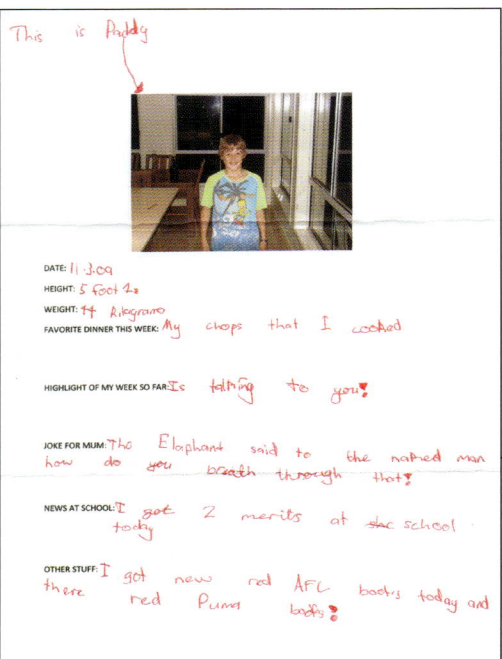

This is Paddy

DATE: 11.3.09
HEIGHT: 5 foot 2.
WEIGHT: 44 kilograms
FAVORITE DINNER THIS WEEK: My chops that I cooked

HIGHLIGHT OF MY WEEK SO FAR: Is talking to you!

JOKE FOR MUM: The Elephant said to the naked man how do you breath through that?

NEWS AT SCHOOL: I got 2 merits at the school today

OTHER STUFF: I got new red AFL boots today and there red Puma boots!

Name: Tom
Age: I dunno
Job: Proctolygist

DATE: 11/3/09
HEIGHT: 5ft,5inch
WEIGHT: 51.8k
FAVORITE DINNER THIS WEEK: Pizza (by Jo)

HIGHLIGHT OF MY WEEK SO FAR: Seeing the superhero movie

JOKE FOR MUM: What did the farmer say to the other farmer A: We're farmers!

NEWS AT SCHOOL: I had to write 5 lots of 9x tables, but they got so fun I wrote 15.

OTHER STUFF: Hi

DATE: 11/3/09
HEIGHT: 5ft 8.25
WEIGHT: 57.5 kg
FAVORITE DINNER THIS WEEK: the pizza I cooked

HIGHLIGHT OF MY WEEK SO FAR: hearing you where one step closer to winning

JOKE FOR MUM: Why did no one want to go out with Australian Idols Disco song A Because he was little disco

NEWS AT SCHOOL: at parent teacher night I heart nothing but good

OTHER STUFF:
I miss you so much I'm talking to a picture of you every night.

love you lots
Joe

> Tuesday 16/6/09
>
> To my dear Princess,
>
> B.T.W. you have become my princess now because you told me you felt like a princess coming home @ Easter.
>
> I am going to rattle off a few phrases or characteristics that describe you, not the old ones like beautiful, hot, wobbly, but the new ones that you have picked up during our journey over the last 3½ months:
>
> ① Famous. You are famous.
> ② Rock solid under pressure.
> ③ Loved by not just the 1000 people that know you, but by millions of people Australia wide. Shit!
> ④ Queen of cupcakes. Lemon Divas.
> ⑤ An exceptional cook. I have always thought a great cook, but you are exceptional.
> ⑥ Someone that inspires children, girls, women, mothers, husbands & blokes.
> ⑦ Someone who I cannot exist without. I find no joy in life without you next to me.
>
> Keep up your awesome work. 16 more sleeps to go. I love you my princess.
>
> Mick xxxx

Mick was missing me as much as I was missing him. He wrote constantly, sending love and encouragement through his letters. My replies were, unsurprisingly, equally heartfelt.

> ~~Friday~~
> Saturday 23rd (?) May
> Prediction. Not sure what will be doing today but pretty sure I'll be tired!
> ♡
> ♡♡

> Mick, Joe, Tom, Paddy, the beautiful men in my life.
>
> I fell in love with the picture on this card because it looks like our family. Big, strong beautiful Dad, intent and focused Mum, walking with three beautiful cubs. The cubs are so protected and loved. Even though there is a stormy sky that family is all right because they are strong and they love each other. Just like us.
>
> Remember to all hug each other every single day. Love each other and laugh together. Tell some crazy jokes at dinner tonight, then write them down for me. I love you all, with every beat my heart makes. So, so much. Love Julie/Mum

Poh takes in the tower of terror – Adriano Zumbo's croquembouche! (AAP)

I was so grateful to go through to the finale with my dear friend, then and now. (© Network 10)

The papers were filled with articles about *MasterChef*. It felt surreal.

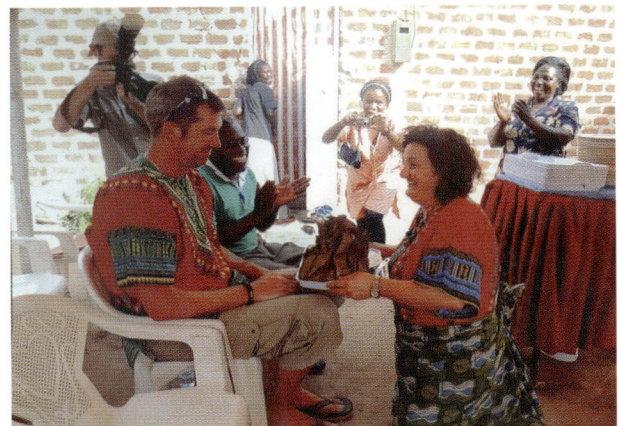

Serving Mick the traditional Ugandan way, on my knees. Don't get used to it!

On tour with my first cookbook, *Our Family Table*. (© Matt Jelonek, Getty Images)

Leaving the jungle after a month, sad to go but excited to get back to some proper food.
(© Nigel West)

My three boys, so proud of their Aunty Deb on her graduation day.

Hanging backstage with Angry Anderson. You know, like you do.

A pinch-me moment – on the cover of the *Australian Women's Weekly*, Christmas 2013. (David Gubert © *Australian Women's Weekly*)

Each month working with *AWW*, I had a different-coloured kitchen as the whole set was styled to best show off the recipes. (© John Paul Urizar, *Australian Women's Weekly*)

You never quite get used to seeing your face mashed up against the back of a van.

Rabs and me in 2018 with our ACRA award for 'Best on-air Team, Regional'.

At the ACRA awards with Rabs. This is his Best Music Presenter award for 2017.

My demolition crew for the Julie's Place kitchen – Paddy, Mick, Tom, mate Dan, brother-in-law Paul, Joe and mate Adam.

Many weeks were spent up a ladder painting the kitchen!

'Sydney Confidential' – the launch party write-up in the newspaper.

Paddy serving at the launch party for Julie's Place.

Janny ready to leap into action during one of my classes.

Julie Wilson, cake decorator and sadly missed friend.

Chef Renee gives me a helping hand after carpal tunnel surgery left me unable to use mine!

Commitment, passion, work ethic, intelligence and kindness: far more than an employee, Chef Renee was the glue that held the whole operation together.

Dinner with some of our friends from the Family Group.

Family Group on one of our weekends away.

A dizzying, wonderful new stage of life: as nanny and poppy to this little scrap, Delilah.

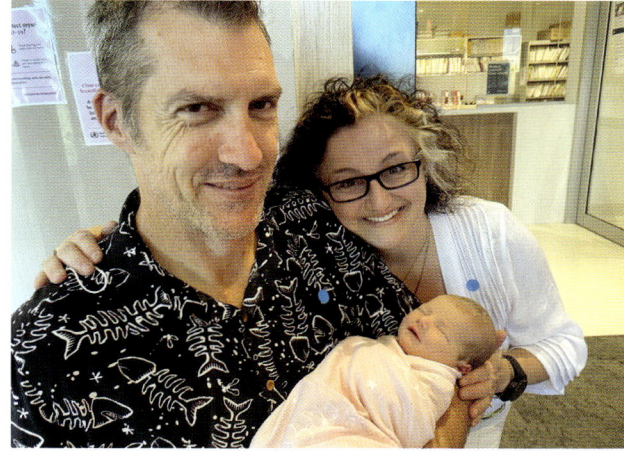

Our trip to Uluru; Paddy, Mick, Delilah, Joe, Tom. How much love can a heart hold?

Standing strong in sisterhood with the beautiful Billie McKay and Mindy Woods. This was a pivotal day for me, not just in the competition but in my life. (© Endemol Shine Australia, photograph by Kelly Gardner)

Cooking on the hibachi, like we all did. The judges loved a bit of real charcoal. (© Endemol Shine Australia, photograph by Kelly Gardner)

Explaining my dish and my food memory to Mel, and to one of my all-time favourite chefs, Rick Stein. (© Endemol Shine Australia, photograph by Carmen Zammit)

That moment when you're cooking for Marco Pierre White, the world's most celebrated chef, and you make him fried chicken . . .
(© Endemol Shine Australia, photograph by Kelly Gardner)

Having Mick and the boys on set in the *MasterChef* kitchen once again, after so many years, was truly a special moment for us all.
(© Endemol Shine Australia, photograph by Carmen Zammit)

Having a chat with Mel as I cooked with truffles in Tasmania. The dish I created on this day was one of my proudest in the competition.
(© Endemol Shine Australia, photograph by Kelly Gardner)

The whisky-themed sticky date pudding that would ultimately send me home. (© Endemol Shine Australia, photograph by Kelly Gardner)

With judges Jock Zonfrillo, Melissa Leong and Andy Allen. I farewelled Season 14 of *MasterChef* in Tasmania after the distillery challenge. (© Endemol Shine Australia, photograph by Kelly Gardner)

Jock. 'Thanks for cooking for us.' What I'd give to do it again. (© Endemol Shine Australia, photograph by Kelly Gardner)

Clockwise from top left: Louise, Vickie, Tash – my closest women friends. They're loving, forgiving, fun, and absolutely essential to a happy life.

Finding my way back to some of the things I loved to do when I was little.

Ticket holders numbers 1 and 2 for the Central Coast Mariners. Come on, you yellow!

Not long after my elimination from Season 14 of *MasterChef*, I was able to have some beautiful family time at the beach with Mick and my boys, and of course Delilah.

Delilah and Poppy at the beach.

One of the great gifts of grandparenting: I fall in love with Mick all over again as I get to know him as a grandfather.

A WHOLE NEW WORLD

Jules remained a part of that kitchen for a long time, figuratively and literally. Occasionally the lights would stutter and the chandelier would turn on all by itself for a few moments. One night, when Julie's best friend, Kelli, came in to do a class with me, the chandelier lit up without being switched on, and stayed on the whole time Kelli was in the room. Make of that what you will. I don't know all the things there are to know in this universe, but I do know this: the energy that my friend brought into that kitchen stayed there for quite a while after she left. Everyone who worked there knew it.

While we were still building the kitchen, I was talking to Pauly Mac. Paul McDonald is a classically trained chef who came on board as soon as we opened, running French technique and bread classes. He took care of many of the kids' classes too, bringing chemistry and delightful chaos to little budding cooks.

Another friend of mine, Mish Tournier, who had worked on my TV show with me, had many years under her belt as a presenter at Sydney Seafood School at the fish markets in Sydney. She agreed to teach seafood masterclasses, pasta, cheese-making and pressure-cooker classes, also areas of expertise for her. Her calm demeanour, beautiful manner and encyclopaedic knowledge were huge assets to the kitchen.

I was teaching mainly cuisine-based classes; feasts from around the world. Lebanese, Thai, French, Italian and more food I loved and obsessed over. Mostly food that lent itself to banquet-style eating. Paella, linguine and confit duck; kofta, flatbread and baba ghanouj; arancini, corn croquettes and lemonade scones. Oh, the things that were cooked in this beautiful kitchen, this squat, ugly building turned into a wonderland of smells and tastes and noise and laughter.

When we opened I didn't have any back-of-house staff. I wasn't sure how many people I would need or what positions they would hold. So before I began the hiring process I put my family to work.

Mick, Joe, Tom and Paddy donned aprons and helped with the classes and all the cleaning and washing up. Before we officially opened, I ran a few dummy classes for my friends and relatives to iron out the bumps.

Back on that huge day after the *MasterChef* finale aired and Poh and I did so many radio interviews we thought our heads would explode, when I spoke with Rod and The Flack at Star 104.5, they told me that the station would provide me with free advertising if I ever opened a restaurant. Rod and The Flack had moved on by the time I was opening Julie's Place, but I called the station anyway to see if the offer was still valid. I was delighted to learn that, even though it was five years after it had been made, and even though I was opening a cooking school and not a restaurant, the station was still willing to advertise it for me. I didn't know it at the time but that phone call, in a very short amount of time, would change my life yet again.

In June 2014 I threw a launch party, inviting media and friends and family. There were speeches and champagne and laughter, canapés and optimism, and we were underway. People could book tickets for classes through our website. In the beginning I didn't want to cancel anything on anyone so we ran classes even if they made a loss, just to have the doors open and attract customers. It was a slow burn; it took a few months for momentum to build, but eventually, we were in full swing.

One afternoon while I was clearing up at the end of the day, a sprightly sparrow-like lady called Janny walked in the door and told me that she had a strong feeling she was meant to be there and she wanted a job. Any kind of job – she just wanted to work here, with me. I was still building my team, so I said yes. She was with me, working her behind off, until the business closed eight years later, through all the highs and lows and fun times.

A WHOLE NEW WORLD

I also found the most beautiful woman to run the office, Shelley. I basically hired her because in her interview she quoted Judge Judy. It was a great decision and she took client enquiries and admin work with enormous enthusiasm and a determination to out-cheerful everyone she dealt with. She succeeded in this one hundred per cent of the time.

After a couple of years I found my amazing second-in-charge, Chef Renee. I knew she was a star; I didn't know yet that she would be the glue that held the business together through all the storms we were yet to weather.

My classes were usually held on Friday nights and weekends. Guests would arrive and gather in the lounge area, where there would be nibbles relevant to the class – bruschetta and olives before the Italian class; tapenade and crostini before the Spanish class; baked camembert and lavosh before the French class; hommous, labneh and flatbread before the Lebanese class.

Then we would cook: four people to a bench, the ingredients pre-measured and all the equipment ready to go. I would demonstrate, then the teams would repeat what I had done while I wandered around the room having a chat and giving a hand. We went back and forth like this for several recipes. Once the cooking was underway we served drinks: wine or beer or soft drinks, tea or coffee.

When everything was cooked, the groups brought their dishes to a big long table and sat and enjoyed the meal they had created. This was always the best part – passing dishes up and down, sharing the food they had cooked with the friends they had arrived with or the friends they had made in the room. The Lebanese Feast was my favourite to teach, and the class that sold out the fastest, followed closely by the Italian Feast and Thai.

I loved teaching these classes, but I hated the anticipation of them. Many was the night I would be in my office listening to people arriving and chatting out in the lounge, my face on the desk trying to slow down my breathing and my heart rate as anxiety coursed through me like electricity. Some days the first steps out to the lounge room to say hello to everyone were the hardest steps I had to make that day.

Once I was underway, though, when my breath had slowed and I was in the swing of the class, I was fine. Happy. Doing what I knew and loved. The energy in the room was always positive and it lifted me up and fed me.

We ran private functions, cooking classes and dinners; there was a monthly supper club, even a book club for a while. I ran recipe-writing workshops and we invited guest presenters, including *MasterChef* alumni, across all kinds of cooking genres. In autumn and spring we put on what we called a twenty-mile lunch, when I would toodle around the coast in my Mini, Alice, remaining within twenty miles of my kitchen, to gather ingredients. I talked to growers and providores and roadside stall sellers, and a menu would grow from these conversations and whatever was in season.

A couple of times a year, spice guru Ian 'Herbie' Hemphill – who with his wife, Liz, had founded their successful business Herbie's Spices in 1997 – would come and host a spice trail lunch. I would cook and he would talk while our guests enjoyed a multi-course feast and stories of spices from all over the world.

One day a gentleman by the name of Pete knocked on my door. Pete was a caseworker with FACS, the department of Family and Community Services (it had been called DoCS but had been rebranded in 2011). Pete wanted to talk to me about the kids in his care, particularly the young adults who were getting ready to leave the care of the department and live independently. He wanted them to have basic cooking skills. That's how it started, anyway; it became so much more.

A WHOLE NEW WORLD

I wrote a course that would span one morning a week for six weeks. We would have eight students in the course, each with a caseworker. Every week we cooked different recipes, and within each menu were the lessons that needed to be taught to these young adults. Hygiene, food storage, budgeting and nutrition were all part of the lesson along with cooking skills. One week we went to the supermarket together to talk about choosing food that is in season, using fresh ingredients over packets, and how to budget.

Many of the kids in the course had never cooked before. Some had, of course, but others had never touched raw meat, or peeled a vegetable, or even been in a kitchen while a meal was being prepared. In the style of all my other classes, each lesson concluded with us all sitting down to the table to share the food the kids had cooked. And that, as always, was where the magic happened.

We had kids who didn't really talk; kids who suffered social anxiety; kids who had no confidence; kids who were angry that they'd had to get out of bed that morning to go to a stupid cooking class; kids who had no idea how to use cutlery or take instructions; kids who refused to eat anything green; kids who had never – not once – sat around a dinner table. Bit by bit, over the six weeks, the walls broke down. Conversations were begun. Connections were made and friendships formed. Like I said, magic.

On the fifth week, after we had cooked and eaten, the kids went through my cookbooks and chose the dishes they wanted to make in week six to show off their new skills. They were allowed to invite a couple of their important people to a banquet lunch. Some invited their case workers or foster parents, some invited their biological grandparents or parents, or siblings.

At the end of week six they were presented with a certificate and a gift. I had long been associated with House stores, having been one of their ambassadors years before and also working with them while I kitted out my kitchen. They allowed me to purchase cooking equipment at cost price so that every student who went through this six-week course left with the tools they needed to have ongoing success when they left their group home or foster home and moved out on their own. They each took away a set of pots and pans, knives and cutting boards and utensils, and a set of my cookbooks.

Quite a few of the graduates from this course went on to work for me. Some stayed a little while, and some for years. A girl from the very first course, Shaylee, stayed with me for the eight years my business ran, and is still part of my family today. For some of these young people, working at the kitchen was kind of a practice run for working in the real world; it was a soft place to land. We gave a fair bit of leeway for lateness, strange clothing choices, overall cluelessness while they learned.

Employing marginalised youth was a lesson for me, too, in patience and compassion. I tended to become a bit irritable if someone didn't know how to do basic stuff like washing dishes in hot soapy water, or setting a table. Or turning up to work on time. Or at all. But the fact of the matter is, you don't know what you're not taught. It was like the kids in the detention centre at Kariong, the boys whose phone-call register was just a list of different prisons containing their parents, uncles, aunts and siblings. Where else were they likely to wind up?

I had two requirements of my team, whether they were the FACS kids or anyone else: that they take pride in what they do, whether it was cleaning or serving or setting up a table, and that they keep their word. Turn up. Be on time so that the team was never left short. These requirements weren't always met, but because they were clear, it was easy to have discussions around them and to explain why they were necessary.

A WHOLE NEW WORLD

It would be lovely to say that everyone who came through my doors to do this course left better off. The reality is that some kids gained a lot and some didn't engage much at all. It's the same for anyone, in anything, really. The more you put in and all that. But it's not possible for someone to put effort and energy into something because I think it's important, if they are having monumental battles on other fronts in their lives. I was happy to have been a small part of these young people's lives, and I felt enormously privileged when they would pop in to tell me about their successes – their latest job, their study, or to show me a new baby. One girl, a beautiful musician, would call in every now and then to play my nan's pianola.

The course ran two or three times a year for several years, until COVID put a stop to it. I honestly believe that in the life of that kitchen, in all the hundreds of classes and thousands of people who came through the doors, the events and the laughter, connection and emotions, the FACS course was the most important thing we ever did.

Baba ghanouj

Lebanese cuisine is vibrant, fresh and packed with flavour. This smoky dip is spectacular as part of a banquet, along with other dips like labneh and hommous, with freshly made flatbread and olives.

Prep time: 10 minutes plus cooling time
Cooking time: 10 minutes
Makes around 3 cups

YOUR TIME STARTS NOW

3 medium eggplants
½ cup tahini
Juice 1 lemon
1 clove garlic
1 teaspoon salt
Olive oil, paprika, chopped parsley and chopped tomato to garnish

To get the smoky flavour into the eggplants, sit them directly onto the gas burner on your cooktop. (If you don't have a gas cooktop, place the eggplants under a hot grill.) Turn the eggplants regularly, until all their skin is charred and they are soft through. Place into a bowl and allow to cool. The skin will peel away easily from the flesh.

Place the eggplant flesh in the bowl of a food processor with the tahini, garlic, lemon juice and salt. Blend thoroughly, scraping down the sides of the bowl occasionally, until smooth and creamy. Place in the serving dish and garnish with olive oil, paprika, chopped flat leaf parsley and chopped tomatoes. Serve at room temperature.

CHAPTER 14

WHERE EVERYBODY KNOWS YOUR NAME

The kitchen had been open for around six months when I received an email from my manager, Caitlin, asking if I would like to be on a new show – an Australian adaptation of the UK reality hit *I'm a Celebrity, Get Me Out of Here!* I had a vague sense of the series: its contestants lived rough in the bush, doing hair-raising activities involving deadly creatures and daredevil stunts, and eating bizarre and disgusting things, all for charity. It seemed participants would do just about anything to earn stars so that their camp-mates would get food for the evening. At any time, if they didn't like the challenge and wanted to bail, all they had to say was, 'I'm a celebrity, get me out of here!' and they'd be off the hook.

'Oh my GOD, I would NEVER go on that show!' I said, after Mick and I watched, with mild horror, some clips from overseas episodes. Mick kind of laugh-snorted and said good-naturedly, 'Yeah, you would.' And he was right. I ended up agreeing to take part in this first Australian series, and in February 2015 off I went to South Africa.

It turned out that I was not going in as part of the starting line-up but as what was called on the show an 'intruder', so I had the opportunity to watch the first couple of episodes before I flew out. I was so glad about this; I was reassured that it was a good-natured, light-hearted show. There didn't seem to be negativity or bitchiness, and I couldn't see any of the gratuitous nudity that seemed to feature in some of the European versions. Among my future campmates in the jungle were Chrissie Swan and Joel Creasey. Actor and broadcast personality Andrew Daddo was in there, along with cricketer Merv Hughes, AFL great Barry Hall, and Maureen McCormick – or as I knew her, Marcia Brady. Also, travel blogger Tyson Mayr, Hi-5 singer Lauren Brand and *The Bachelor* winner Anna Heinrich. It was a colourful group of people – I wondered how I'd get along with them all and where I'd fit into their dynamics.

I was taken to a lodge at a private game park to wait for my turn to go into the 'jungle' – really the veldt – not far outside Kruger National Park. I was supposed to be there for only a couple of days before I entered the camp, but I kept getting the news that my entry was being delayed. I ended up being in the lodge for about a week and a half, participating twice-daily in the dawn and dusk wildlife safaris.

The safari trucks were like utes, with tiered seating in the back and, perched on the bonnet, a tracker. With his eagle eyes he would scan the dirt roads as we travelled slowly along, and point the driver in the direction we should go. Every day was different; being there for over a week meant that I got to go on more than a dozen safaris. I saw some incredible things.

One day our truck found itself in the middle of a herd of elephants. We had been following the trail of destruction that they tend to leave in their path: trees stripped of bark and sometimes branches, or knocked over entirely. Then suddenly there they were, slowly heading towards us along the road, gathered around their babies in a protective guard. The truck stopped as they passed. Our instructions were to remain still; not to stand or shout or wave our arms around. I could have put my hand out and touched one as they flowed either side of the vehicle.

On another day, the tracker found lion paw prints and we followed them. We stopped at one point, and the driver pointed out a little herd of warthogs trotting along in the high grass. He explained that when a lion chooses an animal from a pack, the one it wants to eat, it doesn't deviate from that animal. It homes in with laser focus. The last little warthog to trot past our view stopped, sensing something. An English lady next to me grabbed my sleeve and mouthed 'run', but the little guy hesitated a second too long. He bolted suddenly, and was only out of view for a beat when there was a terrible squealing noise. Moments later the lioness appeared, carrying her catch. We tracked her into a thicket where she stashed the carcass of the warthog. Our driver explained that she had cubs, and now she would fetch them to feed. We followed her as she padded slowly along the road.

At one point we crested a small rise and suddenly had a view of a wide open grassed area. The reason it wasn't covered in scrubby bush, the way the rest of the reserve was, was because it had once been a flower farm. Nature was being allowed to reclaim the area so it would become bushland again eventually, but for now it was like a scene from *The Lion King*. In the gathering dusk, all across this plain, were herds of animals; there were giraffes, gazelles, zebra. And all of them, without exception, froze when the lioness entered the space. They stood stock-still, not wanting to be the creature that drew her attention and ended up being her next meal. Besides an occasionally twitching flank, an involuntary huff of breath, they were still and silent.

They didn't know that the lioness had killed and was not hunting now. She padded slowly, deliberately, her gaze fixed straight ahead. One paw in front of the other, she crossed the grassland as we followed a reasonable distance behind.

I understood, in this moment, the real meaning of the word 'awe'. I thought my heart was going to come out of my chest. I wasn't the only one with tears on my face. It was quite simply the most magnificent thing I have ever seen. I finally understood why the lion is named King of the Jungle. Every creature there knew it, including the humans.

Once she had collected her two cubs, who were rumbling under a big tree and waiting for their mum, the light had faded too much for us to track them back and witness their feeding. The animals in the park were used to the trucks, but only in the day. Shining a light on them at night was not an accepted practice.

On other days I saw a baby hippo, so new it was pink, a baby giraffe, and a fleeting glimpse of a leopard. We saw hyenas and their cubs, zebras standing in the middle of the track, and all kinds of gazelles and birds. It was incredible, and although part of me was keen to get into the *I'm a Celebrity* camp and get on with the show, I will always be grateful for this magical interlude in the South African wilderness.

The day I was being transferred to the camp arrived. I was given no idea what I was in for. A minivan, with its windows completely blacked out with garbage bags, transported me to parts unknown. I was then blindfolded, put on the back of a motorbike, and ridden to the top-secret location of the camp. I have no idea why I needed the blindfold, or the blacked-out windows. I had no clue where

I was and couldn't have found my way back there even if I'd been taking notes.

We had a very strict list of things we could take into the jungle, including limited underwear and swimwear. Everything else we needed would be provided.

I entered the jungle with a fellow intruder, Freddie Flintoff, former captain of the English cricket team and enormous television personality, particularly in the UK. When we first met, he was up a tree, caught in a net. I had to get him down by throwing stuffed monkeys into a basket. If it sounds ridiculous, that's because it was; that was the nature of the show. Absurd fun. Once I'd 'rescued' Freddie, we had to spend the night in a kind of cave, which stank to high heaven. It wasn't a restful night – my homework about this show had led me to believe that the ceiling would open and rats or snakes would come pouring out on top of us from the moment we went to sleep.

However, it was an entertaining night: what I learned about Freddie Flintoff was that he was hilarious. He made me laugh so hard I could hardly breathe, and so even after night one I knew we'd become good friends.

From day two, I started to get to know the others in the camp. Chrissie and Joel were happy to talk about food and recipes with me until the cows came home. Andrew started what we called Craft Club, and made things for us all to do. He whittled me a pair of knitting needles and I knitted things for my campmates using dismantled hessian sacks and other odds and ends.

The fabulous and funny hosts of the show were Julia Morris and Dr Chris Brown. They would appear like magic in the morning to tell us what challenges lay ahead and who would be participating, and to let us know the next person to be eliminated. Their arrival in camp was the only thing that anchored us in time. When we heard their faint cry of 'I'm a celebrity, get me out of heeeeeeeere!' from the distant set, heralding the start of each show, we knew it was evening in Australia and our families would be sitting down to watch the episode as it unfolded.

Being – once again – on the first series of a TV show meant the addressing of some rumours about the production, and the ironing out of a few wrinkles. One of the funnier rumours was that we weren't in Africa at all, but somewhere in the Blue Mountains of New South Wales. (Obviously not the case!) Another was that we were all bussed back to a hotel at the end of each filming day, and fed well, and allowed to sleep in a comfy bed. I wish! We slept on stretchers, in the open air. The show certainly wouldn't have worked if we were comfortable and well fed; we were willing to do just about anything for our diet to be supplemented, which was of course what the producers relied on when they came up with their sadistic concepts for the Tucker Trials.

Our safety briefing before we entered the camp had involved us holding a tarantula to make sure we wouldn't freak out if one crawled over us at any point. We also had the deadliest of snakes pointed out to us, and a lesson on baboons. Baboons are violent. We were instructed not to look them in the eye, and if they came into camp and stole something of ours, we were to let it go. 'They have the power to tear your arms out of the sockets, and they will do so if you challenge them,' the safety officer said matter-of-factly. 'And they become especially angry if a female challenges them.' So, baboons are violent *and* misogynistic. We could hear them fighting at night, and see them too, climbing through the branches above our head.

One day, as we were escorted to the waterfall where we were allowed to swim, we noticed men in the trees. Snipers, in camouflage gear. The producers would not tell us why they were there, so we were never sure if there had been a sighting of some kind of big cat near the camp, or if there were poachers around, or if this was turning into a sort of futuristic game show where if we didn't get enough votes we would be shot instead of sent home. If you keep people in the dark they will come up with some wild theories, that's for sure.

As soon as I arrived I was allocated camp cook, which was okay with me. However, all we had to eat was a small ration of rice and beans, which we had to cook on the campfire. Eventually we were also given a small ration of oats in the morning – I think there were concerns about the amount of weight everyone was losing. One day Barry Hall was sitting on his stretcher, looking sadly at his Christmas ham-sized arms, lamenting, 'Look at me. I'm turning into a javelin.' Joel was fading away to a mosquito-bitten shadow; he, like me, was allergic to the mozzies and none of the products we were given worked at all.

Because of our proximity to Kruger National Park, everything we used, from soap to toothpaste, shampoo, deodorant, detergent and insect repellent, had to be absolutely environmentally friendly. None of it did what it was supposed to do, so we were all mozzie-bitten and stinky with lank hair and dirty dishes. Except Anna, who seemed to have skin that was kissed by an angel even in the absence of any makeup or beauty products.

If the campmates who were voted by the audience to do a challenge succeeded in their task, we were given some other ingredients to supplement our rice and bean diet. We might, for example, get an impala shin, a lemon, a clove of garlic and two apples, or some similarly random group of ingredients. It was like the *MasterChef* mystery box all over again, except when you are cooking for genuinely hungry people, it doesn't much matter whether what you cook is going to go down well. My main problem was the lack of salt – it became my daily request of the producers. I was denied any until someone got hold of a luxury item – a block of Himalayan salt as a beauty product. It was seconded into the kitchen, where I would surreptitiously scrape chunks off it to add to the food.

My most memorable challenge was one with Joel. He had to answer questions about celebrities. If he got one wrong, he was dunked in a pool of stinking goop. If he answered correctly, we gained extra time for me to find stars. These would win us food for camp.

The stars, wooden cut-outs about the size of my hand, were hidden throughout a star-shaped cage, built low to the ground and divided into five sections. The fifth section was boarded up and contained a horror I could not yet see, but which banged and shook as I completed the rest of the challenge. The first section was full of snakes. On my knees, I had to gently move them with my bare hands and untangle strings that were holding the stars together. The second section contained ants, ones that spat acid out of their backsides and left me covered in red welts. The third cage contained rats: I had to push them aside on my hands and knees to find the stars. Compared to the acid-arsed ants, the rats were a breeze. The fourth was the worst: it was filled with elephant poo and intestines of some sort that had been sitting in the sun for enough time to really ripen up, and were covered in swarms of blowflies. In I went, slipping around, trying to find those elusive stars. I retched over and over. If I hadn't been literally starving I would have vomited. The retching was later made into a downloadable ringtone, available for free on 10Play.

Finally the cover was taken off the fifth part of the cage. It was full of alligators. Only small ones, less than a metre long, but their mouths were not taped shut and they weren't restrained in any way other than being in the cage that I was about to enter. Before my time started on this part of the challenge, I was given a safety briefing by the same guy who had told me baboons could rip my arms off. 'Don't make any sudden moves or loud noises – they will bite. We have a medic on standby.' And your time starts . . . now.

I held my breath and entered as stealthily as I could. Reaching for a star, I came eyeball to eyeball with an alligator. 'It's hissing at me,' I whispered to Julia and Dr Chris. 'Oh, that's a bad sign,' said Dr Chris, ever helpful.

I didn't get bitten. I retrieved about three-quarters of the stars on offer. Funnily enough, after crawling around in elephant poo and rancid guts, I didn't have much of an appetite that night.

The strange nature of this television show didn't really faze me, as it had the same surreal quality that my life overall seemed to have had during and since *MasterChef*. If I'd learned anything from my first foray into TV, it was to take on opportunities when they arose. You never know what you'll miss out on if you say no because of fear of the unknown. 'We won't die wondering,' Mick and I said to each other on many occasions.

While I was away, my business was kept ticking over by my team. I hadn't scheduled many classes for that period, knowing I would be gone, and the ones being held were handled by the other instructors.

I was eliminated five days before the finale. I was bummed to leave so close to the finish line. I'd have loved to make it through and earn more money for FightMND, my chosen charity. But my time was up, and after absolutely smashing my first meal of a hamburger and hot chips (which made me feel sick), I packed my bags and headed home to resume my life in the kitchen. I'd been in South Africa for over five weeks, four of them in the camp.

Freddie Flintoff went on to win the title of King of the Jungle. Australians forgave him for being the cheeky, skilled English cricketer who'd beaten us in the Ashes in 2005, having grown to love him for his irreverent humour and shenanigans. I loved him too; I still do. He is kind, decent, funny and genuine – one of the planet's really shiny human beings.

Not long after I returned home from South Africa, I received an unusual request. Shayne Sinclair, a talented young program director at Star 104.5, gave me a call and asked if I would fill in for Mandy on the Craig and Mandy breakfast show one morning, as she was sick. Craig had enjoyed interviewing me previously and had asked for me to sit in.

I happened to be free so I happily agreed, and I had a great morning. I told them to get me in whenever they wanted – I loved it. There was an immediacy about radio; it was nerve-racking but exhilarating, adrenalin-inducing fun.

I kind of fell into a more regular role there. I was invited along again as a guest at a twenty-four-hour outdoor broadcast; to a listener wedding in the park; and whenever I released a new cookbook, of which I had four or five by now, I'd go into the studio for an interview. I became friends with Mandy outside of the radio station – she's a sassy, feisty chick and we hit it off. We would get together reasonably regularly, for coffee or for a long walk around one of the many beautiful beachside locations on the coast. Little did I know that we would end up job-sharing for a while. When Mandy dropped back to three days a week, I took on the role of co-host of the brekky show on Mondays and Fridays.

By this stage another announcer had joined Craig and Mandy in the studio. His name was Dave Rabbetts, but he was known to us all as Rabbit, and he had moved up from Adelaide to the

Star breakfast show. So at either end of the week, I was the third co-host alongside Craig and him.

As well as co-hosting the radio show, Craig was studying law, getting married and planning to move to Melbourne. Mandy was looking for a break from radio – she had kids in high school, and breakfast radio is a tough taskmaster. I was asked if I wanted to come on board full-time as the breakfast co-host. My initial reaction was something along the lines of, 'Haha, that's a really great offer. It doesn't seem like the right thing for me right now but I'll think on it.'

I did think on it, and it didn't seem doable. How would I manage early mornings five days a week, plus the cooking school, plus the *AWW* column, potentially more cookbooks, and the other random and varied things that popped into my life? I asked Mick what he thought. He, being steadfastly who he is, said he would support whatever I wanted to do but that my decision to say no sounded like the sensible one. I gave myself a little more time to think before I gave a definitive answer.

During my thinking time, I was invited to join Craig and Rabbit to MC the Red Hot Summer Tour concert at The Entertainment Grounds in Gosford. These concerts had been touring the country for years and always drew a crowd of people looking for a bit of nostalgia and a great night out. They feature a lineup of acts, mostly from the 1980s and '90s, performing the hits they were best known for back in the day. The lineup for the concert in November of 2015 was epic: Pseudo Echo, Eurogliders, Wendy Matthews, Sharon O'Neill, Mi-Sex, Dragon. It was the soundtrack of my teenage years and twenties; it reminded me of how much I loved music and the way a certain song could light up the dance floor or put me into a deep blue funk. The whole radio opportunity, in fact, felt like a harkening back to my first true love: music.

That night in November, I got to hang backstage with the acts, musical legends from my youth, whom I'd admired for decades. Craig, Rabbit and I introduced them on stage, fired t-shirts into the crowd from a cannon, and danced like maniacs in the wings. Or maybe that was just me. It was surreal – how had this middle-aged cooking-show contestant ended up hanging out backstage with Rose Tattoo? What the actual hell?

About halfway through the concert I rang Mick. 'We have a problem,' I said. He asked me what the problem was. 'I am having too much fun to say no to this opportunity.' Mick, again being steadfastly who he is, told me that I should go with my gut, and if my gut was saying yes, then that's what I should do.

So, my gut and I took on the role of breakfast co-host on Star 104.5.

It felt as though my feet were now very firmly planted on the soil of the Central Coast. I couldn't just take off to parts unknown for random projects and appearances; besides having a business to run, I had a five-day-a-week job to keep me near home. This role came at a time when I really craved that anchoring. The past few years had been exhilarating but a little bit exhausting and bewildering as well. I was looking forward to being more grounded, part of a team, a collegiate group of people all pulling for the same goal. Of course I had that in my own business as well, but there's something quite different about being the employed, not the employer.

The Rabbit and Julie Goodwin show kicked off on 18 January 2016. Looking back at my calendar for that week, I can see that because of the school holidays, the cooking school ran nine classes, six for children and three for adults. I hosted five of them, including two on the weekend. I had also committed to handing out food samples at the Central Coast Stadium before that weekend's Mariners football match. Although in the years that followed I tried to slow things down, this was the new pace. The new normal. My supposedly calmer life.

I loved being on the radio. Early on in the year, Rabbit and I workshopped the show and came up with a list of values for it: positivity, inclusion, humour, kindness. We didn't want to join the ranks of programs that ask people to call in and complain about life. We wanted the good news, the highlights, the relatable, everyday stuff that we all experience and can laugh about.

Every now and then we broached a difficult or serious topic. Once, we made the decision to dedicate a show to the topic of bullying in the schoolyard. We had experts in the studio and across the morning we talked with parents, kids, teachers. It was profound, and all the more so, I believe, because it was such a deliberate departure from our usual banter. Stories were shared, important information was given out.

One of the experts we had in the studio that day was a psychologist by the name of Heather Irvine. She is the daughter of Dr John Irvine, who was a huge influence in Australia on child-raising in the 1990s and used to do segments on the radio when my boys were little. Dr John's brother and Heather's uncle, Dr Warwick Irvine, had helped us enormously with Joe, with navigating his particular needs. He had advocated for Joe, and his kindness, wisdom and appreciation of our gorgeous kid had earned him a place in my heart. Heather, compassionate and articulate on that day in the studio, would become – years in the future – my own psychologist, and steer me on a course that I consider to be nothing less than life-saving.

Rabbit and I not only looked for funny stories, but we also asked people to nominate and recognise local heroes. We created what we called the 'Show Zone' – a bubble that only the show values could enter. The Show Zone existed from 5 a.m. until 9 a.m.

Nothing negative was allowed in, nothing that would bring us down. Of course, life sometimes gets in the way of even the sincerest of ideals, and so it is in radio. Rabs and I agreed that we would check in with each other before we went on air. If we were feeling unwell or unhappy about anything, we'd flag it with each other so we could be aware that one of us might need to be carried a little more that day. But the full discussion would take place after 9 a.m., when the mics were off and the job was done, outside the Show Zone.

I was told, by Rabs and everyone else I worked with, that breakfast radio is usually done a little differently to how we did it. Normally, apparently, there are production meetings to come up with content and to plan the show. We didn't have those. I arrived at 5 a.m. and went through the day's news for any nuggets we could talk about. Rabs turned up right before 6, when we went live on air. We had an electronic calendar and would look for content throughout our days – funny things that had happened at the shops, or at home, or on the road. We'd put a cryptic title into the calendar and when the right time rolled around, away we'd go with our story. Sometimes it turned into a phoner – a question we'd ask the listeners, so they could call in with a relevant tale. We never knew what each other's stories were going to be. We weren't actors so a genuine response was what was needed, not a rehashed or rehearsed one.

In our small radio station, we didn't have a show producer. Rabs panelled, taking care of the desk – the knobs and sliders, as they are known by . . . well, me – and I took care of the phones. During the songs or ad breaks, I'd answer calls, typing in the reason the caller was ringing so it showed up on our screens. Rabs would fire off the music and the ad breaks. In the studio across from us, the newsreader waited for her turn to go on air on the hour and half-hour.

WHERE EVERYBODY KNOWS YOUR NAME

It was a bit of a tightrope performance. You never quite know what will happen when you're live on air. Sometimes a caller will say something so completely different to what you expect, and derail the topic. We had a regular who could talk the leg off an iron pot about any subject; it truly was a gift. Some days one of us would stuff up (almost always me) and say the wrong thing. Sometimes the stories we shared went down such an hilarious path that we couldn't stop laughing.

Always, there was laughter. I arrived ready to be highly amused, and Rabs never let me down. Not just quick on the panelling, he was funny as hell – quick-witted and with a view of things that was outside the box. We developed a great deal of trust between us – I always knew he had my back. Over months, we established an almost psychic set of signals; we could communicate in silence with a glance or a raised eyebrow, the way married couples do. When you spend at least three hours a day, five days a week, in a soundproof booth with someone, you get to know them very well. He was more than my colleague; he was, as we joked, my work husband. Above all, he was, and remains, my friend.

I loved radio, I just loved it. It seemed to come naturally to me, that banter. I felt such a sense of privilege when listeners would call in with their stories. I felt like I knew them, and I know that many felt they knew us as well. For a long time, we signed our show off with the theme song from *Cheers*, 'Where Everybody Knows Your Name'. Sometimes I'd be approached when I was out and about and asked all sorts of questions. 'How's your son's tattoo?' 'Did you ever find the person whose glasses were in your bag?' 'Have you figured out how to open your petrol cap yet?' 'Have you accidentally driven through any parks lately?' Sometimes I would forget that I'd talked about these things on the radio and would marvel that these people knew this stuff about my life.

In 2018, after more than two years on air together, Rabs and I won the Australian Commercial Radio Award (ACRA) for Best On-Air Team (provincial). It was a huge night – the ACRAs are to radio what the Logies are to television. The whole Star team was over the moon: the station won a lot of categories that year. It was a great place, with a fantastically upbeat vibe that came from the head down. Paul Moltzen, Star's general manager, was as beloved a character as you could meet. He had got me into the radio caper to begin with, along with program director Shayne Sinclair.

Of course, even the best jobs have their drawbacks. The hours for breakfast radio are tough: my alarm went off at 4 a.m., which meant going to bed at 8 p.m. Or, I should have gone to bed at 8 p.m. I wasn't very disciplined about it in the early days because I didn't get to see Mick or the boys in the morning and only caught them briefly at night before I was supposed to hit the hay. I did get better at the early bedtimes when I realised how tired I'd started to get.

One of the benefits of this schedule was that I didn't drink very much through these years. Nothing at all during the week. Prior to radio I had become a daily drinker. Not hugely so, but certainly regular: a couple of glasses at night to help shut off my brain so I could get some rest. More on the weekend: on the Friday or Saturday nights I ran classes, I would get home between 11 p.m. and midnight and I'd still have adrenalin racing around my system. Anyone who works in hospitality will likely know what I mean when I say that you can't just go home and fall into bed. It took time – and wine, for me, anyway – to slow down my mind. In hospitality your social life isn't very social. The times when everyone else in the world seemed to be going out and having fun were the times I needed to go to work. In the days before the radio gig began, I'd get home from the cooking school to my quiet, dark house, flop down on the couch while everyone slept, and crack open a bottle of wine. Eventually the muscles in my jaw and shoulders would unclench, the maelstrom of words in my head would abate, my blood would slow down in my veins and I could sleep.

But the 4 a.m. alarm meant I couldn't drink at all on school nights. So I stopped. This ability to change a daily habit into a weekend-only habit allowed me to believe once again that alcohol wasn't really a problem. I could give it up when I wanted to; I could regulate it as I needed to.

Until, of course, I couldn't, and I didn't. But all of that was still mostly ahead of me.

Dukkah

Prep time: 5 minutes
Cooking time: 5 minutes
Makes about ¾ cup

⅓ cup roasted unsalted almonds
⅓ cup sesame seeds
2 tablespoons coriander seeds
2 tablespoons cumin seeds
12 white peppercorns
¼ teaspoon ground hot chillies (optional)
½ teaspoon sea salt flakes

Place almonds in the bowl of a food processor and process until most are about the size of sesame seeds. There will be some bigger pieces and some powder – this is okay.

Heat a large non-stick fry pan or chef's pan over medium-high heat and dry-roast the almonds until golden and aromatic. Remove to a bowl.

YOUR TIME STARTS NOW

Place the sesame seeds in the hot pan and toast until golden, then remove to the bowl.

Place the coriander seeds, cumin seeds and peppercorns into the pan and toast until they are starting to colour and are aromatic. Place into the bowl of the processor with the sea salt and process to a coarse powder.

Place in the bowl with the almonds and sesame seeds, and add the chilli. Mix well and allow to cool before storing in an airtight container.

CHAPTER 15
GOING UNDER

At Star I was part of a beautiful, family-like team, doing a job I truly loved and valued; a job that allowed me creativity and a voice, and made me laugh every day. So when my two-year contract came up for renewal at the beginning of 2018, I gladly signed another one.

My kitchen was ticking along, too. By this stage Chef Renee was running the show and I was turning up mostly to present classes rather than spending whole days prepping the ingredients and setting up the benches. Shelley was running the office like an absolute boss, and with Janny and Shaylee heading up my back-of-house, things seemed to be mostly under control. Or so it seemed, on the surface.

My days remained a lot more regular than they were in the past. For a start, I pretty well always knew where I was going to be each day. A 4 a.m. start, then the fifteen-minute drive into Erina to the radio station. On air from 6 until 9 a.m. Then there'd be a meeting once we'd wrapped up the show. Some days, we'd go and visit an ad client of the station, or film a project we were working on, like the Happiness Project, or a local hero, or a random prize giveaway.

The radio show continued to be rewarding and surprising. Rabbit and I implemented an annual project that we called 'Month of Me'. Each day we challenged ourselves and our listeners to do something a bit differently that day, and invited people to call in and share how the previous day's activity had gone. It could be something like travelling into work a new way. Or paying a compliment to a stranger. Or learning a new skill, or cooking something new for dinner, or making the effort to play a board game. Just little things, mindfulness things, to pull us out of our routines and get us thinking about how we live our daily lives.

We encouraged listeners to dip in and out as they wished: do one activity or do them all. It was amazing how many people let us know that they and their families were going to try to do the activity every day for the whole month. It was absolutely beautiful; the stories were fantastic.

One of the daily activities we suggested was to take care of a medical condition you've been ignoring. I pledged that I was going to deal with dental issues that had needed attention for a while, though I really hate going to the dentist; and that I would get a mammogram, which I had promised a good friend that I would do after she'd had a health scare.

Gosh, we got some wonderful calls about this activity. One listener, a regular caller, also decided to go to the dentist and have her teeth fixed – they had been a source of pain and low self-confidence for years. After she'd done so, she called and told us she felt a million bucks. A couple of people's doctors caught medical conditions that could have become dangerous if they had not been diagnosed. It was definitely one of the less pleasant, harder challenges we set, but the results were quite profound.

Each morning after I was finished with whatever was needed for Star, I would move on to the kitchen. If there wasn't a class there were always still a million other things to do: emails and bills and social media; payroll and meetings with community groups and potential clients; recipes to test and classes to write and graphics to design for marketing. On the nights when no classes were running, I got home in time to cook dinner and fall into bed ready for the next day on air.

Weekends were the bigger classes; they almost always sold out. After a while I realised that teaching on Friday night, Saturday night and Sunday was too much, so I dropped back to two classes or events per weekend. It was still a lot. And so I worked, and drank, and slept, and on Monday morning I would get up at 4 and start all over again.

It was ironic, I thought, that I had taken on both the cooking school and the radio to keep me anchored on the coast, close to home and more available to my family. I was, in fact, less available to them now than I had been for the past few years. Paddy was finishing high school, Tom was working and Joe at university. They all still lived at home, but their lives were hurtling along full-tilt into adulthood. Meanwhile, I was waking and sleeping early during the week, and absent for the weekend.

During this time, days off were rare as hen's teeth. But I was doing what I wanted, wasn't I? I was no longer racing around the countryside from appearance to appearance, away from home. Some days, as I left the radio station I would feel the muscles of my face let go of the smile they had been forming for the past few hours. It would slide right off and I couldn't get it back. Some days I would sneak away for a while: in between leaving the radio and arriving at the kitchen I would go for a drive to a lookout where I could see the ocean. Sometimes I would gaze out over that wide, perfect sweep of blue and wonder how I had got myself into such a pickle. And how on earth could I get out of it? Sometimes, when I was alone like this, I would cry so hard my face ached.

Being on the radio required every bit of energy and focus I could muster. Teaching and interacting with people at the kitchen required energy and focus too – I couldn't show anyone how tired or lacklustre I felt. I couldn't give anyone less than 100 per cent. The result was that by the time I went home at the end of the day, there was just nothing left. No energy. No smiles. No laughter. Zero per cent. The people I loved the most, who loved me the most, the ones I didn't ever have to perform for . . . those people got the least of me. The worst of me. My family only got the dregs I had left after each day of keeping up appearances. It was terrible, and wrong, and it made me feel ashamed of myself.

I finally decided to go to my GP and ask why, when I had such a privileged life and wonderful jobs and a loving family, could I not stop crying every time I was alone? Why was my heart like a big-wave rider, rising and falling with the swell; why was my breath a pendulum, swinging wildly between ragged hyperventilation and seemingly not being able to draw in air at all? What the fuck was wrong with me?

I had a fair idea what the doctor was going to say. I was, finally, ready to hear it and do something about it. I'd never been ready before.

I wasn't ready when I was seventeen, sitting in a hospital bed after taking all the pills I could find in my house.

I wasn't ready when I couldn't study at university and needed to drop out.

I wasn't ready when I had Joe, my first baby, either; when I'd taken my screaming red-faced little bundle to the Tresillian Family

Care Centre to find some help to get him to sleep and the kind-faced nurse told me I had scored very high for postnatal depression.

I wasn't ready when Tom was savaged by a dog on Christmas Day and the world seemed to become a dark and dangerous place.

I wasn't ready when I won *MasterChef* and Nan died and our lives were like socks in a tumbledryer, being flung all over the place, separated from our mates and not knowing which way was up.

Throughout these times I had occasionally sought help from different types of practitioner. Over the years, as far back as my young adulthood, I had tried hypnosis, float tanks, aromatherapy, counselling and psychiatry. Although I was seeking help, I was very conditional about it. I recall my first appointment with a psychiatrist, after Tom's injuries. I said to him, 'Just so you know up front, I am not here to talk about my childhood and you are not to label me with depression.' He answered slowly. 'Okay, if that's what you want, but I have to tell you that I will be limited in the help I can offer you.' And limited he was.

This inability, or unwillingness, to allow myself to be diagnosed with a mental health condition was due, I think, to a number of factors. Partly, it was generational. My nan grew up during the Depression and raised her children during the war. Her family saw terrible hardship; her children were warned not to complain. As were we – raised, and rightly so, to count our blessings and keep our chins up. And these are valuable attitudes, which have served me very well throughout my life. But in holding myself to them, like everything I do, I allowed no nuance: I had to be grateful and count blessings and keep my chin up *no matter what*. And that's when an attitude like this becomes problematic.

Partly, it was the stigma that still, I would argue, surrounds mental health issues. The idea that depression and anxiety are simply an inability to lift yourself up; an unwillingness to just *try*. In the past there was a widely held idea that mental illness equalled weakness, which obviously I had internalised, despite the campaigns to educate us that this isn't the case. And I was not weak. I had never, ever seen myself as weak. Of course, it's not weakness that leads to struggles with mental health, but that was the idea I had in my stubborn skull.

Another reason I had never been willing to accept that there was anything wrong with my mental health was the idea of ingratitude. I held a core belief that complaining about anything at all meant I was ungrateful for all the good things in my life. I was keenly aware that no matter what I was experiencing, there are always people who are worse off, which led me to feel that none of my concerns or issues were valid or had a right to be expressed. I was experiencing 'first world problems'. This can be a pretty insidious label. Sometimes it's used to indicate a self-deprecating, almost humorous acknowledgement that we're complaining about something trivial. But it's also used to shame us into feeling guilty for expressing concern or dissatisfaction about anything at all. Essentially, if you aren't living in a developing nation and afraid for where your next meal is coming from, you have no right to suffer.

Of course, there are people worse off – obviously there are. No matter what we go through, we can find someone who has suffered more, lost more, endured more, had more shocking trauma or a more devastating illness. And I believe in the value of acknowledging our good fortune and the fact that we have privileges that aren't available to many other people.

But there's a balance to be found. We can be grateful, and count our blessings, and acknowledge the plight of others, and still try to face what we're going through ourselves; accept that even though we're not living in the most dire circumstances, there are still issues we have to address, difficult times to work through and problems we need to solve.

One psychologist I met some years before explained it to me through the lens of social comparison theory. This theory is focused on how we compare ourselves to others in terms of looks, talent, salary and so forth. It examines the impact of comparing up – there are always so many people better than me – and comparing down – I am better than so many people. Both of these come with their own problems: if you're always comparing up, you're at risk of suffering low self-esteem, and if you're always comparing down (which ironically often comes from low self-esteem), you're at risk of coming across, in scientific terminology, as an arsehole.

The theory can be loosely applied to your life situation as well. People who are constantly comparing up – everyone has more than me, better houses, better cars, more money and so forth – are generally dissatisfied. And if you're always comparing down – there are people who are so much worse off than me, financially, health-wise, in terms of their human rights – you can feel you have no right to complain about anything at all. This leads to an inability to ask for help without feeling enormous guilt. And that's where I found myself. Comparing down, and ashamed of feeling anything other than tickety-boo 100 per cent of the time.

So I had never been ready to accept a diagnosis, but I was ready now. I knew in my heart what I would be told, what I had vehemently denied for my whole adult life. I was experiencing depression, and anxiety, and I needed a hand. And sure enough, the GP diagnosed depression and anxiety, and I was put on medication.

Within a few weeks, I wasn't crying anymore. Literally, this medication took away the ability to cry *at all*. It was so strange. It would 'round off the edges' was how it was explained to me.

The edges it rounded off were not just the bad feelings but all the feelings. The feelings of dread and helplessness and lack of control were gone; but so were joy, and anticipation, and excitement. And to add insult to injury, my libido.

After six months on this medication, it seemed to stop working abruptly. I was back at square one. Safe to say, it wasn't the right medication for me, and I now know that often it takes a few attempts to get the right medicine in place to balance out those pesky wayward brain chemicals.

I was moved on to a second drug and it worked better, for a little while. But when it stopped, it stopped hard.

I don't want to name these medicines because we all respond differently to different things. Working out what we need is a matter for individuals and their own trusted healthcare providers, and I would hate for anyone to rule out a particular type of treatment for themselves just because it didn't work for me.

Along with medication, I was given plenty of other advice for things to do to try to smooth my pathway a bit. I'm pretty sure we all know what they are: enough sleep, exercise, good nutrition, that ever-elusive work/life balance. Some of these things I already did, some I took on board. Some I ignored. I wasn't fitting in enough exercise, so for a while I began getting up at 3 a.m. and attending a twenty-four-hour gym across from the radio station. Of course, jamming more things into an already packed schedule wasn't the answer. I was supposed to be reducing some of my responsibilities to fit in the other stuff, but I didn't even know where to begin in order to do that.

The madcap shenanigans of radio life continued. Live on air Rabs tried to teach me to drive a manual car. (Fail.) I abseiled off the Crown Plaza in Terrigal to raise funds for the Westpac Rescue Helicopter. Leaning backwards off the roof of a very tall building is one of the most counterintuitive things I have ever done. I am cured of the need to ever do it again.

Not long after that, a listener dared me to skydive to raise more funds for the rescue service. Heights are not my thing, not at all, but what could I do? She dared me. Safe to say, from my memory of the event and also from the video of my terrified, screaming face on the way down, skydiving is also not my jam. I ticked it off my bucket list. I mean, it wasn't on there, but I added it just so I could tick it off, like you do with household chores.

In November 2017, Loyal IT Solutions turned fifteen years old. For our tenth anniversary we'd had a bit of a party at Gosford Golf Club, but now we had beautiful offices to invite people to, and obviously a functioning kitchen underneath. Early in 2018 I finally had a space in the calendar when I could put on a celebration for our clients.

It was a Thursday in April. I went straight from the radio to the kitchen that morning, and got stuck into catering for the event. We had invited our clients, our team and their families, so we were expecting about fifty people. I made grazing tables with hot and cold canapés and we provided all the drinks. Janny worked with me that day and night. We ferried everything from downstairs to the offices upstairs for the two-hour event.

Mick spoke to the room about how we had started our business fifteen years ago, in our lounge room. One of our long-standing clients gave an unscheduled speech as well, talking about Mick and the values we worked and lived by. I was so proud. It was a lovely party. It was the worst night of my life.

In my final reckoning, when my life is played out like a movie and I am forced to view the things I regret, this will be the night that plays over and over and over again. Don't get me wrong, I have done lots of things I regret. Lots of things I'm ashamed of. But on this night, the decisions I made and the actions I took changed everything. My whole idea of who I am in the world, and what my worth is as a human being, went right out the door.

My first mistake was to break my self-imposed rule of not drinking on a school night. Had I not done that, the rest would never have unfolded the way it did. I drank champagne; I did not pay enough attention to how much. I had a vague notion that I would be at the kitchen long after the party finished, cleaning up for at least a couple of hours. I didn't eat; I often didn't eat when I'd spent the day cooking. By then you're over the food you've made. All I had was alcohol.

When the guests left at 7 p.m., I headed downstairs to pitch in with the clean-up. To my surprise and delight, Janny was not just underway, she'd pretty much finished it. I forgot that I had counted on being a couple of hours in the kitchen before I drove home. I forgot that I needed that time, because of the drinks I had consumed. I was just thrilled I would be back in time for my early night so I could get up again the next morning for the breakfast show.

This is incredibly difficult to write. I want to be very clear that nothing in the telling of this story is me trying to make excuses for what I did. I am not trying to explain it away, nor mitigate or minimise it. I am just relaying it. I wish I didn't have to. It was the worst thing I have ever done. But it is a part of my life, a public part, so if I am going to tell my story, this part must be told.

My second mistake that night was getting into my car. I left the kitchen, heading for home, about five minutes away. I did not give a second thought to the fact that I was drink-driving. It didn't occur to me. I can't even make sense of this: Mick and the boys were at that party too, and made their way home together. I could have gone with them. But it didn't occur to me that I needed to – I was hanging around to clean up. I was utterly thoughtless. Unforgivable. Inexcusable.

This was not usual for me, or for us. Neither Mick and I, nor our friends. We always nominated a driver; we were always meticulous about drink-driving. Like all good citizens, we held drink-drivers in contempt; it's indefensible. It's wrong. I was all the way up there on that moral high ground along with most of the population. I can't explain my departure from those values and beliefs on that night. I have tried, but I can't. I just don't know.

Less than 500 metres from the kitchen, I saw the flashing lights of an RBT stop. The realisation didn't so much as dawn on me as douse me in ice water: I was not ready to drive. I pulled off the road. My third mistake.

Somewhere in my head I was thinking, I'll just go back to the kitchen. I shouldn't be driving yet; I'll just go back to the kitchen. It seemed like the obvious thing to do – I won't drive home, I'll go back to the kitchen. I'll just go back. And then I made the final mistake for the evening: I turned my car around.

I had only just turned around when I heard sirens; they pierced my brain and my heart as I realised they were for me. Of course they were for me. I pulled off the highway, turned off my engine, and waited for the police to come.

I expected them to pull up behind me, but somehow they had looped around ahead of me. Headlights came over the slight hill in front of me, crossed onto the wrong side of the road, and screeched to a stop nose-to-nose with my car. I actually thought the police car was going to run head-first into me. In the blinding glare of the headlights and the swirling red and blue, for a moment I believed I was about to die. Later, I wished I had.

I was breathalysed, arrested and taken to the police station in the back of the police car. I called Mick on the way; it was the hardest phone call of my life. He wanted to come to the station; I begged him to wait at home until I knew what would happen.

All the official things were done, then my licence was taken from me, and I called Mick to come and take me home. Shame burned so hot in my chest and face and gut that I could hardly bear it. When I arrived home we called the boys into the lounge room and I told them what I had done. There was no point keeping it from them; I assumed it would be making the rounds in public before too long. And we had always tried to be open and honest with our kids. As much as I wanted to protect them from this, from this knowledge of me, I had to tell them. They knew how serious it was. They knew it wasn't right, and that it wasn't normal. That I had done something very, very wrong. My beautiful boys gathered around me and held me tight. I was so grateful to have their love and forgiveness to hang on to in the coming storm.

At 4 a.m. my alarm went off and Mick drove me into the radio station where I co-hosted the breakfast show.

I'm not quite sure how I made it through that morning. As soon as the show was over I told my bosses what I had done. Then I told Rabs – one of many incredibly difficult conversations of those couple of days. My shame – oh my god, the complete and utter *shame* of it – was unbearable. I was given love and support, far more than I deserved.

The hotline from the police station to the media leaped to life; there's no other way the story could have been picked up so few hours after it had all happened. I called my family – Mum and Dad, Debbie. I called my team at the kitchen. I told them all what I had done and we hunkered down to ride out the storm.

GOING UNDER

In the space of those few minutes, those few decisions, I lost every bit of who I was. I already had some pretty harsh opinions of myself, but I had always believed I was, at least, an upstanding citizen, a rule-keeper, a considerate person. Not always the best person, but at heart a good person. Those beliefs were gone. When I looked in the mirror all I could see was a contemptible, ruinous half-human. A criminal, a hypocrite, a loser. A person with no integrity. No values. No value.

I went to court a few weeks later. I didn't contest anything. I took the prescribed punishment for the offence I had committed: a fine and a six-month suspension of my licence. Joe, Tom and Paddy took turns driving me to work in the early morning. The local Uber drivers, of which there were around five on the Coast, would ask me when I was getting my licence back as they dropped me home.

Being in the courthouse in Gosford was an out-of-body experience. I viewed it as if I were on the ceiling rather than in the packed room. There wasn't a spare seat. Out the front of the building there were news crews, cameras and journalists – the kind of scenes you see at the end of a high-profile murder trial. Gosford was buzzing with excitement at my shame; my fall from grace was hot news.

After my case was heard I could see the media pack from inside the courthouse, lying in wait for me to emerge. I took a deep breath and started down the stairs. 'Hey,' said a gentle voice from behind me. I turned around and there was Mick. He held his hand out to me. I clutched it and we went down the stairs together. I focused only on his hand tightly holding mine as he guided me through the throng, the microphones in my face, weaving in and out of the cameras in our way. He led me across the street to the car park, and he took me home.

YOUR TIME STARTS NOW

On the surface, life carried on. I continued to teach classes at my cooking school and co-host the breakfast show with Rabbit. Beneath the surface, the cracks that had appeared years before were widening. It was getting harder to hold my happy face on, harder to keep the energy going, harder to put my feet on the floor every morning. My work life still left me very little time for my family, and almost none for my friends – my beautiful, steadfast friends. It was just assumed that I would be too busy to go out for coffee, or go to the beach, or go for a bushwalk. And it was a correct assumption.

Late nights after my classes were finished, after everyone had gone to bed, seemed to be the only downtime I got. I would sit up late and drink wine, and feel justified in doing it because it was the only chance I got to relax. It was the only hope I had for everything to slow down, become quiet, to calm my racing brain in order to get some sleep.

My self-talk, the voice that internally narrated my days and nights, was brutal and it was relentless. *Loser. Criminal. Waste of space. Useless. Stupid. Unworthy. Ruiner of everything. Hypocrite. Fraud. Bitch.*

I didn't question the internal narrative; it seemed about right. I deserved all the vitriol that came my way, both from strangers on social media and the non-stranger in my head. I'd earned it. Bought and paid for with my own stupidity, my own hopelessness. My own essential *badness*.

Christmas of 2018 was my last column for the *Australian Women's Weekly*. I was devastated to learn that my contract wouldn't be renewed. It was only a few months shy of my ten-year anniversary and I asked if I could please see out the decade. The request was declined.

Australian Consolidated Press, who had owned the *Weekly*, had sold it to German media giant Bauer a few years previously. On the food team we had noticed the cost-cutting that occurred after the sale: questions were asked about whether we needed pictures of all the food, if pictures could be reused, if cheaper cuts of meat could be subbed in. It was an ongoing battle. My immediate boss, the beautiful Fran Abdallaoui, *AWW*'s food director, told me that she had fought to keep me on the team for a long time, but she had finally lost the fight. I was an expense that was cut.

This is what I was told, but I didn't really believe it. That voice inside gave me what I thought was the more likely reason: it was because of the DUI. It was because I was a useless loser, an unwanted, no-talent, irrelevant, stupid waste of breath.

By the time 2019 rolled around, the medication I was on wasn't coping with my declining state of mind. Of course, I was solely relying on the pills to make me better. I didn't have the time or inclination to commit to other types of help. I understand better now that medication doesn't work in a vacuum; it has to be part of a holistic approach that addresses every part of the mind and body, physically, emotionally, spiritually, psychologically. There is no silver bullet, no magic cure-all pill. Back then I was just irritated that the thing the doctor prescribed seemed to be useless.

I was also having a crisis of faith. Not faith in God so much as faith in the Church I had grown up in. For years I'd been disgusted with the handling of child sex abuse cases by the Catholic Church. Our visit to the Vatican was another blow to my idea of the Church. As we wandered through those luxurious buildings and heard the histories of the popes – some of them so debauched it blew my mind – I couldn't help but wonder, where is Jesus in all of this? Where is that young man, speaking on hilltops, who people came to see because he told great stories? The one who preached kindness, especially to sinners? The one who said it was really hard to get into heaven if you're rich? The one who asked people to take a good hard look at their behaviour and not judge others unless they were beyond reproach themselves?

I couldn't find him in the Vatican. I couldn't find him in the rules we were supposed to obey, or in the attitudes we were supposed to hold towards certain other human beings.

I was once on a panel talk show called *Can of Worms*, where we discussed contentious topics and grappled with ethical conundrums in a comedy format. This was in a time well before the marriage equality plebiscite, and in one episode I expressed my support for marriage equality. I was accused by someone on social media of being a 'pick-and-choose Catholic'. It was intended as an insult, but the more I thought about it, the more I liked it. That's exactly what I was – I picked and chose which of Catholicism's rules to follow and which to question. Another way of putting it was perhaps a thinking Catholic. Or a compassionate Catholic. Or maybe a terrible Catholic. Catholics who attend Mass every week refer to themselves as practising Catholics. I practised and practised for years but never seemed to get any better at it.

Reflecting upon this not-insult, I realised that I had always been a pick-and-choose Catholic, because of how I was raised. My mum was a devout Catholic, but she still questioned so many of the rules and attitudes around the Church. Her father, my larrikin grandfather, used to tell her, 'They're all man-made rules, chook.' Mum taught me that the Bible was something to be read like the newspaper – bits of it are reported second- and third-hand; bits of it are editorial opinion; bits of it are only there for illustrative purposes.

So I based my faith less on what was in the Bible, and the manmade rules of the Church, and more on the teachings of a man who was kind and asked people to love one another. The young rebel Jesus, who stood up to authority and the meaningless traditions of the day; the kind and brave person who rocked the boat and questioned stereotypes. The Jesus who asked people to embrace lepers, tax collectors, prostitutes, sinners. Who are the lepers today? They are the drug addicts, the prisoners, the refugees, the different; the people we judge because we deem ourselves Better Than Them. I looked at my church, and kept asking, where is Jesus in all of this? And I could not find him.

Yes, I am a pick-and-choose Catholic. I picked and chose to use contraception; I chose to live with Mick before we were married; I choose to support humanitarian and human rights, whether or not they are Church-approved; I choose to believe that all religions are different expressions of the same desire to believe in something larger than ourselves. I choose to reject the rules and teachings of the Church that seem to stand in direct defiance of what Jesus taught.

We had sent the boys through Catholic school, and been committed members of the Church ourselves, attending Mass almost every week all of our lives. But in the past few years, with the boys older and work taking over my waking hours, we'd become twice-a-year Catholics – Easter and Christmas, which we kept attending for tradition's sake. I had guilt about this, of course. I'm Catholic, after all.

We were still involved with our Family Group, the families who socialise every month, the village that helped raise our kids. That had always been where I felt that caring for one another could be meaningfully demonstrated instead of just being talked about. Preached about. These people are my parish. The beach, the bush, their homes where we get together, those places ae my church. To me, it turns out, community is the very most important part of the

Church, and my community is still intact even though Mick and I don't attend Mass anymore.

By March 2019, after the findings of the Royal Commission into Institutional Responses to Child Sexual Abuse, I'd finally had enough. It was confirmed by the commission what had long been alleged: that members of the Catholic Church, some very senior, had either engaged in or covered up the ongoing abuse of children. Offenders were hidden, protected, moved around parishes or regions. Victims were utterly disregarded. It was sickening.

I rang my mother and told her, 'Mum, I'm not going to Mass this Easter. I can't bring myself to.' Her response shocked me. My devout mum, who had made us pray the rosary as a family when we were kids, said to me, 'Oh Jules, Dad and I don't go anymore either. Those bastards, protecting the child molesters – bloody disgraceful. Jesus would be spinning in his grave.' It took me a beat to reply, my head going straight to an image of Jesus twirling around in a stony tomb.

It probably seems hard to fathom if you haven't been raised in a church, but it was such a part of my identity. The traditions were important to me. The rituals brought me comfort. The core tenets gave me a rough guide, even if I never followed them to the letter. They were more like a lighthouse, warning me off big rocky cliffs, than a lit path showing me the exact route. It is hard to let those things go.

There are so many good people in the Catholic Church, doing good work, looking after one another and living lives of service. But the organisation itself, in my view, has a rotten core. It pains me to say it and I will need to brace for the vilification that saying it will bring. But it is important in the context of what was happening in my life at the time. Everything was crumbling around me.

GOING UNDER

Or perhaps not around me, but within me. With my core beliefs about myself gone, now my church was also gone as a source of comfort and stability. The earth seemed to be tilting beneath my feet and I became afraid that all the other things I took for granted – my family, my friends, my life – might also be on shifting sands.

In June, the bushfires started. In winter. New South Wales had been ravaged by drought. Ten years of below-average rainfall meant the ground was a tinderbox, ready to go up at the first spark.

As above, so below; as within, so without. I was on a steep downhill run, mentally and now physically. I was stubbornly ignoring all the signs of an impending meltdown. My brain, sick to death of having its warnings ignored, started sending symptoms to the rest of my body. I constantly had cold sores, and ulcers inside my cheeks and on my tongue. Eating was painful. I developed sores on my scalp too. Little things like a cut or a burn, which I frequently accidentally inflicted on myself in minor kitchen incidents, were taking forever to heal up. I started to suffer tinnitus, a screeching in my ears that wouldn't go away, and severe dizzy spells if I turned my head too suddenly one way or another. And my guts were in absolute turmoil. Some days I'd get caught out far from a bathroom. If arse-clenching was an Olympic sport I would have won gold during those days.

I finally understood that if I didn't cut back on my workload, I was going to fall apart. The question was, what would I give up? I didn't want to let go of either the radio or the kitchen; I loved them both. But my whole body was telling me that something had to give. Unfortunately, this realisation came too late to prevent the train wreck that was already in motion.

After a lot of agonising and soul-searching, I decided that I had to keep the kitchen. Not least because I still had to pay it off. If I turned all my energy and focus towards it, it would surely start to pay for itself and provide a decent salary not just to my team, but also to me.

In October I spoke to Moltz and Shayne, and explained I was not coping and would need to leave the show. I told them I would give them as long as they needed to find a replacement; I could work through until the end of 2020 if necessary. After some consideration it was decided that I would see out the year, making the announcement at our last show of 2019. I would then return in 2020 until Easter so that we could find another co-host for Rabs and make the transition as smooth as possible for the listeners.

Then it was time to tell Rabs. I knew he would be devastated. He had often spoken of his wish for our partnership to be long term. We worked so well together; we were great mates and that was evident not only in the friendship we had on air but also outside of work.

A lot of tears were shed in the making of this decision. I was utterly unsure that it was the right one. But I received nothing but love, support and understanding from my colleagues. Even Rabs accepted that it was ultimately the right thing for me to do.

Our last show for the year was Friday 20 December. We did an outdoor broadcast at Coast Bar and Restaurant, a venue on beautiful Brisbane Water. Listeners came along, Santa showed up, breakfast was put on and it was a real party. Towards the end of the show, we announced that I would be finishing up on air, but not until Easter of the following year. There were more tears.

That evening Christmas carols were held in the Central Coast Stadium – the most beautiful stadium in the country, flanked by palm trees with a stunning water view. The view that night was diminished by bushfire smoke. Rabs and I MC'd the evening; we walked around the crowd in between stints on stage and chatted to people and had photos taken. I felt a deep sadness that night, still very unsure if I had made the right choice. Everything had an eerie tinge, too; there was a foreboding feeling in the air. I'm sure this wasn't just because of my deteriorating state of mind. The news cycle was exclusively about the fires. They were all anyone could talk about.

I spent the next day at the kitchen preparing for the Julie's Place Christmas banquet for sixty people on the Sunday.

All this time, the bushfires were gathering momentum. Firefighting and rescue experts, right up to the NSW commissioner, were calling for a response from the government. They asked for climate change to be recognised; they asked for funding for better firefighting capabilities; they emphasised over and over that this bushfire season was like nothing experienced ever before, that the fires were so huge they were creating their own weather events.

These pleas seemed to be falling on deaf ears. The government response to this catastrophic series of fires was scathingly criticised, at the time and for years to come. Possibly the most shocking response was when our country's leader went overseas for a family holiday as the fires raged, and when he was called out on this extraordinary decision, he said, 'I don't hold a hose, mate.'

I was not alone in my feeling of being utterly abandoned by these actions. But for some reason they struck a particularly raw nerve for me. Perhaps it was just this sense that everything was falling apart: the country was on fire, my radio career was gone, my self-worth was gone, my Church was gone. Even the fucking prime minister was gone.

The Gospers Mountain fire was the largest single-origin forest fire in the history of New South Wales; it was Australia's first 'mega-blaze' and one of the world's ten largest bushfires since records began. According to the maps, by the end of November the south-eastern edge of it was only about 15 kilometres as the crow flies from Gosford. Debris rained down into our backyard; blackened leaves and ash that had been propelled high into the sky were caught by the raging winds and came to rest all over the lawn, floating in the pool and settling on the washing. The sky was black and it felt like Armageddon.

Our family Christmas was cancelled. This was a huge deal for us, unprecedented. We all lived far from each other now. Mum and Dad had moved to the south coast some years before, to the paradise in which we had spent our childhood holidays, and where to their golfing friends they now became known as 'lovey and dovey'. My parents had been involved and active in our lives and we missed them, the grandkids especially. Since we still holidayed down the coast, we got to see them regularly.

Debbie and her partner, Kieron, had moved to Bungonia in the Southern Tablelands of New South Wales, where they had bought a barren acreage and turned it into a thriving education centre, running workshops in food security and sustainable, off-grid living.

Our Christmases always took place a couple of days after the 25th, but they *always* took place. We took turns hosting and this was my year. But for us, as for many families in 2019, it wasn't to be. Debbie couldn't leave her farm; Mum and Dad didn't want to leave their home. Those of us on the Central Coast made what we could of the day.

Just after Christmas it became apparent that Mum and Dad were in the path of the fires that were burning along the east coast from Nowra to the Victorian border. The news reports were surreal; even the reporters seemed stunned by the sudden turning of day into night behind them as they spoke wide-eyed into the cameras. Homes were lost, businesses were lost, lives were lost. The fires were outpacing the modelling. On our television screens we saw people huddling on beaches, hosing their homes, comforting each other under a blood-red sky while their whole history burned.

As the fires approached the area where Mum and Dad live, Debbie and I tried to convince them to get out, to come north and stay with me on the Central Coast. Although the Gospers Mountain fire was still a threat, we were in far less danger than the besieged south coast. Being the stubborn old gits that they are, Mum and Dad refused to move. Even when they were evacuated from their house, they got into their caravan and parked themselves at the Narooma Golf Club. Mum sent us a photo of them on New Year's Eve. Their little timber van was perched on a headland overlooking the ocean. The sky was a mass of roiling black and vivid red. It is one of the most terrifying images I have ever seen.

Debbie and I redoubled our efforts to get them to come north. Debbie threatened to drive over there and haul them out herself. Finally, with only one road left open to them, they said goodbye to their home, not knowing if they would ever see it again, and they came to us.

The news cycle was relentless. The looped images will forever be burned into my retinas – a young, long-haired boy clinging to a jetty in Mallacoota; a woman taking off her blouse to wrap it around a burning koala and carry it to safety; footage from inside a fire truck in the midst of a firestorm, the crew futilely trying to hold blankets to the windows.

And in the aftermath, we were shown footage of the people who lived in those places the fire had swept through surveying the wreckage of their lives. We witnessed their exhaustion and devastation. We shared their fury and contempt for the ineffectual politicians who visited these hellscapes, once the danger had passed. Who tried to make up for their utter failure of leadership with a forced handshake, a failed photo op.

It seemed as though my insides were determined to match what was happening around me, as my mind and body continued their downward spiral. The physical symptoms of my impending breakdown, as I now realise they were, were manifesting in a couple of new and awful ways. I had started shaking; I couldn't get a forkful of food to my mouth or hold a pen properly. And I stopped being able to read. This one scared the shit out of me. I tried and tried, but every time I attempted to read something it was as if a swarm of bees was buzzing in my ears and eyes. I couldn't make the words make sense. I couldn't focus. I couldn't *read*. I honestly began to believe that my body was shutting down; that I was slowly, incrementally dying. Not from anything diagnosable or treatable. Just exhaustion, maybe. Or sadness. Or maybe I was simply wearing out; I'd used all the energy allocated to me and now my life force was draining away.

Drinking didn't help, although it felt like it did. I was on leave for the Christmas break, no longer getting up at 4 a.m., so the 'school day' rule didn't apply. Those evening glasses of wine felt like the only thing that could soothe my fizzing brain, when I could release some worry, sink into a TV show, forget about the kitchen and the world, and blot out the insistent internal monologue that didn't stop reminding me I'd ruined everything. Wine put it in the background. Far from being a problem, wine was the solution.

It was a terrible solution, of course, as the next few months would illustrate with alarming clarity. But for now, it was the edge-softener that got me through the night.

GOING UNDER

Mick and I were huge fans of the Central Coast Mariners, the Coast's A-League football team. Our support for them kind of came about by accident. We'd been NRL Wests Tigers supporters forever, and we wanted an NRL team on the Central Coast. When the A-League was established in 2004, we decided to throw our support behind the newly formed soccer team – we figured that if the NRL saw Coasties get behind the Mariners, they would consider putting their new team on the coast. It didn't work; a new team on the Gold Coast was eventually announced. But in the meantime, a funny thing happened: we fell in love with the A-League. We fell in love, more specifically, with the Mariners Football Club. We became members, attended all the home games at our beautiful stadium, and cheered our navy-and-yellow hearts out for these brilliant young athletes. Both of our businesses sponsored the club over the years, as we followed the team's fortunes with passion through its ups and downs. After *MasterChef*, I was invited to be the number one ticket holder for the team, a privileged position that I still hold with great pride.

On Sunday 12 January 2020, Mick and I were heading into a 6 p.m. home game against Melbourne Victory. I had spent the morning cooking, and the afternoon hosting a private party at the kitchen: thirty-five people having a belated Christmas gathering. I got home, changed and we headed off. I was exhausted. I didn't feel like socialising but I was trying to make sure my life had 'balance' – if I cancelled this thing that I loved to do, then, once more, all I was doing was work.

At the game Mick was going to take a bunch of Loyal IT clients to a catered box on the other side of the stadium; I was meeting my friend Louise in the sponsors' lounge, which had a great view of the pitch. There, we'd be given drinks and dinner.

On the footpath outside the gates Mick was quiet. I mean, he's usually pretty quiet, but this silence had a quality about it that made me uneasy. 'Are you okay?' I asked.

'I'm worried about you,' he said. That's all. No recriminations, nothing more than that. *I'm worried about you.*

Of course, he was right to be worried about me. He had told me so before, but I was not receptive to his concern. I was at the bottom of a well with no footholds to climb out. I could see the little speck of light at the top, but it was out of my reach. This was where I lived now, at the bottom of the well.

After Mick had gone to join his clients, I texted Louise and told her I wasn't feeling well and wouldn't be able to meet her. She took her dad to the corporate lounge in my stead. I started walking.

I didn't have a sense of where I was going. I found myself heading to Point Frederick, a posh suburb along Brisbane Water. It was still light, but the streets were empty. I walked down the centre of Albany Street towards Pioneer Cemetery. There was a terrible understanding in my heart, my mind, my soul. It was time to go.

I thought about my boys. Those lovely, beloved little people, who had held on to my hand tight, who came to me when they were hurting and had needed me so much. How proud I was of them; how beautifully they had grown. Their little hands were adult hands now, busy with the industry of their lives, ready to grasp whatever the future would serve up to them. I had done my job and no matter how big of a fuck-up loser piece of shit I was, between Mick and I we had raised wonderful young men. They were all right; they would be all right.

I thought about Mick, this gentle person, intelligent and compassionate and measured, funny and loyal and principled. I thought about how much he had loved me; how unlikely it was to have been so very loved by him. About how I must have used up most of that by now; surely even the fiercest, purest love must be finite in the face of all the damage I had inflicted. He deserved more. He deserved a happy, peaceful life with a wife who wouldn't ruin things the way I ruin things. The way I ruin *everything*.

On that afternoon, walking away from the Mariners match, I believed in my heart that I needed to leave, and leave the people I loved in peace. I needed to be brave enough to let them live the lives they deserved, without worrying about me. Without watching me destroy myself.

Surely I had already had a lifetime's joy, and grief, and wild experiences. Done a lifetime's work. Had a lifetime's worth of risks and laughs and travels and fabulous dinners. A lifetime's worth of living.

My hands, always unattractive with their short fingers and square nails, had scars that told of craft and industry, clumsiness and cookery. Souvenirs of stitches, burns, and lanced infected fingernails; calluses, scabs and sunspots. These hands had held my babies, and held my husband. They had soothed a thousand little wounds and cooked a million or so meals. They had stitched tiny pink roses onto baby singlets through my pregnancies, each time convinced I was going to have a girl. They had planted bulbs and cleaned toilets and ironed shirts and laid flooring. They had drawn pictures and played musical instruments and written letters and dealt cards. My hands looked so much older than the rest of me, and their work was done. My work was done.

This realisation was unbearable and the sadness poured out of me in rivers as I walked towards the cemetery. I knew that I would, once again, be causing pain for the people who loved me; but at least it would be the last time. There would be grief most certainly, but underneath that, there would be relief. I was convinced of that. I was *so sure* of it. My absence would be a relief.

I came to the entrance of Pioneer Park. It was evening but still light. I hadn't seen a single person as I walked up the peninsula, past all the high fences of the huge, expensive homes, but as I got to the entrance of the park I heard a voice ask, 'Are you all right?'

I was startled – I'd been blinded by tears and focused on my feet. A young woman and man were standing there with their dog. The woman was the one who had spoken. I think I shook my head, no. She gave me a hug. I thanked them for stopping and lied that I was all right now. We walked off in different directions.

When I was fourteen, I almost drowned. It was winter and we were on holidays on the south coast, where we always went. I loved the ocean and swam there, even out of season. Even when the beach was unpatrolled. On this particular day, we were the only family on the beach. I didn't see the rip in the water, didn't realise there was one until it had scooped me up and deposited me out to sea. Mum was a dot on the shoreline, waving both her arms madly to get me to come back in. And I tried to come back in – I was a good swimmer. But the rip wasn't letting me go. Eventually I ran out of gas. I couldn't keep moving my arms and legs. The waves started to go over my face; the sun broke through the overcast sky and sent spangles down to where my limbs had stopped moving and I was suspended in the water.

Out of nowhere, an arm reached into the water and hauled me out. It was a man paddling a surf ski. He had seen the situation and come out to rescue me. He also saved Dad, who had tried to swim out to me and got caught in the rip himself. When we had somewhat recovered and went to find this man to say thank you, he had gone for a long walk up the beach, overwhelmed. His wife told us it was his first time on the surf ski.

I look back on this day and still remember what I was thinking as the magically appearing stranger hauled me out of the ocean by my arm. After struggling and struggling and not being able to struggle anymore, I came to a calm, mildly surprising realisation: *It's okay. This is it, no need to fight anymore. And it's not so bad. This is okay.*

I was even happier, though, to bring in that first beautiful lungful of air. I still wish I knew who that man was.

In the cemetery at Pioneer Park, I found a bench seat that had a view of the darkening water. I wondered if it was cold out there today. I wondered how far I would be able to swim. I couldn't work out what to do with my shoes – they were my favourites, a pair of low-rise black sparkly Converse boots. Paddy had given them to me for Christmas. Which would be harder for him to bear: finding them on the shore, or not finding them at all? Would wearing them mean I couldn't swim as far? Did that matter? I couldn't form answers to these questions, and yet it seemed important that I get it all right.

While I was trying to work out what to do with my shoes, and work up the courage to swim, I became aware of some people near the bench. The young woman was back, and her husband, and their dog. They sat down with me and told me they thought they might hang out with me for a while. They told me I seemed like I needed some company.

I'm not sure how long they sat with me but it must have been a couple of hours because it grew dark and I realised the Mariners game would be over. In that time we talked about many things: their young children, and my adult ones; their dog, and my three; all the minutiae of life, which somehow also turns out to be the gold. The small stuff, the beautiful stuff.

We hugged, and cried a little, and parted ways. They knew what they had done. I knew what they had done too.

Larissa, Derek and Bonnie: thank you.

YOUR TIME STARTS NOW

Sausage rolls

The quantity in this recipe is for parties. They are so tasty that it doesn't matter how awfully, catastrophically wrong your party goes, the sausage rolls will still be a hit. They can be frozen when raw and cooked straight from the freezer, if required.

Prep time: 10 minutes
Cooking time: 25 minutes
Makes 72 cocktail sausage rolls

1 kg good quality sausage mince
500 g beef mince
2 brown onions, grated
2 carrots, grated
½ cup tomato sauce
¼ cup French mustard
2 tablespoons curry powder
1 teaspoon salt
½ teaspoon pepper
6 sheets frozen puff pastry
1 egg, beaten

Preheat oven to 200°C.

In a bowl, place all ingredients except for the pastry and egg. Using your hands, work the mixture very well until all combined.

Lay the pastry out on a work surface and cut each sheet in half. Work when the pastry is still a bit firm from the freezer as it is easier to handle.

Divide the sausage mixture into 12 pieces and lay in a line along the length of each pastry half-sheet. Fold the two sides over the sausage mixture and gently press to join.

GOING UNDER

Turn the rolls over, cut into sixths and brush with the egg combined with 1 tablespoon water.

Bake for 20 to 25 minutes until pastry is puffed and golden.

CHAPTER 16

HOW DO YOU MEND A BROKEN HEART?

Later, after I had walked back to the kitchen and Mick had come to pick me up, he asked where I had been. I told him. He stopped the car on the side of the road and said, 'I am not equipped to deal with this. We need professional help.' He turned around and headed to the hospital.

I was utterly spent. I didn't want to be at the hospital. As we waited, seemingly forever, to see someone, I asked him to take me home. I pleaded. Each time, with his face white and his eyes looking straight into mine, he shook his head.

Eventually, a doctor came and asked some questions. Some papers were filled out, some plans were made. And thus I became a client of the mental health system.

The next day, Monday, a member of the acute care mental health team came to our house for a chat. He booked me in to see a psychiatrist at the hospital on Wednesday.

The day after that, I had thirty clients at the kitchen, students from the US on an Australian tour. Back into teaching mode I went: all smiles and energy, and bringing the best I could to these people who had come a long way for this experience. It wasn't their fault I was in the middle of a crisis. Freddie Mercury nailed it in 'The Show Must Go On': no matter how broken I was on the inside, I had to keep that smile on my face.

On Wednesday I kept my appointment with the psychiatrist. Mick came with me. After filling in some questionnaires, the doctor suggested that I go into a psychiatric unit as an inpatient. I kind of laughed in disbelief; it was a ridiculous notion. I explained that I had classes booked at the kitchen, and that I was only a few days off returning to the radio. Going into hospital was not an option, not at all. I turned to Mick, expecting him to agree with me. He didn't. He just looked at me with that white, stressed face, straight into my eyes again, and said, 'It sounds right to me.'

Two weeks, I was told. I would be there for two weeks. Potentially three. It was an outright lie, of course. I was never getting out of there in three weeks, let alone two. That first time, I was in for six.

During the course of this whole process, I learned something really valuable that I think everyone should know. It's to do with private health insurance. Normally, there's a waiting period to add elements to your health plan. If you have basic cover, like we did, and you want to add optometry because your eyes are going to hell, you have to wait for a period of time. It's often a year. But this doesn't apply for mental health issues. It's the law: a waiting period can't be applied if you want to bump up your insurance because of a mental health condition. Because of this law, we were able to use our insurance to get into a private psych unit instead of the one attached to the public hospital. I was so grateful for this, so thankful that we had insurance and were able to access it during this time. And so acutely aware, too, that many people don't have that luxury or that privilege; they are left to take their chances in the under-resourced public sector. As much as I didn't want to go to hospital, I was grateful to be able to choose which one I went to.

The year 2020 had always loomed large in our calendar – it was an important one for many reasons. Firstly, it would be our silver wedding anniversary. It was also the year both Mick and I turned fifty, that Joe turned twenty-five, and Mum turned seventy-five. Lots of significant celebrations. Being in a mental hospital wasn't on my bingo card. Neither was a global pandemic. 2020 turned out to be about the shittiest year in my whole life, and I don't think I am alone in that assessment.

Entering the mental health unit was surreal. It was so far outside what I ever expected to happen in my life. My preconceptions of what it was like inside a mental hospital had mostly been formed by watching movies like *One Flew Over the Cuckoo's Nest*. I hadn't thought for a second about what it might be like to be in that position myself – it just didn't apply to me. Until all at once it did apply to me, and here I was.

At first I was not expected to join the others in the dining room, or to attend the group therapy sessions. I'm not sure if they gave everyone this leeway when they were becoming acclimatised to their new surroundings, or if it was because I had a recognisable face. After a few days, though, the flexibility was removed and I had to face people at mealtimes. We were required to check in to a short session after breakfast, which involved telling everyone how we felt that morning. It was never an overly joyful session – none of us was in hospital because our lives were going exactly to plan.

Morning and afternoon there were group counselling sessions. Some of these were okay. I learned a lot about cognitive behavioural therapy, an element of which is noticing bad thoughts and sending them on their way. I learned to pay attention to the signs of impending panic or sadness, and to work out which feelings attached themselves to those sensations. Then to identify the thoughts that were creating the feelings. And to understand that most of those thoughts were either going over things that had already happened, or worrying about things that had not yet happened. We learned to accept those thoughts without judgement, just let them come and let them go. I put unhelpful thoughts onto leaves in a creek and watch them float downstream; I put unhelpful thoughts into bubbles and watched them drift away into the air.

Being constantly vigilant about the thoughts that are causing the feelings that are causing the problems is exhausting, like that whack-a-mole game where no sooner than you smack one furry little bastard on the head, another one pops up somewhere else.

We had sessions on mindfulness – the art of Now. If you're in the moment, paying attention to exactly what's happening at the present time, you can't be chewing over the past or worrying about the future. A lot of the cognitive behavioural therapy actions we were taught involved bringing us back to the present moment; counting our breaths, naming things in the room, paying attention to each of our senses in turn. These things were quite effective in heading off a full-blown anxiety attack, if you had your wits about you and noticed it coming in time.

Some sessions were brutal – home truths landed like undetonated bombs that went off later in the privacy of my room. Some sessions were fantastic, leaving me feeling like I would have everything under control if I could just master what I had been taught. Some of our teachers were empathetic, kind, inspirational. A couple of them were, in my considered opinion, on the wrong side of the room.

I kept a journal while I was in the hospital. It's a little disjointed, not earth-shattering prose or anything. I was drugged pretty heavily at first, to keep the panic attacks at bay and to ease me into a new antidepressant medication. Writing things down helped me to keep track of the days, which blurred into one another. It helped to somewhat order my thoughts, which were wheeling around in my head like seagulls after a hot chip. It gave me something to do that required me to be at least a little bit compos mentis.

Reading back over the journal entries is hard. They bring back the bewilderment, the sadness and guilt, the helplessness. The anger. All the shitty feelings I had that my life had come to this. That I had *let it* come to this. All the worry I was causing for the people I loved.

It was a dark time, punctuated with light moments. The light moments were not only created by my family and friends, who were able to visit me, but also, to my surprise, quite often by my fellow patients.

January–March 2020
Thursday 16th January
After the psychiatrist I go home to pack, then off to the mental health clinic as an inpatient to get me sorted. They take anything sharp from my bags, all my phone charging cords, my medications. A thorough bag search. It's very confronting. The doorknobs and taps are a weird shape; there are no towel rails. I work out it's so you can't tie anything to them and hang yourself. The doors close but don't lock.

I'm given blood tests. Mick stays all day. He makes phone calls to the radio, the kitchen, Mum and Dad. Others will find out soon enough.

Friday 17th
I see a psychologist, a medical doctor and a psychiatrist today. All the nurses are wonderful. Plans are formulated for new

medication. Everyone's very conscious of my privacy. I don't have to eat in the dining room. I will have to see people eventually. I'm foggy, dopey. Anxiety attacked tonight with sweating, shaking, racing pulse. They gave me more diazepam and put a wet washer on me. The psychologist asked me to write some positive affirmations about being here because currently mostly what I feel is desperately guilty for letting people down.

I write: 'I want to be strong again and I am here to achieve that. I am taking this time away from my work and life so that I can see a bright and happy future. I am looking for different strategies for coping and I want to be the best version of myself for those who love me.'

Mick is here again all day today. He is the bedrock my life is built on. He is my world.

Saturday 18th
Mick here again for the day and he brings my art supplies. I eat in the dining room for the first time at breakfast and there is a bit too much drama. I want to go home. I'm given more valium. The nurse explains the wash effect, which is where they take you off one antidepressant and gradually introduce another, so for a few days you're not really covered by either. Could be why I feel like shit today. They give me a different drug at night. In high doses it's an antipsychotic, but at low doses it's a sedative, so at least I can sleep.

Sunday 19th
Forty-four people come to my kitchen today for high tea. My team, Renee and Leah and Janny, take care of it. I am not there. I sleep a lot today, heavy sleep, new antidepressant maybe, lots of valium, diaz they call it. Meant to be back on the radio tomorrow,

just a few thousand more people to let down, so many messages from listeners excited to have us back.

Paddy and Joe come today, beautiful boys, Mick too. Meat pie and salad for dinner at 5 p.m., lol, probably a good thing as it's 6.15 p.m. and I'm falling asleep again.

Monday 20th
Set an alarm for breakfast. During breakfast I sit alone. Not ready to talk yet. Scrambled eggs, cold toast and tea. Back to the room to sleep. Not doze, proper deep sleep. They keep waking me for obs and valium. Tash comes at 10.30 and brings lollies and love. When she leaves I go back to sleep. Lunch, sleep. Mick at 5.30 after work. I'm so sorry for everything. I've just fucked up everything. Nobody misses me on the radio this morning. Not a single message asking where I am. Like I was never there. That's okay. Maybe disappearing and starting a whole new life doing something else will be easier than I thought. They're fine without me at the kitchen too.

Tuesday the 21st of January 2020
Happy 25th anniversary to the love of my life. I can't believe we're waking up in different beds today. I don't want to get up. The nurse wakes me again at 10 and suggests I come up with some plans for the day, sleeping not being one of them. They have given me colouring-in sheets to do, so that's something, I guess. The medicine has stripped me of the things I am. I don't want to talk to anyone. I sit alone at meals. I can't comfort anyone in distress or offer kind words. The best bits of me have sailed away on a cloud of whatever the fuck it is they're giving me. I'm left here, empty in my heart, of no use to the people here around me or the people on the outside who love me.

HOW DO YOU MEND A BROKEN HEART?

The world turns without me, it's doing quite well, thank you very much.

P.S. I dream I am shot, but when I wake up I've spilt my cup of tea all over my chest. Also, there are no pink Mentos in this packet. What the FUCK.

Wednesday 22nd
I have challenged myself to take all meals in the dining room. Breakfast is at 7. I have to set an alarm. I haven't had to set an alarm that late since I started radio. It must be the drugs. Today I go on the group walk and manage to say a few words. Nothing of consequence. Mainly my name, to a lady who forgets it every few minutes. Lunch in the dining room, rissoles and gravy. I forget to order vegetables so it just looks like three brown cricket balls on a plate, with gravy on them. The food is actually better than I expected. Paddy comes to visit, stays for one and three-quarter hours.

Mick comes tonight too after work. We eat dinner at five, turkey with mash and gravy. I have to stock up on Jatz crackers and cheese so I can have another dinner at real dinner time. They're trying to get me to join groups but today's group was preparing for discharge and I'm not being discharged. Tomorrow's is managing anger but I don't have any fucking anger issues so they can shove that right up their arse.

Tuesday 23rd
Bad night's sleep. Up at 7 for the biggest plate of baked beans you ever saw. Lucky I'm in my own room. I don't do the walk today because it's going to be 41 degrees and despite my current dwelling I'm not actually a lunatic. Meds are messing with me. They make me feel a bit drunk so that's actually pretty cool. Rabs called this

morning. I don't think I have a job there anymore. There's only so long they can wait for me. I am sad but I understand.

Colouring-in therapy is coming along swimmingly. Lunch at 12, turkey and mash. I think it's the first time I've spoken to someone at a meal. After lunch there is group, 'Shame and Guilt', I'd better check that one out since those are my middle names. Silent tears just come out of my eyes as soon as it starts but nobody notices. I don't have to say much. Half an hour break, then art and craft time. I'm trying to be normal and involved, so I join in. I make a 25th anniversary card for Mick. It is, with 100% sincerity, the shittest card I've ever made. It will be the perfect memento of the fact that I spent our 25th wedding anniversary in a mental hospital.

Mick comes in again. He says I'm more myself today. I'm glad he thinks so; it makes him happy. I've had a lot less valium, so that's probably it. Dinner is honey chicken, not crash hot, but I steal cheese so I'll have a snack for later.

I'm resigned to the fact that I'll be here for a while. I'm going with the flow and whatever waits for me when I come out will be what I have to work with. This time 11 days ago I was seriously contemplating sinking into the dark and quiet of the Brisbane Water. I at least feel a bit better than that.

Friday 24th
I'm supposed to be teaching an Italian class tonight. Renee will do it for me. Bless her. I slept poorly last night but this morning feel much more lucid and able to talk to other people. Boy, there must have been heavy drugs in the first few days. I could hardly walk straight or talk or even look anyone in the eye. Now I know a few names and I've had some conversations. Only one person seems to have recognised me from the TV, but she's a bit manic and has

been told by the nurses to pull her head in. I don't mind, I like her. I'm glad to be mostly incognito and not have to answer 15 million questions about Masterchef.

Saturday 25th
I dream I am trying to teach a duck to swim and it just can't get the hang of it so I sticky-tape it to a pool noodle. I wonder what Freud would make of that.

As much as I would give to be in my own bed tonight, I've surrendered myself to this process. This weird, watershed time in my life. Eventually it will be done and I'll be better for it. In the meantime I need to exercise. The meds make me want to eat for Australia.

Monday 27th
We watch the Kyrgios–Nadal match for a spot in the quarters. Kyrgios goes down 3–1 but not without an incredible fight. I watch it with a couple of the others in here and Mick stays for a while. It feels good and normal to have a laugh. Everyone here has their own shit going on. I hope they all turn out okay. I hope we all turn out okay.

Tuesday 28th
Breakfast is tinned spaghetti on toast. I wonder why I never have that at home. I'm going on the walk today, I need it. I feel like a complete fuck-up right now. Like I ruin everything good. Like I take up too much space and I poison the space with my mess. The walk is unbearably hot and humid. It's not a long walk, just to the shops and back.

Afterwards I see the psychiatrist and she bans me from daytime naps. Noooo! Also no screen time for half an hour before bed.

Nooooooo! So I'll read and draw and do crosswords and listen to sleepy meditations.

But the great news is I've been granted two hours per day to go unaccompanied to the local leisure centre to use the gym and the pool.

Group today is about dealing with unhelpful thoughts. It is actually amazing to hear other people's thoughts echoing mine and realising that I'm not alone. There are some people here who are really suffering outwardly and those that appear fine and happy but whose wounds must be on the inside. It is a really profound session. I probably should go to more.

I do go to the leisure centre and sign up for a two-week membership. I buy some goggles and swim and go to the gym. It feels powerful and positive and I'll try to do it every day.

Wednesday 29th
I swear that every day I have to look at yesterday's entry to see what the day and date are. I can't keep it straight in my head. Good brekkie, good chats. As soon as I walk out into the corridor my mood crashes and I can hardly keep my eyes open. I can't wait for them to get this medication sorted. Right now I'm like Dr Jekyll and Mr Hyde except sad instead of homicidal.

Group this morning is quite intense. It is about anxiety. By the end of it, every single one of us in the group is experiencing anxiety, so if that's a measure of success, I guess it is a successful group.

After lunch, I catch an Uber to the leisure centre. I swim thirty laps of the Olympic pool. I've never done that many before but by God it is beautiful. My mind is totally focused on breathing in and bubbling out and counting my strokes. I think I just nailed mindfulness!

HOW DO YOU MEND A BROKEN HEART?

I tick off every single thing on my goals list and also strip and remake my bed and do a load of washing. Maybe they're slipping a bit of pseudoephedrine in with my pills. And of course, my favourite time of day is when Mick visits. We sit and catch up on each other's days, and laugh and reassure each other. I love him more than I can ever express, my rock and my heart.

Thursday 30th
Today's group is about self-compassion. The first handout had a graphic on it that knocks me absolutely sideways. It's a quote by Jack Kornfield: 'If your compassion does not include yourself, it is incomplete.' I start crying, because being a compassionate person was something I took pride in. I thought I was good at it, something I believed was an important part of me. And now I learn that just because I hate myself, I'm not really that great at being a compassionate person. Thanks a lot, Jack. Way to kick a girl when she's down.

After lunch, I go to the leisure centre for a swim. The Uber driver recognises me from the radio. I swim thirty laps again, in less time. I love it so much. Then the Uber driver back to the hospital recognises me from Masterchef. My stay in hospital is probably not going to remain private for much longer.

Rough evening; I know one of the women who comes in to visit a relative. I feel exposed, as though I don't have any privacy. I wonder how long before the news is public that I am in a psych unit.

Tuesday 4th February
A weird night full of bad dreams. Group this morning is all about resilience. I've always prided myself on being resilient. It's a core value of mine in fact, and I define it as being strong, able

to *withstand, able to carry on. What I learn today is that resilience also means the ability to adapt to change. Like the Eiffel Tower or Statue of Liberty, designed to expand and contract with the temperature, and bend with the wind, without breaking. Like trees, built by Mother Nature to withstand storms. Resilience isn't rigid strength, it's flexibility. Another thing that I thought was a defining characteristic of mine, but that I've been getting so horribly wrong.*

Lunch is a saltless spinach and feta filo. Should have stuck to the sandwiches.

Wednesday 5th
Brekkie is bacon and avo toast. I try to cut my lemon to put a squeeze of juice on the avo, but we only get butter knives here and they are so blunt you could ride bare-arsed to London on them. Check-in is fine, I clocked my mood as a seven after the best night's sleep I've had since I came. I think it has to do with the fitted sheets Mick brought from home so I don't wake up looking like a mummy all trussed up in the sheet.

Our group today is about gratitude which is actually something I do practise daily with Mick. Some days we forget but our general rule is that we text each other every day with something we are grateful for. Small, big, whatever, just a moment of the day that we set aside to think about positive things. It's one of the many reasons I love him.

I got to swim this afternoon. It is a pure and true exercise in mindfulness. There's nothing but counting strokes, moving through the water, the tiles on the bottom of the pool, the only sound my own breath, bubbling to the surface. It is pure therapy and I love it.

Tonight Mick gets here early and sits with us at the dining table. It is nice for him to join in on what really is a family experience. There is plenty of laughing, chatting about the food (roast turkey and mash), hearing from the new lady who just arrived. I'm learning so much from the facilitators and counsellors here but, really, I think my biggest lessons have come from my fellow patients. All of us dealing with one thing or another. They are so brave. They are fighting for their best lives. That's what we're doing. It's all we want.

Thursday 6th
Rabs comes in today and smuggles in cheese and crackers. He was going to glad-wrap them around his torso under his hoodie but he forgot his hoodie. It doesn't matter, I'm actually allowed to have cheese and crackers, he doesn't need to smuggle them. It is great to see him. We yap on for an hour and a half. A replacement for me on the breakfast show has been found. It looks like I will only return now to welcome her, and say goodbye. I have a lot of hugely conflicting emotions about this, but I'll leave those to sort out later when they've completed the grease and oil change on my brain.

There's a beautiful lady in here, it's not her first time at the rodeo, and I've found her honesty and insight and wisdom to be a really important part of my beginning to heal in here. Today she asks if I have a sec. She's been debating whether to tell me something. She doesn't want to upset or trigger me, but she's decided she wants to let me know.

'Thankful Thursday saved my life,' she said. Thankful Thursday is a regular spot on our brekky show where we ask listeners to call up with something they are grateful for. She was going to pick up her car from a service, and had decided it was her last day. She had picked out a tree along Wilford Barrett Drive. When she got in her car, the mechanic had changed it from her station, the ABC,

to Star 104.5. Rabs and I were doing our Thankful Thursday segment.

Apparently on this day I had said something like, 'Even when things are hard there's always something, even if it's small, that we can be thankful for.'

She said, 'Anyway, I drove past the tree.'

I tell her she's obviously meant to be here. We both are. Thank God for the mechanic who changed the radio station. Thank God for a radio station that supports our show in doing positive things. Thank God the timing worked out. Thank God for the two strangers and their lovely dog who found themselves on a footpath between me and Brisbane Water. Not everything is accidental.

Friday 7th
It's pouring here. Blessed cleansing rain. May it soak deep into the earth to the deepest roots of the trees and give them the strength and sustenance they need for the coming battle with their own atmosphere.

Today is a busy one with both psychologists and psychiatrists visiting. I hope to get some kind of idea what might be happening with me in here. There won't be a walk this morning, but I'm not keen on group tai chi, so I'll have a little extra downtime. Yay! Tonight, Mick is taking me out for dinner as part of doctor-prescribed re-entry into normal life by doing normal things, like a space shuttle returning to Earth's atmosphere. I hope I don't burn up.

I miss my house, my bed, my best friend and lover next to me in the bed, stacks on with the dogs every time I sit down, cooking in my kitchen, the boys breezing in and out of the house with or without friends and girlfriends like it's a cross between some college dorm and Central Station. I want to drive my car and run errands and use scissors without having to ask permission.

HOW DO YOU MEND A BROKEN HEART?

It has poured all day. Sydney has flooded, towns in NSW have recorded their highest rainfall since records began. Parts of the coast are underwater.

I have a check-in with the psychologist. She thinks maybe groups aren't the best thing for me anymore; she noticed that I was being funny, and was worried that I might be in performance mode. She's probably right. Note to self: be unfunny. I saw the psychiatrist as well, it looks like I'm in here for another week and a half at least.

Fuck.

Sunday 9th
It has been pouring all night and there is howling wind as well. In the evening the power goes out. Thankfully I have a little charger pack for my phone. It's as black as the inside of a cow in my room. Power is set to come on at 11 p.m. so all is good.

Monday 10th
The first thing I do this morning when I wake up is flick the bedside light switch. Still no power. In a hospital! They've somehow supplied an urn of hot water to the dining room so we can have a reasonably warm cuppa. The windows don't open in the rooms here so without aircon it's a bit stuffy, but that's the worst of it for the moment. Power comes back on after breakfast and before check-in.

I try to do a meditation from an app on my phone instead of going to groups but I fall asleep instead. They wake me for lunch and I eat fast (roast veal and salad) then go back to my room. I still feel really tired, deep in my bones, like I'm wearing heavy wet woollen clothes.

I'm worried about Mick on the flooded roads coming to see me but he insists on still coming. I'm too selfish to insist that he not come. I need a hug from him tonight. I physically need it. I don't achieve anything today beyond a hot shower and crawling back into bed, and for once I actually feel grateful to be in a place where I can just do that. Normally on days like these I have to wear this wet woollen suit out into the world, to work, to parties, to the supermarket. I have to arrange my face into appropriate expressions and strive to focus on what people are saying so that I can make passable responses.

So, as much as I'd like to be home, on a real blue day like today, I'm glad I could be here.

Tuesday 11th
I have a meeting with the psychologist and the psychiatrist to discuss doing my final show on the radio. To say goodbye to the listeners, and my colleagues. They were a little shocked at the date I proposed, 21st of February, but I made my case and it's on.

We're starting to build a discharge strategy, how life will be when I get back home. It's a bit daunting. Anyway, I'm in for another two weeks, best case. I am a bit disheartened by this. I want to be at home, but I want to be well at home. I want to be excited about the things I've chosen to do with my life, rather than feeling dread about every class, meeting, business lunch, social event. It was the only goal I could articulate when I arrived here: I want to feel joy again.

Wednesday 12th
Mick came last night, as he does every single night, after work. I ordered sandwiches with my dinner last night. I like to have a snack organised as he's always starving when he gets here and he's having dinner quite late every night. I can't talk him out of coming every day. I hate being a burden but he insists it's for his own benefit.

HOW DO YOU MEND A BROKEN HEART?

I feel giddy and weird this morning but I'm going to push through that today. Sleeping the day away sounds like heaven but I'm not evolved enough yet to not feel guilty about doing it. So today is going to be an active, productive, positive, achieving type day. That's the plan. I manage check-in then the walk. The walk is a shock. We only go a short way to the shops – only two of about eight are open. The hairdresser and the bottle shop. The water from the lake is up to the path outside. All the businesses have sandbags in their doorways. The footpath is covered with seaweed. The roads are underwater and barricaded shut. I feel so sorry for the business owners and their mostly casual workers. I also feel quite sorry for myself. I was hoping for a coffee.

I go to morning group where we work on a wheel of wellness where you assess six areas of your life – emotional, physical, occupational, spiritual, social, family and intellectual. Then you fill in a pie chart according to how you're tracking in that department. Then you contemplate how smoothly your wheel would roll. My wheel is pretty wonky. No wonder it's been a bit of a bumpy ride lately.

After lunch (little sandwiches) I email back and forth with Shelley at the kitchen then wag afternoon groups to swim laps at the pool.

One of the things I've been working on with this psych and in groups is the nasty little voice that speaks in my head and undermines everything I do. At its best it's disappointed, at its worst it's a vicious bile-spewing troll. The pool is as close to zen as I can get. It's repetitive, it's tiring. I'm a bit obsessive about counting things, so that takes most of my concentration, but today I noticed the voice creeping in, especially when there's more than one person in the lane.

'You're too slow for this lane, you're in the way, the instructors are probably laughing at your technique,' and so on. Not overly *vicious but unhelpful, and giving me that familiar knot in my stomach. I decided that while I'm in the pool, while I'm weightless and moving regularly and strong, the voice is banned, just not allowed, not while I'm in the water. So every time it creeps in I do the thing we've been taught to do in here, to notice the voice and let it go, to put it on a leaf in a stream, or imagine it as a radio chattering away in the background, or give it a funny voice so it loses its sting. I start out by trying Donald Trump's voice, but it is too depressingly close to the way he actually speaks. And anyway, I don't want him in my head, I've got enough shit going on.*

So that's my plan. If I can neutralise the nasty voice while I'm in the pool, then I can start to do it in other situations.

Dinner is corned beef with white sauce and salad. Not my favourite.

Thursday 13th
Four weeks today. When they initially told me I'd be here for three weeks, possibly two, I freaked out. I couldn't see how it'd be possible. I've at least one week and five days to go. God.

Mornings are still tricky, hungover from the sleeping pill they give me at night. I need to get that sorted.

Lunch is roast lamb and salad, no potato. I've eaten so much mashed potato in here that if they cut me open I think that's all there will be.

Friday 14th
Mick and I exchange our usual morning texts. We don't really do the whole V-Day thing, but I don't dump on it either. Any chance to focus on who you love for a sec is good in my books. I have made him a card. Lots of therapeutic art going on in here. I go to check-in, still groggy from last night's sleeping pill, and I go for the walk.

HOW DO YOU MEND A BROKEN HEART?

The mood crashes and I don't go to morning group. After lunch (prawn curry), I have a quick nap. I'm a rule breaker and a rebel, that's for sure. The psychiatrist comes to see me and she's now fully on board with the final show next Friday.

Sunday 16th
Today marks one month since I arrived here. In one way it feels like a blur, days and weekends running into each other. In another way I barely recall sleeping between my own sheets. Time is a bit warped and strange. One week and two days to go, hopefully.

Monday 17th
Happy 23rd birthday to Tom, my beautiful middle boy. For his birthday we're giving him some travel cash, redeemable right before he travels so he doesn't blow it all by the weekend, and have lined up window tinting for his new car. He'll be pretty excited about that.

I'm really low this morning, tired and flat. I have an actual to-do list today. The real world is creeping back in. I skip morning group to get some stuff done. Lunch is butter chicken and rice, pretty good. I go to afternoon group but am just tired and cranky and not that into it.

I'm allowed out for a family dinner. We eat steaks and have a birthday cake. I drink ginger ale and too much water, I'll be up and down like a yo-yo all night. Tom is happy, the boys make me laugh so much. Even when I'm feeling disconnected and sad and a bit stunned at the turn my life has taken, they can crack me up. I love them like oxygen.

And shouldn't that love be enough? How can a person with so much love all around them be here in this hospital, in this state, in tears, in fright? Shouldn't all that love be enough?

YOUR TIME STARTS NOW

On Friday 21 February, I did my final show on the radio. Mick picked me up very early in the morning. I went into the studio, put on my headphones and turned the volume up loud for the last time. I explained that I wasn't returning at Easter as I had planned; we kept the show light, though, and I posted a statement with more detail around my reasons onto our Facebook page. It began:

A special note from Julie:

If you're a regular listener of our show you may have noticed that I have been missing in action this year. I didn't want to go into too much detail on the show this morning. Being the last Rabbit and Julie Goodwin breakfast show we wanted to keep it fun and positive, a celebration as well as a goodbye.

But I did want to provide a bit more information for anyone who is interested. I went on to outline, in detail, what had happened, the mental illnesses I was facing and the treatment as well. I described what I was going through just in case it resonated with anyone else who might need to hear it. I finished this long statement by saying:

I have a lot more to learn, and a lot of work to do, but one thing I do know is this: if the comment 'I don't know how you manage it all' comes my way again, I won't be taking it as a compliment. I'll be taking it as a warning sign that I perhaps need to step back and take stock. Before I break again.

The biggest lesson I've learned, and this is what I'd like to pass on: treat yourself the way you would treat someone you love. Don't work more than you would allow your partner or child to work. Don't speak to yourself with harsh words you'd never use towards your friends or colleagues. Be as kind to yourself as you try to be to others.

HOW DO YOU MEND A BROKEN HEART?

And if you're overwhelmed, if you're struggling, ask for help. Do it before you can no longer hear the logical voices, the clear and good voices. Do it before it's too hard to see a way forward. If you won't do it for yourself, do it for the ones who love you the most.

Love, Julie

No one needs to face their problems alone.

Help is available. Call Lifeline on 13 11 14

The support was enormous, and overwhelming. At the end of the broadcast, we signed off with the *Cheers* theme song. It was, to put it quite mildly, emotional.

My colleagues at the station had a guard of honour for me to walk out the door; they gave me gifts and wished me well. I got back in Mick's car, and returned to the psychiatric unit to continue treatment and try to work out what life would look like from now on.

On Tuesday 25 February, I was discharged from the hospital.

Curried mango chutney

This chutney is not only great with curry or on sandwiches and burgers, it also has the ability to transform a cheese platter into a memorable evening watching the Australian Open with fellow travellers on a rocky road. Such is the power of my favourite condiment.

Prep and cooking time: 40 minutes
Makes: 4 cups

1 kg ripe mango flesh, roughly chopped
2 birdseye chillies, stalks removed

YOUR TIME STARTS NOW

¼ cup fresh ginger, peeled and sliced
3 cloves garlic, peeled
1 brown onion, peeled and quartered
1 red capsicum, seeded and cut into chunks
3 tablespoons olive oil
200 ml white wine vinegar
150 ml pineapple juice
¾ cup brown sugar
2 tablespoons curry powder
⅔ cup raisins

Place chillies, ginger, garlic, onion and capsicum in the bowl of a mini food processor and process until finely chopped.

Place this mixture in a pan with olive oil over medium heat. Stir for around 3 minutes or until soft and fragrant.

Add the mango, pineapple juice, vinegar, sugar, curry powder and raisins. Mix well and bring the mixture to the boil.

Reduce to a simmer and reduce for around half an hour or until required consistency is reached. Spoon into sterilised jars.

CHAPTER 17
LEARN TO FLY

I was so determined that things would be fine from that moment on. I did all the discharge activities, including providing my doctors with an hour-by-hour breakdown of how I would be spending my days in the coming weeks. Every single thing was colour-coded and put into my calendar: breakfast, lunch and dinner, gym and pool, relaxing time, social time, bed time. I engaged a new psychologist, someone outside of the hospital.

Two weekends after I returned home I was teaching again. For my first couple of classes Renee came to the kitchen. She had run everything while I was in the hospital, and she wanted to be there to step in in case I didn't feel up to taking a whole class. Only after I was underway, comfortably in the saddle again, did she go home. Mick came in as well; he hung out in the office for the whole four-hour class.

It was an apocalyptic time. I had gone into the hospital amid the fires; while I was there came the floods; upon emerging there was the pestilence. News was making the rounds about a disease sweeping the globe, a novel coronavirus. It seemed at first as though this was going to be one of those stories about a problem in another place on the planet, a story that might impact Australia in only a small way or barely at all. A news item of interest but not immediate concern.

It didn't seem that way for long: by February COVID-19 had already hit our shores and by the end of March we were in lockdown.

It seemed as though Australians had been spared a more rapid and devastating start to the pandemic because tourism was at an all-time low due to the bushfires. Nobody in their right mind was booking flights to this burned-to-a-crisp country. But before long we seemed to have caught up with the world, and a zero-COVID suppression strategy was adopted by the government.

Two of my boys were overseas at this time. Joe was in Greece with friends, and Paddy was in the USA with his girlfriend, both on holidays that had been saved up for and long anticipated. Joe got home as scheduled, with two hours to spare before he was caught up in the quarantine rules. Paddy was not so lucky. Only halfway through his trip, the US was closing business and cancelling the basketball and football games he had bought tickets to see. Mid-March the government called for Australians abroad to come home. It took a few days for Paddy to get a flight, and it cost him hundreds of dollars. Upon arrival home he had to quarantine for two weeks.

I was so disappointed for him. At the time we didn't really know how this virus was going to affect the world; how our lives would be impacted for years to come – the carnage that was coming our way. At the time, it just seemed like the worst bad luck and a real blow to Paddy on his first, long-anticipated overseas trip without his parents.

By then, the restrictions upon businesses meant that running our classes was no longer possible. We could only have one person to a bench if we were to abide by the new social distancing rules, and that meant we couldn't hit break-even. So, a few days before New South Wales was shut down, we postponed all our scheduled classes and events and closed our doors.

I couldn't believe it. I had really struggled with the decision between leaving the radio and closing down my business. I'd left the radio and now my business was closed anyway. I wallowed in a bit of self-pity, but not for too long. With Renee in my corner, and half of my team eventually covered by the JobKeeper scheme, we decided to use the shutdown time to get the kitchen back into tip-top shape, deep-clean everything, and come up with some new class ideas. We also looked at how we could continue to keep our team working and our business in people's minds for when we reopened.

Renee put together a whole lot of cooking science classes for children and these were provided for free on our Facebook page. Parents home-schooling their children were on a keen lookout at the time for different things to do to, and these fitted the bill perfectly.

We also started making boxed dinners. We started with TGIF boxes, a choice of luxurious cheese or mezze platters that could be purchased online and picked up from the kitchen on Thursdays or Fridays. There was a great deal of satisfaction in creating these boxes. We could spend time cooking treats we didn't normally have time to cook. Terrines, lavosh and crackers, chutneys, pates and dolmades, flatbreads, dips and pickles. It was fun. During this time the liquor laws were changed so that our on-premise licence also allowed us to sell takeaway wine and beer, and we could add that as an option to our Friday platters.

As we came up to Mother's Day, people were still not allowed to go out, so we decided to create and deliver a range of options for the day: mezze platters, Devonshire teas, and the full high tea option. These were prepared and cooked by Renee and me, and delivered to the door by her husband, Mitch, as well as Mick and my boys. It was absolute chaos. Orders kept coming in right up to the last minute. At the end of the day we were completely knackered; all the boys had driven the length and breadth of the coast. We had baked thousands of scones, made hundreds of finger sandwiches, cupcakes, flatbreads, vats of dips, pickles and chutneys. To this day, I can make Renee's eye twitch by mentioning Mother's Day orders.

In the second lockdown we did whole dinners, which became a staple for many families: we had regulars calling by for the lasagne with garlic bread, or the chicken, cheese and mushroom strudel with salad, or the old-school cottage pie. Our dinner project allowed us to have an ongoing conversation with our online community as each week we posted what the specials would be. It felt important to stay in touch, so that when the world opened back up, those relationships would be intact.

It was important for me to keep a bit busy, too. All my meticulously laid plans for self-care and exercise went out the window as pools and gyms, spas and eventually psych offices, closed their doors. You can, at least, have a psych appointment over the phone, but you can't swim thirty laps.

Mick was still going to work – he and Loyal IT fell under 'essential services', especially as so many people needed help setting up new computer equipment and software to work from home. While my hospitality business closed its doors, the IT business could hardly keep up with everybody's changing circumstances.

One morning after Mother's Day, Tom told us that he needed to have a serious conversation with us when Mick got home that night. Mick and I went over the possibilities of what Tom would say, so we could make a good-parent response rather than a shocked-parent response, which can often have elements that are regrettable. We were pretty sure we had worked out what he wanted to tell us.

I had frequently worried that my Catholic-raised heart might be warped out of shape when it came to outdated ideas of morality, but I needn't have. There was nothing but an almost overwhelming swell of pride and pure joy when Tommy told us what we had already guessed: we were going to be grandparents.

Tom then called his brothers down and gave them the news. Paddy fist-pumped and said, 'Yeaaaaah, I always wanted to be an uncle, I'm gonna be the best!' Joe went pale for a moment, a bit shocked until he registered that this was happy news, at which point he congratulated Tom. There were brother-hugs all round. Then Paddy piped up, 'Wait – does this mean you guys have had sex?'

As the three of them headed upstairs to their rooms, I heard Paddy ask, 'Can I tell my girlfriend?'

Tom said, yeah, sure he could. Joe then asked, 'If I get a girlfriend, can I tell her too?' They all laughed; brothers sharing a moment. Mick and I hugged and laughed together on the couch and my heart was full. It wasn't just the news of a new life on the way, it was my family, dealing with something unexpected in the only way they knew how. With love, and support, and dumb jokes. How I love them.

And I loved Crystal too, the girl who would be mother to our grandchild. Tom's long-time girlfriend was a ray of sunshine. She slotted so well into our family, with a bright sense of humour and a kind heart. She balanced Tom out and made him happy. It was a relief. I've always known that the day will come when the boys will choose who they want to spend their lives with, and I've known as well that I won't get much of a say. In fact, I know that if I want a relationship with them through their adulthood, I had better keep firmly to myself any negative opinions I might have.

I remember a woman coming to one of my book signings and asking me to sign a book to 'The best daughter-in-law ever'. I made a light-hearted comment that she must have an uncommonly good relationship with her daughter-in-law. She said something that really stayed with me: 'She is my son's choice. I had my choice of life partner, and my parents didn't get a say. She is his choice, and I don't get a say. It's his life. So I either love her and get along with her, or I lose him.'

I was determined to adopt this attitude, and Crystal makes it easy to do. She is Tom's choice of a life partner, but she would also be my choice for him, if I got one.

***

I wish I could say that this beautiful news was my turning point, the cure for everything, and we all lived happily ever after. But this is not a fairytale or a Hollywood movie, and real life is far more complex than that. There were still battles ahead.

Grandparenting would begin in January of 2021. Meanwhile, I was swinging between feeling frustrated that my business was on hold, and relieved that I had a little reprieve from the real world crashing in on me again.

I had cut right back on drinking after my stay in hospital, at least for a little while. Drinking wasn't one of the things they'd talked about in there, though for me it would have been helpful if they had. I knew it wasn't optimal for me to drink at all – far from it. I knew it didn't go well with the antidepressants I was on. But it still gave me that quietening that I needed, and eventually it grew into a larger habit again.

LEARN TO FLY

I was at the point where I knew I shouldn't drink, but I didn't want to stop. I knew I *should* want to stop. But for all the reasons I, and I am sure others, tell ourselves – 'I need it, I deserve it, it helps smooth off the edges, it's my way of winding down at the end of the day' – I didn't want to stop.

I moved to the stage where I didn't want to stop, but I *wanted* to want to stop. Because if I wanted to, I could, of course. I had done it before and I could do it again. But I didn't want to. I just *wished* I wanted to. It's an incremental difference, but you can see it if you look.

Then I got to the stage when I wanted to stop, and made plans to stop. Plans that kept getting delayed for one reason or another. A particularly bad day. A particularly good day. A reason to celebrate. A worry to ignore. A birthday. A weekend. A day ending in y.

Eventually I wanted to stop enough to try to actually stop. And I found I couldn't.

Like many people, our significant celebrations in 2020 were truncated in ways we never could have imagined even a year before. Mick hadn't really wanted a fiftieth party, so we'd planned a trip instead. It never came to pass. Instead, I made an Italian-themed dinner for him, based on our magical trip with the boys.

I felt sorriest for the people whose weddings, meticulously planned and hugely anticipated, had to be postponed; and for people who had to attend funerals via Zoom, or those who could not hold the hands or touch the faces of their loved ones in hospitals as they died.

It was such a surreal time. People posted videos online of deserted streets in the top tourist spots of Italy; cafés in France and pubs in Ireland with their doors closed. Debates raged and citizens turned on each other over views on masks, vaccinations, whether someone was breaking the lockdown laws. Borders between states closed and opened and closed again, and the rules changed at a head-spinning pace. As with all disasters on this earth, it brought out the best in us and it brought out the worst in us. There was kindness and connection, anger and isolation, stories of hope and of unspeakable sadness. Mental health disorders were going through the roof as we all in our own way struggled to survive.

By October I was on a steep downhill run again. I was doing everything in my power – my power not being great at that point – to follow the rules set down for me by the doctors, and yet I was sliding backwards. It was a helpless, hopeless feeling. I knew what I had to do to be well. I had to stop drinking, for a start. And I had to exercise. And practise gratitude. And use my newly acquired cognitive behavioural therapy skills to keep the bad thoughts at bay. But sometimes, as I had been learning over the past few years, there is a vast gap between knowing what you have to do, and being able to do it.

I went back to the hospital. This stay really was just for two weeks. It was a different experience this time around. We couldn't all eat together in the dining room, and groups were half-sized so we only had them half as frequently. We had to wear masks if we were outside our own bedrooms, or if anyone had to enter them. No visitors were allowed, which made me lonely but also alleviated my guilt about Mick having to come every night after work.

I went back with a fair bit of anger: this shit wasn't working. I needed better drugs, or better doctors, or a better plan. *I did (almost) everything you asked, and it didn't bloody work. Here I am – fix me, and do a better job this time, if you don't mind.*

I was angry, too, that this hospital would not address my drinking or any other kind of addictive behaviour. I knew that many of my fellow patients were struggling, as I was, with one addiction or another, and that this was having an adverse impact on their mental health. Of course it was! And yet it wasn't spoken of.

One day in groups we were talking about our responses when we get stressed. The whiteboard was divided into columns for positive responses and negative responses. 'I go for a walk,' said one guy. *Go for a walk* was written on the positive side.

'I get angry and lose my temper,' said someone else. *Lose temper* was written up, on the negative side.

'I cry,' someone said. *Cry* was written on the board.

'I have a glass of wine,' I said. The group leader wrote *unhelpful coping behaviours* on the negative side of the white board.

I had lost count of how many times I had tried to bring this up, and I was frustrated by the euphemisms. I was here to get help. My hand went back up. 'I would like to know why we don't seem to be allowed to talk about drinking,' I said.

'What do you mean?' asked the therapist.

'Well, every time I mention drinking, the subject is changed. I need help with it. Is it a rule here? Is there some reason we can't talk about it?' I genuinely wanted to know.

After a second, the facilitator said, 'Sure, we can talk about it.'

She left *unhelpful coping behaviours* on the board, and underneath it, wrote *'drinking'*. In inverted commas, like it was imaginary. The conversation very quickly turned back to noticing unhelpful thoughts and sending them floating away in a fucking bubble. We never spoke about 'drinking' again.

I got out of hospital the day before my fiftieth birthday. I was advised to stay there longer, but I honestly couldn't see the point. My medication was not being changed; we were going over the same topics in group therapy; and I wasn't getting any help with the one thing that I thought might help turn this whole messy ship around. Besides, I had already spent my twenty-fifth wedding anniversary in this place. The idea of having my fiftieth birthday in here, without visitors, was more than I could bear. So I checked out.

We celebrated my birthday at the cooking school: as a food venue, we could have a few more people there than were allowed into our home. Mick, the boys and my closest friends came, and the boys cooked a three-course meal – Tom on entrée with a spiced pumpkin soup, Joe on main with his signature chicken schnitzel and potato bake, and Paddy on dessert with sticky date pudding. Mick oversaw the whole operation, and they did a beautiful job. I was still wrecked, exhausted, overwhelmed and low, but I felt very loved that night.

I tried and failed again to stop drinking. It was infuriating – when I was in the hospital I had no access to alcohol at all, and yet I wasn't thinking about it or missing it. I was just there, and wine wasn't. But once I was out in the world, there it was again. It probably didn't help that I owned my own licensed premises, that I had a coolroom full of wine and no clients to give it to.

I decided, to Mick's great relief, to find a different hospital. One that would help me with my mental health, but that was also equipped to address addiction. Once again I thanked heaven for health insurance, and made arrangements to go into a private facility on the Northern Beaches of Sydney. So off I went, once again in a state of weary surprise that my life had come to this: not just a psych unit this time. Rehab.

Mick took the morning off work and drove me there. He was not allowed to stay inside, so after an anguished goodbye from me he drove home again. As I waited in the foyer to be admitted, I noticed the signs painted across all the walls. 'You are miracle' one said. I snorted. Some miracle. Another proclaimed that this centre was focused on a twelve-step program. I nearly bolted out of the door. I did not view my experience with AA more than fifteen years before as a positive one, so this information left me cold.

But I had committed to this. I had promised Mick I would give it everything, and I knew that I did not have an infinite well of chances to dip into here. Something had to change, and that something was me.

The place was completely different to the previous hospital. That facility had been focused on mental health, and had basically ignored addictions; this place was almost the other way around. It was much stricter, too.

Once again I was searched, as was all of my luggage. My razor, tweezers and any other sharp implements were put into safe storage. We would be allowed a phone call every couple of days, on an old-school phone inside a little booth next to the common room. That phone cut out automatically after fifteen minutes. We couldn't have visitors.

So, no phones, nor television or computers, and the only books we could bring in were of an approved self-help nature. Anything addictive was banned. Obviously no drugs or alcohol were permitted, but also no cigarettes, caffeine, sugar; and no exercise was allowed either. This was to try to prevent anyone swapping one addiction for another, as addicted people so often do. If you've ever tried to even cut back on drinking, you will understand how difficult it is to forgo sugar: the craving is so powerful.

We were only allowed to eat in the dining room, at mealtimes. No food was allowed outside the dining room. Of course, when you feed adults their dinner in the afternoon, they are going to conceal cheese and crackers in their pockets for later. It's a law of nature.

I quickly realised that among the herbal teas available to us, there was green tea. I don't think anyone had cottoned on to the fact that green tea has quite a good amount of caffeine in it. Needless to say, my morning beverage was the strongest green tea I could wring out of those bags. It was no double-shot flat white with one sugar, but it did the job.

For the first few days I was monitored often – my blood pressure, temperature and pulse. I had Vitamin B injections in my backside, and lined up with everyone else for medication in the morning and evening.

Each morning all of the patients in the hospital sat in a large circle. We went around the circle and gave our name, why we were here, and what emotions we were feeling in that moment. The approved emotions were up on the wall in picture form.

Hi, I am Julie, and I am here for depression, anxiety and alcohol abuse. Today I feel sad/happy/excited/ashamed.

As the days and weeks went by, and people were given extra diagnoses by the psychiatrists, their lists grew longer. Some were adding seven or eight issues after their name, as though we were in a kind of psychiatric pissing contest. I could have added complex PTSD, perfectionism, work addiction and unrelenting standards schema – all diagnoses I had been labelled with throughout this medical pilgrimage. But I kept it simple – my three were hard enough to come to terms with. Depression. Anxiety. Alcohol abuse.

The days were full, starting early and not finishing until late in the evening. We attended lectures and workshops, group therapy sessions and twelve-step meetings according to our issues. Some of us went to Alcoholics Anonymous. Some went to Narcotics Anonymous. Some went to Gamblers Anonymous and others to Sex Addicts Anonymous. There were a couple of other meetings as well – I can't remember them all. They were held via Zoom, mostly, with a limited number of people in the room. We were still in the pandemic.

It was via these Zoom meetings that I found a group which met online at 7 a.m. every day. After I left the hospital they became a very important community for me for a while.

Twice a day there was a walk to the nearby beach. Because of COVID, the walking group could only be small. I got out on the walks as often as I could – the beach is my spiritual home. The ocean is the most calming thing in the whole world to me. Unfortunately we weren't allowed to get more than our feet wet; and after sitting on the same rock morning and afternoon for two weeks, I was told that I was not allowed to sit down either. Because of the no-exercise rule, nobody was allowed to run on the beach, just walk up and down. This wasn't problematic for me, I'm not built for running. But I have to say, being told I was not allowed to was the biggest motivator to run I have ever experienced. Occasionally I would do some sit-ups in my room, just to break the no-exercise rule, because I thought it was dumb. I had so many plans for when I got out of there and was allowed to swim and go for unsupervised walks and pat my dogs and do the things I loved again.

Group therapy was extremely intense. It was different from the previous hospital. We were in the same group for our entire stay, for a start. The group changed as some people finished their program and new people arrived, but it was mostly static. We got to know each other well, as you do in those kind of settings. We had to write out our life from birth to twenty years of age, highlighting any traumas, and share the whole thing. This was, as you can imagine, incredibly difficult. Some people handled it better than others; it required a level of trust and vulnerability that is hard to achieve in a room full of relative strangers. But the walls did eventually break down, due simply to the fact that we recognised we were all there as flawed human beings who were not at their best point in life.

I learned something interesting about all of those people, and came to a realisation: not one of us had a past that was free of trauma.

It's like that old saying – not all dogs are German Shepherds, but all German Shepherds are dogs. Not everyone who has experienced trauma ends up as an addict, but all addicts have trauma.

I know this to be true. Something causes addiction, and it's not just lack of character or inherent weakness. Addiction happens because there's a disconnect between who we want to be and how we behave. And, put very simply, that disconnect, that disintegration, comes from experiencing trauma.

Nobody wants it. Nobody becomes addicted to drugs or alcohol or sex or work or overeating or gambling, or any of the thousands of other things you can become addicted to, because they think it makes their life better. Nobody wakes up in the morning thinking, 'Today I want to disappoint my family, infuriate my partner, annoy my co-workers and not turn up for my friends.' Nobody starts their day deciding to let people down, piss people off, do a second-rate job, spend money they don't have. But so many of us go to bed having done just that.

Finding out why, and healing that why, is the answer; it's the answer I didn't even know I was seeking and I didn't come across it for a long time. I didn't find it in this rehab, although I did gain some useful tools and knowledge there. And even more importantly I gained some friends, fellow travellers who understood at a cellular level what it meant to feels this shame and hopelessness and grief. People who I am still in contact with today, many of whom agree that the experience inside this hospital was itself traumatic. Others who swear by it and say that it saved their lives. Horses for courses, as they say. There's no one-size-fits-all solution to mental health or addiction problems, and it takes trial and error to find out what works for you.

In the third week of my stay in the rehab, I was selected, along with five others, to take part in a more intensive program. We spent an entire week together, in a small room, and went very deeply into our oldest traumas. We were not required to attend any lectures, meetings or groups during this time, and we sat separately from the other patients at mealtimes. The facilitator took each of us through a process of semi-hypnotism, to the place and time of our worst childhood memories, and made us verbalise them. And speak to the people who had perpetrated them. And speak to the people who should have protected us. It was fucking brutal. Doing it was brutal. Witnessing it while the others did it was brutal.

After completing the three-week program in the hospital, I went to a sort of halfway house next door for two weeks to learn how to assimilate back into my normal life. In this house, we were allowed our phones in common areas, and we could go out on walks by ourselves.

I was due to arrive home on Christmas Eve 2020. Mick and the boys were going to take care of cooking the Christmas Eve dinner, and I had talked them through each step of doing so. I used some of my downtime to do online Christmas shopping so that Mick wouldn't have to deal with that all by himself, on top of everything else.

Just days before I was due to be discharged, there was a COVID outbreak on the Northern Beaches. Restrictions were immediately reintroduced. Police were stationed at the Spit Bridge to stop anyone other than residents from entering the area. I was terrified I would be unable to get home, and terrified that if anyone from my family was to come and pick me up they would be in trouble from the police. So I checked out a couple of days early and hired an Uber to take me home. I didn't tell anyone I was coming. Mick's face when I walked through the door, the hug I had been yearning for, was the only Christmas present I needed.

I am not sorry that I attended this rehab. I consider it a part of the path I had to walk down to get where I am now. But I will say this: when I stood on the footpath outside the halfway house, waiting for the Uber to take me home, I felt naked. Not just naked, flayed. Like I had been skinned, scrubbed raw, and thrust out into the bright sunlight, body and soul exposed. It would take a long time for that feeling to subside.

Chicken, cheese and mushroom strudel

A hearty, warming retro dish, this chicken strudel is a crowd-pleaser.

Prep time: 15 minutes
Cooking time: about 40 minutes
Serves 6 as a main meal

1 tablespoon olive oil
800 g chicken thigh fillet, cut into 3 cm cubes
200 g button mushrooms, sliced
3 cloves garlic
2 tablespoons plain flour
1¼ cups milk
1 tablespoon Dijon or French mustard
½ teaspoon sea salt
¼ teaspoon ground white pepper
1 cup tasty cheese
4 shallots, finely sliced
2 sheets frozen puff pastry
1 egg, beaten

Preheat oven to 200°C.

Heat 1 teaspoon of the oil in a large, heavy-based fry pan and brown half the chicken. Remove to a bowl and repeat with another teaspoon of oil and the remaining chicken. (At this stage the meat only needs to have some golden colour, not be cooked all the way through.)

Heat the remaining oil in the pan and sauté the mushrooms and garlic until the garlic is fragrant and translucent, and the mushrooms have gone a light golden colour. (They will release liquid as they cook; continue to cook until this liquid evaporates.)

Return the chicken to the pan and sprinkle flour over the top. Stir to coat the chicken. Add the milk a quarter of a cup at a time, allowing the sauce to cook and thicken in between each addition. When all the milk is added, bring the sauce to a simmer and add the mustard, salt, pepper and ⅔ of the cheese. Simmer for a few minutes or until the chicken is cooked through. Remove to a bowl and allow to cool.

Place two sheets of puff pastry on a sheet of baking paper on a large cutting board. Brush 1 cm of the edge of one sheet with a little egg, and overlap the other sheet over it. Press to join the sheets together into a large rectangle. Turn the rectangle so it is vertical on the bench. Using the back of a butter knife or a skewer, make faint lines on the pastry dividing it into equal thirds. Cut off the top two corners to form a point. At the base, cut a square out of the left and right thirds of the pastry. It should now resemble the shape of a big straight Christmas tree.

Make incisions about 1.5 cm apart, following the line of the upper point of the pastry, starting at the middle third line and going to the edge. Once cut, lift the baking paper onto a large baking tray.

Place the cooled chicken mixture along the middle third of the pastry, stopping short of the pointy and square-cut end. Sprinkle with the sliced shallots and the remaining cheese.

Fold the pointy end over the chicken mixture and, alternating from left to right, fold the strips of pastry over the chicken mixture. It will look a bit like a braid. Fold the square end of the pastry over.

Brush liberally with egg and bake for 20 to 25 minutes, or until a deep golden brown. Lovely served hot or at room temperature.

CHAPTER 18

MAD WORLD

Our 2021 began with so much promise. Mick and I were days away from becoming grandparents, and we had planned a trip to the Red Centre in just a few months. Chef Renee was still managing the cooking school and she had taken care of the whole Christmas period, our busiest time. I was looking forward, albeit with some trepidation, to getting back to work and easing some of her load.

After I got home I contacted the psychologist I had been seeing weekly since the beginning of 2020, having paused our appointments to go to the rehab in Sydney. I'm not sure if there was bad blood because I had sought a different treatment, or if the shortage of psychologists was just that severe, but I was told I couldn't have an appointment until May.

I couldn't wait five months – regular counselling was a strongly recommended part of recovery and I needed all the help I could get. I looked up the list of psychologists in my area and saw a name there that was immediately familiar: Heather Irvine. She had been the one who'd come onto Rabs' and my bullying segment on the breakfast show. The one whose uncle had helped Joe all those years ago.

I contacted her office and was able to get an appointment. And so we embarked on a course that would, with time and work and tears and laughter, finally start to draw me back into the light. But that happened a little bit later on.

In setting myself up to carry out all the recommendations that would make me well, I started ocean swimming. I'd always loved the thought of it but been too nervous to try it by myself. One night on the local news I saw an old mate, the former mayor of Gosford and a past coach of the Central Coast Mariners, with a ragtag bunch of middle-aged blokes, doing an ocean swim. They called themselves the Scozzies – Scots and Aussies – and were swimming every day at Terrigal Beach. The swims began when a couple of them had decided to get out of their own blue funk by starting the day with a swim and a coffee at the Surf Café, and had grown from there.

I texted Lawrie. 'How far is it out to that buoy you guys swim to?'

'Come down at 6 tomorrow and find out for yourself' was the answer.

I did, and I found something I loved even more than pool swimming. Most days I only made it a few hundred metres; not as far as I went in the pool but it's a little bit harder in the sea. Especially if it's a choppy day. I made it part of my routine and, back then, I went four or five times a week.

Another thing I was doing was attending daily AA meetings online. It was a firm recommendation at the rehab that we complete ninety meetings in ninety days, starting from when we were in the hospital. I ended up doing 150 meetings in 150 days, or very close to it – the only ones I missed were during a television filming commitment, and a couple of times while I was out of range on a road trip.

The online breakfast meeting was a completely different experience to the first time I had been to AA. There were a lot more women, for a start. In fact, being online meant I could have joined a group for only women, if I'd wanted. Or a group in the US or Ireland. Or any number of different iterations of the old traditional meeting. We still all had one thing in common, though: a wish to stop drinking.

The 7 a.m. group suited me very nicely. It fitted in after my morning swim, and was done in time for me to have the day clear ahead. I really liked the group; it was supportive and welcoming. It was forgiving, on those occasions when any one of us stumbled and had to reset our day-count to zero. It was people just sharing their experiences; not trying for shock value to relate how dreadful things had got for them; just a frank and honest discussion about the reasons they didn't want to drink anymore, and the benefits they each saw in their lives from being sober.

Once again I was in the privileged position of hearing other peoples' stories, and these stories were real and raw. They were relatable, cautionary tales, heartbreaking, hopeful and honest.

On 16 January 2021 our granddaughter, Delilah Marlene, was born. The whole time we knew she was on the way, I was a bundle of nervous energy. I prayed as hard as I ever had in my life. *Please let everything go well. Please let them be all right. Please let them be safe. Please let us in to see them.*

Because of the stinking pandemic, we weren't allowed to be at the hospital. We had to wait, with bated breath and crossed fingers and toes, until we were called in. Finally, we were told we could visit Tom and Crystal's freshly formed little family in a lounge area outside the maternity ward. Mick and I got the chance, for just a few minutes, to hold this astonishingly small scrap of a person;

a wrapped bundle of perfectly formed, brand new humanity; this tiny little girl.

To say she stole our hearts doesn't adequately describe it, and it sounds clichéd. But she did. We were both instantly lost, drowned in love of a new kind. And somehow, at the same time, elevated. This new status – grandparenthood – the gut-level understanding of the importance of it, of the role we would play in her life, hit like a thunderclap.

I remember when I first became a mother suddenly having a deeper understanding of my own mother and how much she loved me. And now, holding my grandchild, all at once I truly understood how much my nan had loved me too. I missed her in that moment, profoundly, yet somehow felt her there as well. And I understood, also, how much I would come to mean to this precious girl – if I was around. If I stayed. If I was an involved presence in her life. Suddenly, nothing in the whole world seemed more important.

I wish with all my heart that I could write, here on this page, in this moment '. . . and they all lived happily ever after'. Because that would make for a tidy story arc, wouldn't it? It would be a nice place to finish, comforting and warm; everything turns out all right. But once again, this isn't a fairytale; or if it is, there are a few more brambly forests and wicked wolves to conquer before we ride off into the sunset. Don't be disheartened, though. There is a sunset and we do ride off into it, kind of. So please bear with me a little longer, and weather a couple more storms with me first.

At the end of February, I went away for two weeks to film a television program for SBS called *Could You Survive on the Breadline?* I stayed in emergency accommodation and over the two weeks, I visited and stayed with various families living on different kinds of welfare. I was given the equivalent of the JobSeeker payment to live on, around $42 per day. But that was really the smaller part of the program. The most important part was meeting many different people and hearing their stories; learning about how they made their meagre government payments stretch to cover their household expenses, food, bills, clothing, schooling, and on and on and on.

I met one woman who had a café but she'd had to close it down. She reminded me of me. Her business dreams were so similar to mine, and her story broke my heart.

One of the families I visited didn't end up in the final cut for the show and I was so disappointed. This amazing young woman, a single mum of an eight-year-old girl with autism, was doing everything in her power to keep her household running. Her budget was watertight; shopping with her was like a military operation. She was studying to become a pastry chef. Every single dollar was accounted for, which was great while things were running smoothly. But things don't always run smoothly. She was delaying medical appointments, mechanical appointments and juggling the bills. Some weeks she had to choose between buying toothpaste or dishwashing liquid.

I was only a few weeks out of hospital when I went away for this show. I'm not sure it was a smart idea. But once again I was doing that 'comparing down' thing. I was asked to help shine a light on the circumstances of people who were really struggling. Not dole-bludgers, not people gaming the system, not people 'blowing it all on cigarettes and booze', but people genuinely trying to make their lives work at a basic, hierarchy-of-needs level: food, shelter, safety. I had no right, no right whatsoever, to complain that I was feeling low or might be unable to handle the assignment. There were days when I felt so defeated by it all, and days when I missed my family desperately. I saw out the two weeks and was guilt-ridden but relieved to return home.

When the show went to air, there was a small but noisy cabal of people baying for blood. They didn't like the premise of the program: they called it 'poverty porn', a term that I found deeply offensive. Never once in my whole life have I sought to belittle disadvantaged people. And I never once even remotely suggested that two weeks of living in emergency accommodation with a $42 a day budget was the same as living in those circumstances long term. Quite the contrary – I frequently voiced my understanding that it was nothing like real life.

These commentators did not seem to understand that, whether they liked the way the show was presented or not, it was doing exactly what it had set out to do: it was generating conversation. People who had not previously appreciated how dire the situation is for those trying to survive on government assistance were actually taking notice. Like it or hate it, we were talking about poverty in Australia. And isn't that the point of this kind of TV? To shine a light, spark a conversation, in the hope of effecting change? That's why I agreed to be a part of the program.

I was still learning, though, slow learner that I am in these affairs, how frustrating and hurtful online commentary can be. Especially when you're banned by your family from feeding the trolls.

In April Mick and I set off on a two-month road trip. We'd planned it after our big trip in 2020 was cancelled, wanting something to look forward to.

We headed south first, to pick up Poppy Roy's caravan from Mum and Dad on the south coast. That expertly crafted, lovingly maintained caravan had never been out of registration, having been used regularly for all of its life. First with Nan and Poppy Roy and their kids, then with Mum and Dad and us kids, and now Mick and I were taking her for a whirl.

Dad gave Mick a crash course in towing and we were off. We headed up through country New South Wales, then across to the Queensland coast and up again to Far North Queensland. There, we turned west, through Mount Isa to Alice Springs and north to Darwin.

All the way we stayed in campgrounds and caravan parks. One night we stayed at a site on the banks of the Mary River. We lit a campfire and I cooked a chicken biryani in my big cast iron skillet. Mick played his twelve-string guitar in the firelight. It was such a beautiful, clear night that we decided to bring our blankets outside and sleep under the stars. About ten minutes after we made that decision, the stars began to disappear behind a thick layer of cloud. Next minute it was pelting with rain and we were scrambling to get ourselves and all our stuff into the van and out of the deluge.

There were certainly times on the trip when I felt a bit wistful for a glass of wine; it was how we travelled, usually. How a lot of people travel, especially the grey nomads in the caravan parks. Late afternoon out comes the cheese and the beverages. But the wistfulness actually didn't last too long; all I had to do was follow that line of thought to its logical conclusion. It wasn't going to be good for me. I drank many, many cups of tea. We played a lot of cards, too, and I feel as though this account of my life would be incomplete if I did not mention that I gave Mick an absolute hiding in euchre that trip.

I was still attending the online AA breakfast meeting each day. We were usually up, packed and ready to roll by 7. I'd join the meeting until 8 while Mick went for a walk or pottered around, then we'd hit the road. I only missed a couple of days during the trip, when we were so far out in the wilderness we had no phone reception at all.

MAD WORLD

The Northern Territory is absolutely magical. There is something about the light there – it's golden, it makes everything gleam. There's a feeling that's somehow ancient, spiritual. The landscape is wide and open, the towns tiny and hundreds of kilometres apart. Darwin, sweltering and humid, with so much history, has a unique personality among Australian capital cities. The Mindil Beach Sunset Market is magical – all the food hawkers, musicians, flame throwers and performers. And the best show of all: the sun setting over the ocean as hundreds of people gather on the beach to watch.

We headed back south, towards the red heart of the country. We were missing the family so much, but especially that new little baby of ours. We had arranged for the boys to fly out, with their partners and of course Delilah, and meet us at Uluru. Mick and I had always planned to take the boys around Australia, the way my parents had done with me. But starting up your own business pretty much puts an end to those plans. When a business is young it can't survive any neglect. It becomes its own kind of child, needing more attention than you ever thought possible. So we were keen to show them what we could now that we had the opportunity.

On our way down to the rock to meet the boys, about a week before they were due to fly over, we had a bit of a disaster: our car, a Chrysler van, died. The transmission had decided it was retiring. We were in a place called Renner Springs at the time, which is essentially a truck stop with a few power poles for camping. We needed to get a towie from Tennant Creek, who had to tow the car as well as the caravan back to town. We rode with him in the cab of the truck.

In Tennant Creek, mechanics tried to fix the car, but basically if you have anything other than a Toyota in the centre of Australia, you're out of luck. I was starting to freak out that we weren't going to get to Uluru to meet the boys. I was ready to start walking if I needed to.

Eventually we found a hire car and we got there in time to spend five magical days together. I couldn't let go of Delilah; I couldn't stop kissing her teeny four-month-old face. As a family we toured Kata Tjuta; we watched the sun rise over Uluru one day and set over it another; we took a chopper flight over the rock as well, with Delilah in enormous noise-cancelling headphones sleeping peacefully through the whole thing.

We were lucky to be there at the end of one of the most abundant wet seasons the region had seen in years, and the desert was flourishing. The water was flowing, not only here at Uluru but also up in Katherine, Kakadu and all through the gorges of the West MacDonnell Ranges, Tjoritja. It was glorious; it looked so different to the dry Red Centre I remembered from when I was eleven. The boys loved it; we all did. It was definitely a trip for the family memory album. We are so very fortunate.

After we said farewell to the family, Mick and I took a bus back to Tennant Creek. The car and caravan were sitting in a depot waiting to be towed to Adelaide, the nearest place that could deal with a Chrysler transmission. From there we got onto another bus, an overnighter to Adelaide. We missed a few stops on our trip because of this development, but there were few other options open to us. And, hey, it's all part of the adventure, right?

We got the caravan towed to a campground and stayed there, waiting for the car to be fixed. After a week, the mechanic told us that he would need to get a part from overseas. Estimated arrival time, ten weeks. So, with weary resignation, we booked the car onto its third big towing adventure, back to Gosford. We could have flown around the world on the money this was all costing,

MAD WORLD

if we'd been allowed overseas. I was grateful that we could access what we needed to get the car home at all.

Mum and Dad had to come to Adelaide to rescue us, and their caravan, and bring us home. It was not quite the ending of the trip we had envisioned, but it didn't take away from all the magic that we saw and experienced in those two months. It was, in fact, a lot of fun.

Going down an opal mine in Lightning Ridge; watching the sun set over Rockhampton Downs; swimming in Bitter Springs and cruising through the wetlands in Kakadu; dawn over the West MacDonnell Ranges: these were just a few of the many highlights of this incredible journey. Best of all, I was with my favourite human being, and I even got to see my other favourite human beings along the way.

Back home we were straight into the thick of it. Mick had been sorely missed at work. It was a long time for the owner to be away and his team were glad to have him back. I returned to the kitchen. The restrictions had eased, and we could run cooking classes again.

The timing of our trip was fortuitous: less than three weeks after we got home another lockdown was declared, on 9 July. It came with almost no notice. I was teaching a Lebanese Feast class. We had sat down at the table to eat when the news came through at about 2 p.m. Janny had seen it on her phone. Lockdown was to begin at 5 p.m. I was the one to tell the attendees of the class. There was disappointment around the table that weekend plans would need to be cancelled; there was devastation for one group who realised an upcoming wedding was now in question.

This 2021 lockdown was only meant to last two weeks, but as the health advice changed it was extended further and further out.

In the end, it lasted 107 days. Once 70 per cent of the population had received the vaccine, 'freedom day' was declared, in October. Vaccines were hard to come by for a long while. There was any number of dramas about who ordered what when, and who was going to be vaccinated as a priority, and which vaccine was best for which age group. I believe most Australians, whatever their views, acted in good faith during that time. But it was hard to keep up with all the advice and what was going on; there was simultaneously too much and too little information, depending which way your face was pointed on any given day. We did our best. Most of us did our best.

At the kitchen we postponed class after class. Eventually we had to cancel and refund tickets – we couldn't keep postponing indefinitely and there was no knowing when we'd be open again. These were refunds we could scarcely afford. Like any other small hospitality business, we were not thriving during all this upheaval and uncertainty. It was disheartening, to say the very least.

A couple of weeks into lockdown, my brain took me further off the rails than I had ever been. This time it wasn't a slow descent, it was instant. And I didn't see it coming; I'd thought I was doing pretty well. I wish I could explain it, but I can't.

Mick came home one day and knew he needed to take me to the hospital again. This time, I was put straight into the mental health unit of a public hospital in the middle of the night, and held under the *Mental Health Act*. Involuntarily.

It's so tempting to leave this out; it would be much easier to skip over it as a repetitious, almost boring part of the story. For the love of god, what now, I can almost hear you say. But I have to include this part, just as I did all the other parts. Without it, it might seem that recovery from a mental illness is a straight line from unwell to well, as long as you do all the things you're supposed to. And that just isn't necessarily true. I *was* doing all the things. *All* of them. I wasn't drinking, I was attending AA daily. I was exercising. We had just returned from weeks in nature and time-out from work. I was taking medication, doing meditation, getting therapy. And to top it all off, I had a granddaughter – a child who filled my heart so full I thought it would burst. It still seems inconceivable to me that I could have been hit by this bus once again, with all the good things that were happening in my life.

But – and it still hurts me to remember it and say it – the decline was real. And recovery is not a straight line. It's a cliff with a trampoline at the bottom. It's cruel and fickle. It takes concentrated effort and even when you can manage a concentrated effort, sometimes it still doesn't work. You keep falling off that cliff and, if you're lucky, you keep hitting the trampoline. Not everyone is lucky.

With all respect and compassion to the staff who work in mental health wards in public hospitals and do their best, I have to say this: the ward I found myself on was bloody dire. How anyone was meant to get well there was beyond me. The food alone – oh my god. It was inedible slime that differed from day to day only in shades of brown. Most days it had been sitting in its plastic bowl for so long that the gravy had welded to the plastic. I didn't see a fresh vegetable in there, not once. Mick started dropping off salads to be delivered to me for lunch – I wasn't allowed to see him but he could deliver them to the front desk. I lived on those and chocolate bars out of the vending machine. They were brown too, but at least I could chew them. This isn't hyperbole. I took photos.

The food was one thing, the mood was another. It was . . . depressing, is what it was. There wasn't a sense of hope, of advancement or healing. Not in my view, anyway.

After three days of being held involuntarily, I asked to be released so I could go home. Three days, I'd been told, is how long they could hold me against my will, and those three days were up. I was, however, informed that my case had been reassessed and instead of being considered a mentally disordered person, I was now considered a mentally ill person. It is, I think, mainly a legal distinction. It meant I could be kept indefinitely, until I was reviewed by the Mental Health Review Tribunal. A panel would then decide the best course of action for me. I was stunned by this. I was frightened. Mick was shocked too: what had seemed like the right thing to do a few days before, now meant that my welfare was out of our hands and in those of 'the system', subject to the judgement of strangers.

I was told that if I found a place in a private mental health unit, I could go there. But I would not be released to go home. Mick kicked into action, making phone calls and trying to get me in anywhere, anywhere at all but there. He got me onto a waiting list at another local private hospital, a different one to the one I'd been in the year before.

One morning at breakfast, I was sitting near a woman who was asking the nurse to please be allowed to go home. She must not have had the option of going to a private hospital. The response was that she would have to wait and see what happened at the tribunal. The woman wept helplessly. I wanted to cry too. I was, once again, so grateful to have private health care, and at the same time keenly aware of the inequity here. This other woman would have to take her chances in the public system. I hope with all my heart she got the outcome she wanted.

There, and there, and there but for the grace of god go I.

After eight days on the public mental health ward, I was released to the care of a private hospital for a three-week stay.

It was determined very quickly once I got there that my medication was no longer effective and that I'd need a long time to wean off it; it was, they told me, the 'worst one to come off'.

Three weeks in relative comfort in terms of the accommodation and the meals; three weeks of head spins and nausea as I was taken off one medicine and put on to another. Three weeks of dialectic behavioural therapy, and more cognitive behavioural therapy, and aquatherapy, and occupational therapy. Three more weeks of Renee running my business without me, cooking meals for people to pick up in this latest lockdown, keeping the team in action. It seemed that there was no end to the pain and inconvenience I could visit on the people who loved me.

When I got out this time, there had been a rather beautiful change at home. Tom and Crystal had decided to give up their townhouse and move in with us so we could all be together during lockdown. I had been so worried about not seeing the baby; FaceTime is fantastic but real-life cuddles are so much better. I couldn't have been more thrilled with this news. My whole family, with its incredible new addition, under the one roof. I didn't take this for granted. I knew that it would probably be the last time we would all live in the same house, these boys of mine, my trinity of sons. I marvelled anew at how different and alike they are, the contradictions and similarities in them.

One has a degree. One is sporty. One is artistic, but will never tell you so. One is political. One is competitive. One is in a job that he is too gentle for. One works outdoors, one works indoors, one alternates. One plays video games. One plays AFL. One plays with his daughter.

Two are very tall. Two are tattooed. Two are in long-term relationships. Two still live at home. Two work night shift. Two have dark brown eyes like their father. Two eat mashed potato.

Three are intelligent. Three are funny, and kind. Three can cook. Three know what consent means. Three like to hang out together. Three grew in my belly. Three are the most important thing I'll ever do, the loves of my life, my very heart.

YOUR TIME STARTS NOW

I held on to this time together, this unexpected silver lining in a dark time, like Rose to that door in *Titanic*. But unlike poor Rose, my door had enough room for us all.

I started to see Heather more frequently. This last episode had terrified me with its stealth and swiftness, so I was frightened that it might happen again, but hopeful that with my new medication and more regular therapy from someone I trusted and was bonding with, I might just be coming out of the woods. Now, surrounded by family and with everything in place, I thought that maybe I could really begin to heal.

Three weeks after I got out of hospital, I received a phone call that would change my life all over again.

Chicken biryani

I love to eat well, even when we're camping. I always have my huge cast-iron pan to use on the fire, and I carry a box with all my most frequently used dried herbs and spices. Although not traditional, this biryani is ideal for a night by the campfire.

Prep time: 20 minutes
Cooking time: 45 minutes
Serves 4

½ cup slivered almonds
800 g chicken thigh fillet, cut up into small (3 cm) pieces
2 tablespoons olive oil
2 brown onions, diced
2 cloves garlic, diced
2 teaspoons garam masala

MAD WORLD

2 teaspoons ground turmeric
1 cup basmati rice
6 small curry leaves
1 x 400 g tin tomatoes
2 cups chicken stock
¼ cup coriander leaves

Heat a large cast-iron pan over medium-high heat and add the almonds. Toast until they are a light golden brown and remove from the pan.

Add 1 tablespoon of oil to the hot pan. Sauté the chicken until golden and remove to a bowl.

Reduce the heat to medium and add the second tablespoon of oil to the pan. Sauté the onions and garlic for 1 to 2 minutes until soft and fragrant. Add the garam masala, turmeric and uncooked rice and stir for a further minute.

Add the curry leaves, tomatoes and stock. Increase the heat to high and bring to the boil. Reduce the heat to medium-low and place a lid, a timber breadboard or a piece of aluminium foil on top.

Cook, covered and stirring occasionally, for at least 5 minutes or until all the liquid has absorbed and the rice is al dente. You may need to stir constantly in the last few minutes as the biryani dries out.

The dish is ready when it is quite dry. Serve scattered with the almonds and coriander leaves.

CHAPTER 19
ALL YOU NEED IS LOVE

The phone call came while I was still raw and reeling from the last stay in hospital. Most of my time was being spent on the rounds of things I had to do to keep my brain on track. My routine was three swims and three gym sessions per week, plus some time for art, therapy, and lots and lots of time for family and baby Delilah. We were still in lockdown, and I was comforted and grateful that we were all under one roof.

The best part of my day was after dinner. It was Delilah and Julie time; I'd take her out to the backyard while the others washed up. I'd walk her around, singing to her and winding her down for bedtime. I sang Mama Cass, and Billie Holiday, and Ella Fitzgerald into her small, perfect ear. She knew and loved this routine; sometimes she'd sing along with me, making toneless, breathy noises as her little arms and legs relaxed, her grip on me loosened and she grew heavy in my arms.

I had stopped going to AA. This was not a decision I took lightly, and there will be many members of AA who read this and shake their heads sadly, certain that it means I am on the way to a relapse. I had my own concerns that in ceasing the meetings, a part of me was trying to pave the way to take up drinking again. But I had a feeling in my gut that I had given what I had to give, and taken what I had to take, from this stage in my quest for recovery.

I will always owe a debt of gratitude to the people who I met at both the online and face-to-face meetings. These are people who not only openly tell their stories, but share themselves at their most vulnerable, or most destructive, or most despairing. They share themselves rising out of agony and finding meaning and happiness again. They offer not only the worst that they've done but the best as well, their strongest and proudest moments. They offer hope. It is an incredibly brave thing to do. It is generous and cathartic and at times almost impossibly hard.

Listening is a privilege, and a lesson in compassion. All German Shepherds are dogs; all addicts have trauma.

After daily meetings for five months, I decided that I no longer needed to begin every day focused on alcohol. I didn't want to say 'I am an alcoholic' every morning. I didn't want to count days either, although I know that for many people those milestones are so important and bring a justifiable sense of pride.

I have broken the habit of drinking, and I am no longer white-knuckling it one day at a time. I just don't drink. I don't know exactly how many days it's been, but it's more than three years since I stopped. And my god is my life better for it. I'm not puritanical, I don't preach, I don't tell anyone else what to do. When I am out for dinner I don't announce that I don't drink. I just don't drink. Every now and then, the thought creeps in – at a wedding, or a special event – that it would be nice to join in with a celebratory beverage. But the truth is, it wouldn't be nice. I know that it would open a door that took a really long time, and a lot of heartache, to close.

I once heard a guy tell a story at an AA meeting: 'I have a friend who asks if I ever miss a nice glass of red wine with a steak,' he said. 'And I tell him, a glass of red wine with a steak will see me in six months dragging myself in from the wilderness, looking like roadkill, and having to start all over again.'

This is what I think of when I have a niggling idea that a drink might be nice, the way other people have one. I'm not other people; I can't have one. I don't want to go back into the wilderness. I don't need to: as a result of therapy, the parts of me that needed to be numb don't need to be numb anymore.

'Julie? It's Marty Benson here, director of content at Endemol-Shine. We're doing a *MasterChef* "Fans and Favourites" series of the show next year, and we'd like you to be part of it.'

I am sure there was more preamble to the call than this, but that's how I remember it – kind of like a bucket of cold water to the face.

I was very blunt, very clear: 'I have been unwell and I think this would be a bad idea.'

'Don't answer me now,' Marty said. 'I'll call you back tomorrow and answer any questions you have. Have a think, have a chat to your family, and we'll talk tomorrow.'

Tomorrow! Ha. What difference would a day make? I was still only just beginning to build up the ability to cook again, to work and be independent.

Coming out of my last stint in hospital, I had lost the confidence to go into the kitchen by myself; in fact, I was afraid to be by myself at all. At some point, surely, life would return to normal and I could be a functioning human being again, but it was taking time. Mick was accompanying me into the kitchen for a couple of hours on the weekend then taking me home again. COVID rules meant we were still unable to run classes.

By the time I got the phone call from Marty I had worked up to about half a day a week in the kitchen, but not yet on my own. It had become a daunting place, representative of the struggle to keep my head above water, to perform, to achieve more in a day than a day would allow. The idea of going back to the *MasterChef* kitchen was ridiculous. Impossible. Unthinkable . . . a little bit intriguing . . . a little bit . . .

What *was* that feeling? That little bubble in my gut? Could it be . . . *excitement*?

I realised with surprise that I was excited. I spoke to Mick. And he, once again, put his faith in me to make a good decision. God knows why. I felt myself leaning towards a yes. I spoke to the boys. They were behind me. I spoke to Heather. She looked a little shocked. She told me it was like I had said I wanted to run a marathon with two broken legs, but that she too would be behind me all the way.

They all presented me with one condition: if I were to accept the offer, I had to be allowed to do everything I needed to do to stay well.

When Marty called me back the next day, I found it very easy to tell him what I needed; it was pretty straightforward. I said I understood that a big production like *MasterChef* couldn't shape itself around the needs of one contestant. At the same time, I couldn't put myself into a high-stress situation, away from my family, without safeguards in place. I couldn't risk ending up back where I'd been; I couldn't do it to my family.

It's interesting, from the perspective of a person who has always struggled to lay down boundaries, how easy it was for me to lay them down now. It was simple. If these things can't happen, then this scenario cannot take place.

I told Marty what I needed to be well: eight hours of sleep per night, the ability to get to a pool to swim, access to my family via technology, access to Heather for regular appointments.

As I'd heard from more recent contestants, the production had changed a lot over the years. For one thing, it was now filmed in Melbourne. COVID meant that we no longer shared one big house, but had apartments. Some of the contestants would share with someone else, some would have their own space. Filming was mainly within business hours. There would be exceptions to this, but Marty reassured me that most nights I'd be able to get the sleep I needed. Contestants were now allowed to have technology with them – phones, computers, everything. Not inside the studio, of course, but at all other times.

I would be allowed to drive my car to Melbourne so that some days before filming I could get up and go swimming. I would have time allotted to talk to Heather regularly. Weekends would, for the most part, be our own. There was a psychologist available to us at all times in Melbourne.

Twenty-four of us were to be brought into the kitchen: twelve of us previous contestants and twelve newcomers. The details were cloaked in secrecy for now, with more information to come.

We would be facing the new judges – new to me, anyway, as they had already filmed two seasons and had embedded themselves with the Australian viewing public. Andy Allen, Melissa Leong and Jock Zonfrillo had replaced the widely loved Gary, Matt and George. I had watched with interest, wondering if the show would survive the exit of this beloved trio. In a stroke of what I considered to be genius, for the first season with Andy, Mel and Jock, the theme was 'Back to Win' – favourite personalities from past seasons returned to the kitchen for a second chance at winning the title. In the absence of familiar judges, we were gifted familiar contestants.

With my decision made at the end of August, I would be leaving home to start filming at the end of November. For the next three months, I prepared myself to go back to *MasterChef*. Gradually, my kitchen became a safe space for me again. My obsession with food, dormant for a couple of years by now, uncoiled in my gut and reclaimed its place. I studied, and practised; I researched and memorised recipes, and ate, and cooked. I cooked and cooked and cooked, just like I did back when my house was new and *MasterChef* Australia was not yet born.

I thought I had lost it, my passion. I thought that in the wash-up of all the things that had happened, I'd let go of food, of cooking – those parts of my life that had brought me joy and purpose. Even before Marty's call, I had been tentatively looking for them again. I would need that passion in order to go back to my cooking school when the world was normal. I would need to have found the arcing creative spark, the fizzing connection, the uplift and wonder that cooking had always brought. I didn't know if I would.

But as the weeks went by, I became more and more excited about cooking, and to go to Melbourne, back into that arena, where my career in food began. Back to *MasterChef*.

In November I packed my little Mini to the roof. I held my beautiful ten-month-old granddaughter and wept, and I left for Melbourne.

I had packed my clothes and all my favourite cooking kit, including my beautiful pink stand mixer and a massive stack of cookbooks.

I'd also packed my art stuff. During some of my stays in hospital I had been encouraged back to activities I had loved doing when

I was a kid – before the adult world crashed in and took over. I'd always loved to draw. I'd tried to make time for it over the years, but never managed. I had so many blank notebooks and watercolour sketchpads and beautiful pens and pencils and paints given to me as gifts or that I had bought for myself. But I was too busy – and too afraid – to use them.

I now know that the fear of messing up a pristine piece of paper, or starting a fresh sketchbook only to spoil it with something sub par, was part of the psychology that needed untangling in my head. It's called a schema of unrelenting standards, or more broadly and commonly, perfectionism.

Perfectionism doesn't mean that you are perfect. Hell, no! Put simply, it's the fear of doing anything imperfectly. This leads to two extremes. One is that you work and strive and yearn for perfection, and always feel like a failure because perfection isn't actually achievable. Perfectionism is what drove me relentlessly in my parenting, my personal life, my career. The other extreme is that you are so immobilised by fear of making a mistake, of doing something imperfectly, that you do not start at all. And that was what stopped me from making art.

Just knowing you have this trait, this overarching theme or schema, doesn't mean you know what to do about it or how to relieve yourself of it. You can know in your bones that your behaviour isn't just striving, it's driving you into the ground, and still not know how to stop it. That understanding would come later for me, in therapy. In the meantime I just wanted to find a way back to art.

I eventually found a solution. I cut up pieces of watercolour paper into tiny squares, 7x7 centimetres, and used them for drawing and painting. I called it tiny art. If I messed up something that small, it didn't matter, I could just move on to the next little square. After many months and hundreds of pieces of tiny art, I was able to move on to slightly bigger projects.

Another thing I had been doing as therapy was making jewellery from polymer clay. This was pure fun, a return to early childhood. It was like mucking around with playdough, except when you're done you can turn the results into useful things like food-themed earrings and necklaces. By the time I headed to Melbourne I had quite a collection of food jewellery, and I took my polymer clay supplies with me so I could keep making things if there was some downtime to fill.

My apartment had everything I needed, including a little kitchen, a bathtub, and a balcony with views over Albert Park Golf Course. I set everything up so it felt as close to home as possible, and spent the weekend getting to know my surroundings and joining the nearby aquatic centre. On Monday, we got into it.

I will never forget that first day. I had been to the Melbourne studio plenty of times, as a guest at the finales and occasionally as part of the show, but walking in as a contestant was . . . well, it was terrifying.

Of the three new judges, I already knew Andy from when he'd been a contestant. He'd won season 4 and we had been at a few of the same events, including *MasterChef* finales, over the years. I knew him to be friendly, funny and kind. I knew he had worked so hard on his season to learn and grow, and he had a soft spot for anyone willing to listen and take new things on board.

I'd watched Mel and Jock in the previous couple of seasons. Mel seemed the softer of them; her heart was always right there on her sleeve. She was the one, I thought, who would connect with the stories behind the food. She was the one who would understand the importance of a dish's history and place in a family, a culture.

Jock seemed the slightly harsher critic from my observations – not mean but *blunt*, and just as honest when he was delighted by a dish. He was the one who would not be impressed by tricky techniques unless the result was delicious food. He was the one, I thought, who might be the hardest to win over.

The three of them had done an incredible job of taking over from Gary, George and Matt. A lot of pundits didn't give Andy, Mel and Jock a chance; those of us who loved the show held our breath to see if it would survive this upheaval. The original three were so beloved, such a part of the brand, so *integral* to *MasterChef* that it seemed impossible it could survive without them. But Andy, Mel and Jock had made the roles their own. Not carbon copies of the originals, but their own personalities and their own dynamics, and their own ways of interacting with each other, the contestants and the viewers.

The 'Fans', new contestants, and the 'Favourites', the old contestants, were kept separate from one another right up until the first day of filming: the new guys didn't know who the old guys were going to be.

Those first hours on set were a little bit overwhelming for all of us. The Fans were bussed to the studios hours before the 'Faves'. They were standing there, at the head of the room, as we returning contestants were introduced in ones, twos and threes into the kitchen. I entered with Billie McKay and Sashi Cheliah, two other previous *MasterChef* winners.

There was some banter, some 'getting-to-know-you', before the first challenge kicked off. Andy asked the youngest contestant, Montana, how old she was when I'd won my season of *MasterChef*. She'd been a little kid. I was swiftly cast as the veteran in the room, which seemed reasonable considering I was thirty-eight the first time round and was an actual grandmother now.

ALL YOU NEED IS LOVE

The judges took turns asking around the room how we felt to either be standing here for the first time or to be returning. Jock asked me, 'Julie, how are you feeling?'

I said, 'Oh, I'm brickin' it,' which was true, but not something I expected them to put to air – let alone as a promo for the first episode.

Our first challenge was for an immunity pin – three were on offer. We were asked to cook a dish that played to our strengths. The way the challenges were run had changed: in series 1, when the challenge began, our only option was to run to the pantry. Now, when a challenge began, we could run to the pantry, or the equipment shelves, or to the garden. However, those words, which Jock said for the first time this season, 'Your time starts . . . now!' triggered exactly the same adrenalin rush.

Being back in the pantry, wheeling around looking for ingredients and ideas, gave me a cold and terrible feeling: *this is a mistake.* My heart was banging in an awfully familiar way, my ears were full of white noise and my eyes unable to see what I needed. My old friend anxiety had jumped straight back on in there, twisting my guts and making my hands shake. What the bloody hell, I thought, was I doing?

Once I was back at my bench, though, I somehow got on with it. I let muscle memory take over. I had chosen food I cooked frequently and knew like the back of my hand – a bunch of recipes from my Lebanese Feast class at the cooking school.

On that first day, probably because I was the first-ever winner, I was called up first for my dish to be tasted. I carried to the judges a huge timber board loaded with food. I'd cooked shish tawook (marinated chicken skewers), a rice dish, flatbread, fattoush salad and toum garlic sauce. Walking up, I had the same feeling in my guts I'd had all those years ago. Dread is probably the right word for it. I felt like a fish out of water, here among all these previous competitors and new contenders.

Watching Andy, Mel and Jock taste, waiting for their appraisal, was excruciating.

Jock, with his thick Scottish accent, spoke first. 'Julie! You're a competent cook, clearly. Right? I just want to talk about what I'm feeling from you, watching you cook today, and watching you stand now. I feel that you think, that because you are the OG, and you were the winner from such a time ago, that you feel as if you're not at a standard as the years that have come after you. Is that fair?'

Talk about hitting the nail on the head. 'That's absolutely true, yes,' I replied, sounding more confident than I felt.

'What I'm gonna tell you, and I need it to just wash through your brain, is: you're not an OG. You're a winner. But what you are, more importantly, is a classic. Okay? And classics don't get old. Classics are very hard to beat. And time and time again, the classics rise to the top.'

Mel and Andy went on to say very kind things about my food. But, once I'd found out from the young contestants what OG meant, it was Jock's words that stayed with me. They made me realise I was going to be able to cook the way I loved here in this kitchen. I wasn't going to be reinvented into a fine-dining hatted chef; I didn't have to offer a modern interpretation of every dish I cooked. There would be challenges ahead, I was sure, which would call on those abilities, but in between those challenges I felt I had permission to cook the food I loved to cook. The favourites. The classics. His words were a kindness and a gift. They didn't remove the stress but they did relieve it.

We settled into the rhythm of the competition. I wasn't the only one who experienced nerves and anxiety; really, I think just about anyone would have such feelings in this environment.

ALL YOU NEED IS LOVE

There was lots of down-time between cooking and judging, and then between judging and the verdict. We hung out in the green room, a demountable building where we could chill out and make a cuppa or a toastie. Some people read books or worked on their computers, others kicked a footy around outside, others played music or games on their phone. But mostly we talked; and what we talked about was food. We were a varied group with many different cooking styles and influences. Some of us focused on our cultural heritage – and what an array. Vietnam, Malaysia, Sri Lanka, Scotland, Italy, Venezuela, India and Argentina were some of the countries being showcased. Some of us were experimental, taking risks and learning on the go. Some of us were established professionals, with an inner reservoir of experience and recipes to draw from.

It's rare situation to have so much time to hang out with people who are as impassioned by cookery and food as you are, and it's fascinating to me that when people are in a strange situation together, they bond very quickly and strongly – and being a *MasterChef* contestant is certainly a strange situation. Great friendships grew over those few months; from the first day, the conversation flowed fast and rich among us. Everyone was willing to share ideas and techniques. Some of the new guys – the Fans – were so keen to learn, and had a million questions. On the weekends, we cooked in our apartments and shared the results. Occasionally, we would book the rooftop space and have a party on the weekends. All of us would prepare something to share, we'd put on music, have a swim or a dance, and let off steam. The food at these gatherings was, as you would expect, epic.

We were testing for COVID daily. Inevitably, the virus hit the production. I was one of the first to go down among the cast and I went down hard. It was my first COVID infection and I was utterly miserable; I've never been a great patient and being away from home made me feel very sorry for myself. Filming was suspended for two weeks as the virus rolled through more than half the cast and crew. During the time I was holed up in my little apartment by myself, I'd get texts from my fellow contestants as they left meals outside my door. Food people show love with food – and boy did I feel loved. If you ever get sick and need meals delivered, I recommend getting them delivered by *MasterChef* contestants.

One of the contestants who made me feel truly at home was Tommy Pham, a wonderful Vietnamese cook. He was staying in his apartment with his pregnant wife, Wendy, and their adorable toddler, Miles. Miles would come and visit 'Uncle Julie', as he called me. Tommy apologised and said he was trying to get Miles to say Aunty instead. 'I'm Aunty to a fair few people,' I said. 'I'm only Uncle to one.' So I remain to this day, Miles's and now his baby brother Hugo's Uncle Julie.

Before and after contracting the virus, I was swimming as often as the filming schedule allowed: some days we started too early but if I could realistically get to the pool and back before the bus left for the studio, I was there. Friend and fellow contestant Michael Weldon loved to swim too, so we would often go together. I had a fantastic pair of waterproof headphones so I'd lose myself in the music and the water before the stressful business of the day began. It was nice to have someone to debrief with as well, on our way to the pool, outside the busyness of the green room and the studio.

Outside of the kitchen I was keeping up my important routines. I went to sleep each night with a meditation in my headphones, and started the day that way as well. When filming times permitted, I spoke to Delilah most evenings before she went to bed. She totally understood FaceTime and would babble away happily to me and give me slobbery kisses through the phone. I also got to see my Melbourne-based brother-in-law and his beautiful family. Ben, Alix and Isha had been isolated by the lockdowns that Melbourne experienced and we had not seen each other in three years. I visited them nearly every weekend while I was filming. I was exercising and getting enough sleep and doing little bits of art when I could. There were even a couple of days when the other contestants came to my unit and we made polymer clay jewellery together.

I saw Heather nearly every week, via Zoom. She had been my therapist for around a year by this time, which was longer than I had ever seen anyone in the brain department. I had let go of my notion that therapy was a kind of self-indulgent navel-gazing. I now realise that taking time out to examine what caused my breakdown saved my life.

Heather was helping me to understand what had happened to me through a model of therapy known as Internal Family Systems (IFS). Simply put, this model regards us all as having different parts within ourselves. If you've ever said, 'Part of me thinks I should do x, and another part thinks I should do y,' then you'll have the gist of it: we all have factions within ourselves that try, in their own way, to help us function.

Bear with me while I try to explain this; it's hard to capture all the nuances of a whole model of therapy in a few paragraphs, and I am aware that it may come across as sounding a bit weird. I'd also like to say that this is the model of therapy that has helped me, after trying many others. It's like finding the right medication, or the right exercise – there's more than one way to tie your shoes. Every person will have their own combination of treatments that resonate for them.

According to the IFS model, our parts present themselves differently in different people, and they play different roles in our behaviour. IFS therapy is about finding out which parts are causing the pain, or distress, or discomfort, or addiction, or dysfunction, and helping to reintegrate them into a healthy whole human – the Self. The IFS model groups these parts into three categories: exiles, managers and firefighters.

Exiles are often our vulnerable parts, those we put away, out of sight, out of mind, because we cannot process the trauma they went through. They are still there, though, trying to help in their own way, no matter how destructive that may turn out to be.

Managers are those parts of us that keep us going, keep us on the job; but, like managers in our external lives, our internal managers can be perfectionists, and hold unrealistic expectations.

Then there are the firefighters. These are the parts that come charging in with extreme solutions to the pain we are experiencing. Firefighters will do anything to stop the hurt – addiction, self-harm, self-destruction.

When I looked back over my life, at its distinct cycles and seasons, my parts began to become clear to me.

The youngest is Seven. Seven had already lost a parent; seven was terrified of being left again. Seven knew that being good at school, cheerful and helpful, were ways to be loved and to make sure that nobody would leave ever again.

Seven was also abused, and felt ashamed, ruined, dirty. So Seven was exiled, banished from the memory bank, in order that Eight, Nine and Ten and so forth could survive.

Seven's way of helping was to be a clever, shiny, un-leavable little person. Seven was compliant and eager to please, never saying no, never wanting to let anyone down. I can look at my adulthood and see very clearly where Seven stepped in to help: all the times I put other people's needs ahead of my own, the times I said yes to things even though there was not one shred of time or energy to do them.

The next part that has its own clear face and role is Seventeen. Seventeen had honed a desire to be clever and shiny into a fierce competitiveness. Academically, in public speaking and music contests, Seventeen wanted to excel and was relentless in pursuing that. Seventeen drew all of her value from external accolades and achievements. Certificates. Awards. Recognition. Results. These are the things that motivated Seventeen. Failure was not an option.

Seventeen was a manager, until she wasn't. She managed the schoolwork, the extracurricular activities. She demanded excellence and was blistering in her self-loathing when excellence was not achieved. But all of this didn't change the fact that she remembered the exiled Seven and why Seven had been put away in that box on a high shelf. So Seventeen became a firefighter and she tried to self-destruct.

The next distinct part I call Young Mum. Here she is with three small boys, an indescribably fierce love for them burning in her chest. She is terrified that she'll get something wrong, that she won't give them the home they deserve, that fundamental mistakes will be made that will scar them forever. She wants to try to contribute financially to the household even though raising three babies is a more-than-full-time job. She is a manager. She irons tiny clothes and makes healthy snacks and tries, and fails, to do everything perfectly.

Next is the part I call Post-*MasterChef*. This is the thirty-eight-year-old who was catapulted from a suburban life into the glare of the public eye, into a thousand new opportunities. This part said yes to just about everything, and harboured the fear of losing it all. This part is a manager; she gets it done. But she is 'helped' by Seven, wanting to be loved, not wanting to be left.

And the final distinctive part that I can identify in this room of mine, this brain, I call Forty-Nine. I probably shouldn't call her that because she was stepping in for a couple of years before that, but forty-nine is when she took her help to the next level. Forty-Nine is pure firefighter. She stepped in because Seven couldn't say no, and Seventeen still wanted to be the best, and Young Mum had guilt about the children, and Post-*MasterChef* was trying to keep all the plates spinning in the air. Forty-Nine helped by bringing the wine. She provided the relief. She numbed the stress. And when that solution didn't work, she brought the next solution to the table: to get rid of the pain entirely.

I struggled with the IFS concept for a bit. I was confused – if I only tried hard at school so people wouldn't leave me, if I was only a helpful person because I thought that was how to be loved, then was I just a bundle of fears and reactions in a skin sack? If I am just the sum of my traumas and triumphs, who am *I*?

In this type of therapy, once we have identified all the parts, we need to introduce them to the adult in the room. This is the Self, or what I refer to as Today Me, for want of a better name. The grown-up, the one who holds all the parts. The real me, the one who I would be underneath all the coping mechanisms.

It helps me to get my head around all of this if I think of my life as a bus, and the parts as passengers. Today Me, the adult, is meant to be driving. But Today Me does not always have the wheel. Whenever things start to go wrong – an anxiety attack, for example, I can have a look at who's driving the bus and suddenly the way I'm feeling makes sense.

If those anxiety symptoms kick in while I'm waiting for a dish to be judged, for example, I can see that Seven – who just wants to be loved – and Seventeen – who wants to win at any cost – are fighting over the wheel. It's no wonder we're all over the road. It's my job, Today Me, to gently take the wheel back; to say to Seven and Seventeen, 'It's all right. I see you and I hear you and you matter. But I've got this. You're safe, you can relax, it's okay.'

ALL YOU NEED IS LOVE

Being back in the *MasterChef* environment was a pretty hefty test of the therapy I was undergoing. Early in the season I was really bad at regulating my feelings: if you watched any of it you'll know that I cried at the drop of a hat, whether I was happy or sad or stressed or excited. My eyes were like little sprinklers.

Commentary on socials was predictably pretty brutal – some of it, anyway. I was accused over and over of trying to be emotionally manipulative, of throwing myself an ongoing pity-party, of 'milking' the fact that I'd had depression and anxiety. The opposite was true, actually. I was trying very hard to contain my runaway emotions. It's embarrassing being a grown-ass woman with no control over your own face. But I didn't always succeed very well. That was partly because my brain was still a soft-boiled egg, and partly because it's just who I am.

The competition rolled on, and the green room became less crowded as we said goodbye to our friends on a regular basis. The elimination process is swift and brutal. The friendships are real and the goodbyes are emotional. And the bonds last.

Most of the Favourites I already knew, either briefly from meeting them at their own season finale, or from working with them on other projects. There were those whose food careers I had followed with admiration from afar, and those who I counted as friends. Alvin Quah and I had had an uproariously funny time working together with an appliance brand many years before, and I was delighted to find out he would be on this season. I fell in love with Aldo Ortado, the effervescent Italian, when I saw him in season 10. With his flowing Fabio-style locks and delicious accent, I could have watched him all day, and I howled with dismay when he was eliminated from his season. Meeting him now, and being on the receiving end of his bone-crushing bear hugs, was a bucket-list item ticked off.

Aldo was great friends with Sarah Todd from series 6. Impossibly beautiful and poised, Sarah's undeniable talent lay in the dishes she had perfected in her time as a restaurateur in India.

Billie McKay had been on series 7; she'd won it in an epic showdown against Georgia Barnes, in which she'd had to reproduce a dish by Heston Blumenthal. We all knew her as a cool operator, an absolute machine in the kitchen, and in reality the one to beat. It was a treat to get to know her for real; warm, funny and just as prone to nerves as the rest of us – but way, way better at hiding it.

Mindy Woods had been on the season that Andy won, series 4. I remembered watching her, this proud Bundjalung woman with joy and attitude just radiating off her. In the intervening years she'd gone on to open her award-winning Byron Bay restaurant, Karkalla, which showcases Indigenous and local ingredients.

The Fans, the newbies, left their impression too, and getting to know them was its own source of interest and laughter. I was struck early by the enthusiasm of Daniel Lamble, a fireman from the Northern Territory. On the weekends, at night, whenever he had the chance, Dan would ask questions of the people around him; he would practise, try new things, seek advice. His eagerness was infectious. In my view he had a very real chance at winning – I told him this early in the piece, and I believed it.

The competition went for me the way it had done the first time around: I won some, I lost some. I very rarely sailed through the middle; that was how it felt, anyway. One day I might be cooking a paella using randomly selected ingredients and winning an immunity pin, the next day I might be cooking from a rainbow mystery box a colourfully confusing dish that landed me in an elimination. I rode out the highs and the lows with the support of my friends, and I kept on swimming.

Some of the most memorable moments for me this time around came from the guest judges – two in particular. One day we walked into the kitchen to a stunning display of images of a chef who had struck fear and awe into the hearts of so many over the years: Marco Pierre White. And there he was, standing at the head of the room like some iconic apparition. My heart was clanging like a bell and I shook my head in wonder at this competition, which kept delivering surprises and experiences far beyond my expectations.

Marco's challenge was centred around his favourite condiments. He had brought mustards, vinegars, liquors, jams, and we were to create a dish that used at least two of them. I noted with delight that there were ingredients that echoed my chilli plum sauce, although for a redcurrant jelly rather than plum, so I set about making it, along with crispy fried chicken wings. About halfway through cooking, too late to change my dish, the absurdity of what I was doing struck me: I was making fried chicken for arguably the most legendary chef alive.

When he visited my bench during the cook to ask about my dish, and during the tasting, he was kind to me. He liked my fried chicken and licked the sauce off his fingers, which is one of the most surreal *MasterChef* moments in all my years of surreal *MasterChef* moments. On that day, Harry was sent home, an enthusiastic and passionate young cook who I liked immensely.

Another pinch-me day in season 14 was when Rick Stein came to visit. I had long watched his shows, and admired his ever-so-honest approach to cooking. He made a fish curry for us. It was so simple, and so delicious. He tasked us with creating a dish from a travel memory. The decision of what to make was not hard for me: I went straight back to Paris, to the fragrant fug of Polidor with its warm, generous provincial French dishes. I made coq au vin, employing every technique I had learned in this kitchen to create a sauce that was as rich as if it had cooked for hours.

This dish was judged in the tasting room, outside of our view. I didn't get to see the judges' reaction to it until it aired on television. The praise my coq au vin received from Rick Stein on that day is a treasure, a nugget of pure gold that I keep in my heart and turn over and over when I need a little boost. The sad part of that day for me was that Michael left – my swimming companion and good mate.

One day, a few weeks later, we had a later start than usual and I was catching up on a bit of email. Renee had been running the cooking school – again, to my ongoing gratitude – so I didn't have to deal with much at all. But I emailed something to Mick on this day and got an out-of-office reply. It said he was off work, returning in two days' time.

This may not sound like a big deal, but I can tell you it was. Mick didn't take days off lightly. Besides scheduled leave he barely took days off at all, sick days were just about non-existent. And I had only talked to him the night before! Why hadn't he said something about this?

So I called him. The call went to voicemail, and the message said the same thing: 'I am on annual leave for two days.'

I texted: 'You're on annual leave? What's happening?'

Mental health day, came his reply.

'2 days off. Are you sure that's all that's happening? Are you all right? It's really unlike you to take a day off without having your arm twisted?'

No response.

I felt a creeping cold sensation, like someone had injected ice water into my veins. Something was not right. I recalled that a few weeks before, Mick had had a couple of sus-looking moles removed. I tried over and over to call, with no answer. I tried to call all three of the boys, with not a single one of those incorrigible reprobates answering either. I convinced myself that Mick had a bad result. That he was scheduled for surgery. And nobody was telling me, because I'm the delicate mental patient who can't hack the stress. I was beside myself.

I texted again, since Mick seemed to be suffering from a sudden inability to pick up his phone. I told him, 'I'm on the bus now but I'm going to call when I get to the studio, in about 30 minutes, and I'd like you to pick up please.'

This time he replied. 'Please trust that I'm fine. No need to call, get your head where it needs to be for today. Good luck today and we will have a chat tonight.'

Like hell.

'My head won't be fine until I speak to you. I'll call shortly.'

Then I texted again. 'And you'll tell me what's going on.'

In the bus on the way to the studio, I made a decision. If Mick didn't pick up when I called, I was going to get into an Uber and go to the airport. I would go home.

Mindy noticed my distress and came to sit with me while I phoned Mick. He did pick up; as soon as I heard his voice I bawled my eyes out and asked what the hell was going on. He told me he couldn't say. I pleaded. He asked me to trust him. He told me he promised that he was okay, and the baby, and the boys, and the dogs, and everybody else was too. He couldn't tell me what was happening but he would soon.

Mindy and I had a bit of a cry together; we wondered for the eleven hundredth time why we were there, we women with family commitments and businesses to tend to, with worries and concerns far larger than a television show.

I can laugh about this now, but I couldn't then: during this whole exchange, Mick and the boys were mere metres away from me. They had been flown to Melbourne, along with all the other families, to surprise us contestants for a service challenge. We were cooking for them. It's why none of them was answering the phone. The night before, when I had phoned home, they were already in Melbourne; they were having dinner in a noisy restaurant and Mick had to find a quiet corner so I couldn't hear that he wasn't in the house. I never suspected a thing.

Mick told me later that while the families were waiting to go on set, one of the story producers found him, Joe, Tom and Paddy, and said, 'Julie's out there, really upset. Do you have any idea what is going on?' He showed her all the missed calls, and my texts, and she said, 'Ah. I see.' Apparently there was a discussion as to whether I should be told what was happening, but since we were about to get started they decided to let it play out as planned. The judges told us that we would be cooking for very important people – and here they came.

Our families were led in one by one, and there was much hugging and crying and laughter. I think the words I said into Mick's ear as I held him were, 'I'm going to kill you.' Our loved ones had been brought from all over the world. There wasn't a dry eye in the house when Aldo's family arrived. First, his husband appeared, and the next minute, in his ever-so-loud Aldo voice, we heard, 'It's my fockin' mooooommmmmm!' She had been flown out from Italy. He had not seen her in three years.

We cooked a herb-themed three-course meal for our families and served them in the beautiful garden restaurant that had been set up. After filming, we only had a few minutes with them before they were all whisked away to a hotel, and then back home. It was such a lift. I was thrilled for my boys to have had a small piece of this experience, the way they'd had thirteen years before. They had the best time, hanging out in the secret building with all the other families. They loved watching the challenge from the gantry. Seeing them not only gave me an enormous boost, it also allowed me to reset, refocus and keep going.

Not long after this, the remaining contestants decided that we needed to have a party. Specifically, a dress-up party. A dress-up *karaoke* party. I found a local company that hired out a karaoke rig. Our house coordinator, Cliff, who along with his co-coordinator, Megan, looked after all of us and our various complaints and needs, booked the party room and ordered dinner. We closed the curtains, agreed to leave our phones turned off, and had one of the best nights I can remember. We ate pizza and chicken wings, and sang for hours and hours. Far from being shy, everyone wanted a crack at the karaoke machine. Sassy, shimmying Venezuelan mama Keyma and Aldo performed the Gaga/Cooper duet 'Shallow', Alvin did something by the Backstreet Boys. Mindy and her wife, Shell, sang a few duets, Dan got us all belting out 'The Gambler'. I did some Bette Midler and Mama Cass. My throat caught on 'Dream a Little Dream of Me': it's what I'd sing Delilah to sleep with when I was with her. But I think the most astonishing performance was by Billie: she pulled the hood of a bathrobe low over her face and sang, word-perfect and without missing a beat, Eminem's 'Lose Yourself'.

Not long after this, the tide turned again, as it always does in *MasterChef*, and I found myself in a pressure test against Mindy and Billie. It was a bit of an odd time; the mojo was not great. Seeing our families had been a highlight, but had also served to remind us how much we missed them. A sense of homesickness had set in among some of us – most of us, I would venture to say. The mood, as changeable as the weather in this fantastical television world, always ebbed and flowed, and right then it was at an ebb.

Billie, Mindy and I were separated from the rest of the contestants as always happens to those in a pressure test. As we talked, we made a decision; a pact. We were not going into this test with a feeling of doom and gloom, but one of celebration. For one of us, it would be the last day, and we were buggered if we weren't going to make it a great one.

We were not going to operate from fear today. Whatever came our way, we would approach it with joy, power and sisterhood. I put on my kick-arse playlist of strong women singing strong songs and we danced it out. Katy, Christina, Taylor, Destiny's Child sang us into the kitchen, where we stood, feeling confident and proud.

We could not have been more delighted when Kirsten Tibballs walked through the doors – the chocolate queen. Another skilled, intelligent, accomplished woman. It was like we had summoned her and the universe delivered.

A strange thing happened that morning. It was something to do with our pact; our determination to go out on a high. As I stood there at the front of the room, with Mindy and Billie alongside me ready to see what we would be cooking, I felt . . . *calm*, I suppose. For the first time since I had returned to this kitchen, I could feel my two feet planted on the ground in my boots. I could feel my back, straight and strong, and my head clear and serene. It was a most unusual way for me to be, especially on what we called Black Apron Day.

The dessert we had to replicate was a 'cherry on top' cake of many layers and textures. It was a work of art, and tasted like heaven. There were twelve elements and sixty ingredients in this behemoth of a recipe. It also involved tempering chocolate, one of my least favourite things to do. We were given a ridiculously short amount of time – just three and a quarter hours – to make it.

Jock said, 'Good luck – your time starts . . . now!' and we were away. We called to each other through the cook, checked in, made sure we were cooking with as much joy and presence as we could. Which was harder for Mindy than Billie and I, after she cut herself and was held up waiting for first aid.

Time was up, and our three cakes were finished. I noticed that one corner of mine had a little downhill slump to it. I remembered that the appearance of this cake was an important part of the judging criteria, and I felt in my bones that I was going home. I felt it with the same sense of calm with which I had started the day.

Usually between cooking and judging, I might shoot Mick a text to let him know how I thought I'd gone. Today, I called him.

'I'm done, babe, I messed up my cake. We're not judged yet but I'm coming home.'

'Oh Jules. I'm so sorry,' he said.

'I'm not.' I wasn't even crying. 'It was an awesome day. I did the very best I could. I am ready to come home. And I don't have a single regret.'

One of us, then, started crying. It still wasn't me. 'I'm so proud of you,' he said.

'I am too,' I replied.

I had finally worked out what I was looking for when I'd agreed to come back on this show. And it turns out, it wasn't to win at all. Well, not in the trophy sense. It was to be able to stand with my boots planted on the ground, my back straight, and my head calm. It was to feel the joy that comes from connection, and using your hands, and being part of a group. It was to feel fully alive again.

Long story short, the inside of my cake made up for the outside and I wasn't eliminated after all. Mindy was; and, strong, proud, extraordinary woman that she is – fierce Indigenous advocate, voice of calm and positivity, sister to us all – she left with the same incredible attitude that she arrived with.

The six of us who remained packed our bags and were flown to Tasmania for Finals Week. I had won immunity for the first challenge, having cooked a decent orange upside-down cake with an orange and ginger ice cream the week before. In Freycinet National Park on the east coast, we farmed oysters and the others cooked outside of Devil's Corner winery. The air was like cut glass and the wind whipped the heat out from under the pans.

Alvin, not being able to summon enough fire under the wok for his Singapore oyster omelette, was sent home at the end of that day.

So now there were five of us: Billie and Sarah, Dan and Keyma, and me. We were taken to The Truffle Farm, near Deloraine, where we hunted truffles with truffle-hunting dogs. In the crisp afternoon, we gently prised the earthy nuggets from the rich soil to cook with in the next challenge.

The dish I created with the truffles was one of my proudest in the competition. I layered delicate quail breasts with truffle, wrapped them in guanciale (cured pork fat), and served them on a truffled celeriac puree with a rich quail jus and glazed grapes. It was so pretty, so delicate, beautifully cooked, and could have come to you in a restaurant. I very, very rarely made delicate food so I was thrilled with this dish. I seemed to have taken that calm from the cake challenge and carried it over into this one.

The next day, our challenge was to be in a distillery. The smell of alcohol was overwhelming in the air; if you'd struck a match, I reckon the whole place would have gone up. We were to cook with gin or whisky.

Production, knowing my situation, had arranged for some non-alcoholic whisky to be delivered to the distillery and offered me that to use. I was given a say in how it would be portrayed, too;

whether I wanted to speak on air about using a non-alcoholic spirit and why, or whether to decant it into one of the distillery's whisky bottles and leave it unspoken.

After a lot of deliberation, I elected to use the actual whisky. No substitute would taste the same. I didn't want to go home because I didn't hero the hero ingredient.

I drew the short straw for this challenge – the short straw for me, anyway: dessert. We had to cook for thirty-odd people. I made a whisky date pudding with whisky caramel sauce, and whisky chilli ice cream. I was thrilled to pieces with all my flavours. But I had cooked my pudding on the bottom rack of the oven, and it had burned. I am still asked, 'Why didn't you just cut the burned bit off?' And the honest answer is, I didn't think I needed to. I call these lapses in judgement '*MasterChef* Brain'. They occur frequently for me, even when I am not on *MasterChef*. This lapse cost me the competition.

Two memories from this night stay with me. The first one is when the five of us were waiting for the verdict on our dishes. We were under a marquee in the garden of the distillery; it was getting dark and we were cold, trying to rug up in whatever we could find. I don't think any of us really knew what the result was going to be. I found an extract from Theodore Roosevelt's speech 'The Man in the Arena', and read it out to these four beautiful people:

> It is not the critic who counts . . . The credit belongs to the man who is actually in the arena, whose face is marred by dust and sweat and blood; who strives valiantly . . . who at the best knows in the end the triumph of high achievement, and who at the worst, if he fails, at least fails while daring greatly.

It was getting a bit emotional then, so Dan, who always carried a little Bluetooth speaker with him, started playing 'Hakuna Matata' and we all sang and danced and laughed our heads off.

The second memory is from after I had been eliminated but before I ran away up the long gravel driveway. It was Jock's hug, and then him saying, 'Thanks for cooking for us.'

I told him, 'It's been an honour.'

And it truly, truly had.

By the time the five of us were flown back to Melbourne from Tasmania, there was no sense in my going home – if I had, I would've had to return to the studio less than twenty-four hours later to attend the finale. So I stayed until the end.

I watched as Keyma took fourth place and joined the rest of us up on the gantry. I cheered on Billie, Sarah and Dan in their service challenge. Dan the fireman, ironically looking like he'd just put out a house fire in his *MasterChef* apron, bowed out after this round. He really was the man in the arena; his face was marred by all sorts of stuff. He had fought valiantly and almost made it to the very end. I had a maternal sort of pride; he reminded me of my boys.

And then I watched Sarah and Billie duke it out for the title, cooking once again a diabolical Heston Blumenthal dessert. I watched Billie, the epitome of grace under fire, make history as the first person to ever win *MasterChef* twice.

When I'd left home, I knew that filming the entire series was going to last six months so the longest I would be gone was six months. When I'd arrived in Melbourne, I didn't know when I would come back. I didn't know *who* I would come back; if I would be in pieces all over again, or if I would be healed, or something in between. In the end, I was gone for the whole six months. And when I returned home it was, once again, to a rapidly changing life.

ALL YOU NEED IS LOVE

Coq au vin

Here is one of the lovely meals we enjoyed in Paris. This is the recipe to use if you are making coq au vin in the traditional way, with time up your sleeve. If you are making it in the *MasterChef* kitchen, especially if it is for one of your food heroes such as Rick Stein, you will need to pull some strings and get it done faster. If not, take your time and enjoy the process.

Prep time: 30 minutes
Cooking time: 2 hours 10 minutes
Serves 4

¼ cup plain flour
½ teaspoon salt
¼ teaspoon ground white pepper
1.2 kg chicken pieces – leg, thigh, wings
1 tablespoon olive oil
150 g speck, cut into batons
20 pearl onions
8 button mushrooms, sliced
8 girolle mushrooms, sliced
2 cloves garlic, chopped
1 teaspoon thyme leaves, finely chopped
1 tablespoon tomato paste
30 ml Armagnac
375 ml red wine
1 bay leaf

Preheat the oven to 140°C.

Combine the flour, salt and pepper in a bowl. Coat the chicken pieces thoroughly in the flour. Place the olive oil in a fry pan over medium-high heat, and when it is hot, brown the chicken on all sides. Transfer the chicken to a casserole dish.

Place the speck in the hot pan and cook for about a minute, until it starts to turn golden. Add the onions, mushrooms, garlic and thyme leaves and sauté for 3 to 4 minutes, until softened and fragrant.

Add the tomato paste and cook, stirring, for a further minute.

Pour the Armagnac into the pan, followed by the red wine. Bring to the boil, then pour the mixture over the chicken in the casserole dish. Add the bay leaf.

Cover with a lid and cook for 1 ½ hours in the oven. Remove the lid and cook for a further half an hour.

If the sauce is too thin at this stage, remove the chicken pieces and turn the oven up to 180°C. Cook the sauce, uncovered, for another 10 to 15 minutes before returning the chicken to the casserole dish to serve.

CHAPTER 20

TIMES LIKE THESE

On Easter Monday of 2022, *MasterChef* season 14 went to air on Channel 10. There had been intense promotion for the show. I was confronted by my picture on billboards and bus stops and trams; in fact, my enormous head, along with Billie and Sashi's, seemed to be all over Melbourne. The show's creators had accomplished the almost impossible task of securing the rights to The Beatles' 'All You Need Is Love' as the theme song for the promotion. It set the tone for the series; it was a warm reassurance about the loving heart of *MasterChef*.

Once the show was on air, we all had to brace for the social media fallout. It's just an inevitable part of being in the public consciousness. You'd think something as innocent and fun as a cooking show wouldn't invite nastiness, but people get pretty invested in their TV shows. As I knew, they can get extremely heated about what's unfolding in a competition, even one as collegiate as *MasterChef*. All sorts of nonsense was published.

The *Daily Mail* ran an article late in the competition that a promo for the finale contained 'clues' I would win – along with a bevy of other inaccurate and poorly thought-out rubbish.

Pundits – in the press and on social media – targeted me as being given chances, as the show being rigged in my favour. Not very original, guys – check the notes from thirteen years prior. None of it was true then either. No, I was not 'manipulating' the judges to get chances: I was simply still a messy human, flour on my face, buttons done up wrong, sweaty, teary. The auto-dishevel function that I suffered from as a child has well and truly followed me into adulthood. (So much so that once, when I sat for a portrait for an artist friend who was entering the Archibald Prize, he painted me with my bra strap sticking out. 'Could you not have edited that out?' I asked him. 'I could,' he said, 'but then it wouldn't be you.')

I urged the newbies, the Fans, not to look at social media. They ignored my advice and I did too. It's hard not to look.

Having come out of the gates pretty strongly to win the first weekly immunity of the season, I was overwhelmed not just by the win or the judges' comments on my paella, but by the love and encouragement and support from all the other contestants. I spoke that day about having had a tough couple of years. I spoke about depression and anxiety; I spoke about how the call to return to *MasterChef* had been like a tap on the shoulder from the universe.

After this episode went to air, I started to receive messages. They came from everywhere, through many different channels. It was clear that what I'd said had resonated with so many people who'd gone through or were going through the same thing, and these messages gave me a small insight into how common it is to have these struggles. How hard it is to talk about them, until someone else does first.

Once *MasterChef* was on air, our classes at the school began to sell out faster than we could put them online. I had planned for a five-week handover at the kitchen on my return. Renee had been running the show, but she was leaving to go on maternity leave.

That apart, it was hard to staff the classes – my beautiful team had had to find jobs outside of the hospitality sector during COVID, so now the kitchen had to fit in around their shifts at other jobs. They gave me the very best they could.

We had spent all of Renee's pregnancy trying to find a replacement for her, but there was none to be found. A week before I returned home, beautiful little Lachlan made his entrance into the world six weeks early. The first concern was, of course, his health and wellbeing. The second concern, for me, was no handover period – just jumping straight in with both feet.

At the same time, Joe, who up until then had been working in the office with me, landed his dream job in television, one that he had been seeking for a very long time. He offered not to take it, to stay with me instead since I would be on my own. I've sometimes not felt like the best mum in the world, but I've also never felt like the kind of mum who would stop their child from actually taking their dream job.

So here was I. All the work I had done on setting boundaries, and fitting important things into the day, and making time for exercise and art and craft and time in nature, and being present for my family – all in one fell swoop it was out the window. Gone. My small business had become so very, very small: except for my loyal little band of back-of-house staff, there was just me. Me and the emails, and the phones, and the queries, and the gift vouchers. Me and the ordering, and the deliveries, and the bills. Me and the coolroom full of wine and the edges of my vision starting to darken again.

I was still seeing Heather, still working on those Internal Family Systems, so I looked around my bus.

Seven was trying to take the wheel, saying, 'You have to make this work. People are excited to come; they want to see you – you can't let them down. Keep going, you can do it!'

Seventeen was also grabbing at the wheel, saying, 'Yes, you have to keep going! You cannot close your business – that is failure! We don't fail! Keep going, you *can* do it!'

Forty-Nine was there too, standing quietly to the side. She wasn't yelling at me like Seven and Seventeen were. She was saying quietly, 'You know how I can help. I can numb it out. I can make it all go away. Just let me drive for a minute; it'll be so easy.'

All parts of the one whole. But us parts needed an adult behind the wheel of this bus; it had left enough wreckage in the rearview mirror. Today Me, the grown-up, my Self, knew deep down what I had to do. I had so many reasons to keep on keeping on: the money it would cost to close down and repay all of those classes and vouchers; the wounded pride; the sheer guilt of letting people down.

But, as the ever-pragmatic Heather pointed out, 'It's not brain surgery you're cancelling, Julie, it's a cooking class. People will survive.' She also said, 'Not letting people down is a terrible reason to keep doing something that is going to make you sick.'

Mick and I crunched the numbers. They hurt but we could manoeuvre to make sure everyone was looked after and paid back. I visited Renee to tell her personally: it was her business too – more than mine in these last years. I offered it to her, the world's most unwieldly gift, but with her new baby it just couldn't work.

With grief and relief, more than eight years after we opened our doors, I closed my kitchen.

Eight months more after we closed down, Renee and I were in the kitchen sorting through some stuff, tidying up and getting ready for a Mother's Day 2023 gift fair. It was Renee's idea. The kitchen had closed so abruptly. The tables full of beautiful homewares and giftwares sat untouched. The pianola sat silent; the walls of appliances abandoned. So we were stocktaking for our one-day gift fair when the phone call came. It was Caitlin, my manager. She had terrible news: Jock had died.

Like every other person who heard the news that day, I couldn't take it in. Renee and I held on to each other in shock. Only a few months before, Jock had been giving me advice on writing an autobiography, the book you're reading now. I had read his. I asked him how to write about the hard stuff. He was generous with his time and advice.

It was unfathomable. Heartbreaking, unreal, could not be true. But it was true; impossible to reconcile with reality, and yet true.

I couldn't even begin to know what a terrible shock this must be to his family. His friends. His workmates. I was not a big part of Jock's life; I was one of many contestants whom he mentored. But he left an indelible impact on me. He was a large part of the coming back to life that *MasterChef* Fans and Favourites represented to me. It's just not fair and it will never be fair.

'So, what are you up to these days?' I get asked. In a funny turn of events, I am almost back where I was when I first won *MasterChef*, albeit on a smaller scale. But I am a lot more discerning now about what I take on. Work-wise, no two weeks are the same. I might be filming a piece of Instagram content for a product I like, or I might be heading off to do a demo at a food festival, or I might be giving a keynote address at a conference. I might be doing an event with Beyond Blue, a charity who I have aligned with in the aftermath of my own mental health encounter. Sometimes, like now, I write.

I am seeing so much more of my family than I have for years. Tom, Crystal and Delilah moved out of our house when lockdown lifted, but they moved five minutes down the road. We all play a part in raising Delilah: picking her up from daycare, playing with her in our backyard, dinners and sleepovers with her – they are the very best part of every week.

I am also painting. Not tiny art anymore, either. I had been following the online artistic journey of a woman I knew; I'd met her when she was a huge presence – the OG – in the blogging world. Kayte Murphy, or Mrs Woog as she was known, had her own tales to tell and had taken up painting. She saw something I posted online and invited me to her place for an art session. With Today Me, the grown-up, firmly behind the wheel of the bus, I accepted the offer for a couple of days of nothing but pure art therapy.

I had a bit of a nervy turn when, after dabbling at a small picture, Kayte waltzed in with an enormous canvas and told me to go for it. I had never painted on a stretched canvas before; it was daunting, and then liberating. It was just the most wonderful feeling. Freedom. When I was done, Kayte told me that she really liked it. I think her words were, 'Pack your bags and fuck off out of my house.' Now we have these sessions on the regular. She has helped me to put my art online and I have even sold a few paintings here and there.

My kitchen, my closed-down cooking school, has become a dual-purpose space. The kitchen end still has fully functional appliances, and it's also set up for filming and photography, so I can still make a living there. But the rest of it, the rest of that space that became such a mixed bag of emotions for me, is now a studio. There, I paint and draw and make jewellery. The wall of cooking utensils has become an art playground – I paint with pastry brushes and icing spatulas and egg flips. One of my slow cookers is dedicated to soap-making, and another to making encaustic paint. In the office there is one whole desk dedicated to gift-wrapping and another area for my card-making supplies. Can you imagine?

And I still, in this kitchen, cook. I develop recipes, I make dinners, and I indulge that reawakened love I have for delicious food, and feeding it to the people I love best.

I still swim in the ocean several times a week. I meet Mick at the gym a couple of times a week as well. I'm never going to be a swimsuit model (except that one time, LOL); it's not about that. I accept that I am short and sturdy, but I am also strong. My body is strong. As the months go by, and I keep doing the things that matter, my mind is getting stronger too.

And my spirit is strong. I didn't lose it in the shedding of my formal religion. Around that time, I did a lot of reading – once I could read again – about the brain. Books about neurology and breathing and cold water therapy; Buddhist guides to recovery from addiction, the law of attraction, sleep studies; the biographies of people who had suffered from mental health issues. I wanted to understand all the things I could about the connections between our physical, mental and spiritual health. And I found a curious thing. There are a lot of parallels between them. Or maybe it's a lot of crossovers.

There is scientific evidence now of the benefits of gratitude, and of seeking out and expressing emotions such as awe. Or, as it's called in the Church, thanks and praise. I have a theory – and I don't intend to press it onto you or anyone else, so there's no need to smash it to smithereens, unless you really must. It's this: God, the Universe, Mother Nature, Intelligent Design, Science . . . they are all words that describe aspects of the same thing: this incredible earth and the space it is in and the endlessly fascinating creatures that inhabit it. The creativity that springs from those creatures, our capacity for wonder.

I wish that we could all be a little bit more tolerant of different beliefs from our own. Being cynical, crapping on someone else's ideology, is so easy. It's lazy, really. It's so much harder, but so much more interesting, to be a little open to other possibilities than to hold a conviction that we are the only ones who are right. Lots of people – and lots of institutions, religions and organisations too – are guilty of this. How wonderful it would be if we could approach the world with curiosity rather than assumptions; if we could come with our mind open to possibility rather than an impulse to disbelieve, dismiss, disparage.

These days, my god doesn't hang out in a church. My god is in the sky and in the ocean and in the eyes of the people I love. My god is in the details, in the scientific explanations, as well as the inexplicable feelings that they evoke.

I can look at a rainbow and know that it is the result of light refracting off droplets of water. I can simultaneously allow myself to be uplifted by the sight, to feel optimism and promise in the simple beauty of that refracted light. I can hold two thoughts in my head at the same time; more than one thing can be true. I choose awe over cynicism and I believe I am richer for it.

Another area of my life has improved dramatically since I stopped flogging myself to death: I can see my friends again. Tash, who started coming over when our babies were born, texts me every single day. *Every day* she checks in on me. Vickie, who I met right before I gave birth to Joe, and Louise, who I met right after, are over the moon that I can every now and then meet them for coffee. I can duck down south to see my parents. I can go to many more of Debbie's and my nieces' and nephews' special occasions. I am more present to all of the people in my life. I am wide open to the happiness that comes along with loving, and being loved.

I look around my bus these days, and sitting neatly in the seats are those parts of mine. They were so tired, but they have laid their burdens down now.

Seven knows it wasn't her fault. She knows, because I tell her, that it all turns out okay: she is going to be loved, and loved, and loved more than any single human being has a right to expect.

Seventeen knows that she can stop struggling so hard to control everything, to make everything right. To win everything. To get perfect marks. She knows, because I tell her, that everything is going to be all right; that success doesn't always mean coming first; that there are so many ways of winning that don't involve beating someone else. And that she is going to win, in all the ways that really matter.

Young Mum is fucking exhausted; she's asleep. But when she's awake, she knows that she was in fact an awesome mum. That she kept three rowdy, blazingly glorious little boys alive; she gave them a home and a family that nurtured them through everything they needed to be nurtured through. She knows, because I tell her, that they turn out to be magnificent young men. She's so proud of them, that they contribute to the world in wonderful ways.

Post-*MasterChef* hopped up for a sec, thinking she was taking the wheel again after *MasterChef* series 14. Fair enough, I guess. But she knows now that she can relax. The opportunities don't disappear. Fabulous things will still come along, but we have choices now; we don't have to accept all of them. She knows, because I tell her, that we can take our time and embrace the opportunities that give us true purpose, or true joy.

And here she is: Forty-Nine. The one who tried so hard to fight the fires, to put out the blazes with booze and deep water. The one who knew exactly how to numb the panic and pain; who knew how to soothe the racing heart. She was the one who wanted so badly for me to say, no, no, I can't keep up this pace. No, I can't take on another commitment. No, I can't manage all of that. She knows, because I tell her, that I am driving the bus now. I have taken the burden away from her, and found something surprising. She is now the one who sets boundaries. She is the one who says no. She is the one who stands behind my shoulder when I am not paying enough attention to the road, and reminds me what the alternatives are.

Also here in my bus are the wise guides of my life. Mick, always my steadying influence, my greatest supporter, the person who walked with me through the nightmare and kept walking out the other side. My boys, whose hands have held on to me since they were born and whose hearts hold on to me now. My nan is there: she is a beautiful golden glow that permeates my life and dances around my spirit when I am being a nan myself. And there, beyond them, is my family of origin: Mum and Dad, Debbie, nieces and nephews, my beautiful in-laws, my extended family, my friends, old and new. My colleagues, current and past. Heather, who has coached me through the hardest place in my whole life in a way that your nearest and dearest just cannot do.

My bus is in order, and I am at the wheel, and I have a map. This is not to say that there will never be a detour or a ditch, that there will never be an accident or a catastrophe. There's no crystal ball. Just my bus and all its inhabitants, and Today Me at the wheel.

~

If I were to describe to you my perfect moment, it is this.

I am lying on the swing in our backyard, the long one shaped like a boat. Delilah is on top of me, also on her back. Her sweaty little head with its wispy curls is tucked under my chin. Mick, Poppy, is pushing us gently. I know Delilah is awake only because her small head moves side to side as she studies the spangled sun through the needles of our huge, ancient Norfolk Island pine.

TIMES LIKE THESE

In this moment, there is no thinking about earlier in the day, no worrying about later. There is only now. Babies are so good at now. In this moment, Delilah's sticky little hands splay out to her sides, and her full weight sinks into me as she drifts into a doze.

It is warm, and bright, and utterly perfect. It is the only thing that matters.

In this moment, I fully know and understand something: it doesn't matter what has passed, it cannot be changed. It doesn't matter what's coming, it cannot be foreseen. There is only this moment.

Your time starts now.

ACKNOWLEDGEMENTS

I would like to thank and acknowledge the team at Penguin Random House for taking a chance on a cookbook author to write something other than recipes. Special thanks to Ali Urquhart and Catherine Hill, whose job seems to be not only to edit text but to gently hold the hand of an author new in the genre, who is quite fragile and also quite demanding. Thanks to Steve Brown for the cover photography, to Adam Laszczuk, who designed the cover, and to all those at PRH who have worked so hard to birth my book.

I would like to thank my management team, One Management, particularly Caitlin Sullivan. She, and Lisa, have been looking after me since I climbed aboard the crazy *MasterChef* ride. I have so much gratitude.

Thanks to my Family Group, my swimming buddies, my art buddies and my wider community. Thanks to my team at Julie's Place: you made the dream absolutely come true. Thanks to my former colleagues at Star, especially my co-host Rabbit, for your love, support and understanding. Thanks to those in the mental health system who care so very much for their patients and our outcomes.

I am blessed indeed to be, and have been, surrounded by such wonderful people.

Thanks to my *MasterChef* colleagues, the judges and contestants, for being integral to the whole experience each time; for being a part of something that has shaped my whole life.

Thanks to my dearest friends, you brilliant people – life would be so poor without you.

The greatest thanks must go to my family. Writing these things down involves some difficult discussions and asks courage of the people closest to me. And I have witnessed that courage in spades.

My sons – thank you, I love you, your constant encouragement, support and forgiveness are so important to me. To the partners you have chosen – thank you for loving my boys.

Thank you, Delilah, for being joy personified.

A general acknowledgement must go here, too. Not all of every story can be told in one book. Firstly, because if it were, the book would be so heavy you'd get arm strain trying to hold it up in bed. Secondly, in this case, because not all stories are mine to tell. If you're left wondering, 'But wait . . . whatever happened to . . .?' all I can do is draw on one of my favourite books in the world, and say, 'But that is another story, and shall be told another time.'

And of course, as the book begins, so it shall end: with Mick. This – the book, as well as the past little while – was hardest of all on you. Thank you for loving me back to life, to our beautiful life.

With love,

Julie

Powered by Penguin

Looking for more great reads, exclusive content and book giveaways?
Subscribe to our weekly newsletter.

Scan the QR code or visit penguin.com.au/signup